Praise for *A Guide to the New Ruins of Great Britain*

'An excellent vade-mecum for the disgruntled urban flaneur.' Keith Miller, *Times Literary Supplement* Books of the Year

'An exhilarating book. Owen Hatherley brings to bear a quizzing eye, venomous wit, supple prose, refusal to curry favour, rejection of received ideas, exhaustive knowledge and all-round bolshiness. This book is as much a marker for an era as *English Journey* and *Outrage* were.' Jonathan Meades

'The latest heir to Ruskin … Hatherley blasts the architectural style of New Labour Britain. Whatever your pet-hate, Hatherley will probably have some enjoyably cruel words for it.' Boyd Tonkin, *Independent*

'Compendious, erudite and witty … a man to watch.' Ken Worpole, *openDemocracy.net*

'Witty, occasionally bleak but immensely readable.' *Architects' Journal*

'This is an important book that is entirely worthy of the arguments it sets out to provoke.' Patrick Wright, *Architecture Today*

'Owen Hatherley is a fulminating critic-cum-flaneur … This is fear and loathing in Lost Albion riffed by a quainter version of Hunter S. Thompson.' Jay Merrick, *Independent*

'A gem of a book.' Kevin Orr, *Socialist Review*

'Wonderfully provocative … Intensely passionate and bitter (I was reminded at times of the thunderous laments of the Victorian sage Thomas Carlyle) … Hatherley's book is terrifying in its exposure of the human cost of the mistakes that have been made.' Rupert Christiansen, *Daily Telegraph*

'Hatherley is a formidable new voice … this surgical evisceration of the cityscapes of Blairism is required reading.' Hugh Pearman, *RIBA Journal*

'This is the real Britain, and Hatherley is the most informed, opinionated and acerbic guide you could wish for.' Hugh Pearman, *Sunday Times*

'Painted with a raging energy that is exhilarating … [It's] political, sinister, sometimes funny.' *Morning Star*

'Hatherley deserves to be widely read … he has brought a welcome freshness and honesty to architectural criticism." Chris Hall, *Icon*

'In this angry, fiercely funny book, Owen Hatherley steps forward as the Pevsner of the PFI generation, an erudite, urbane guide to the Ballardian wreckage of millennial Britain. Essential reading for anyone who ever feels their blood start to boil when they hear the word "regeneration." ' Hari Kunzru

OWEN HATHERLEY is the author of the acclaimed *Militant Modernism*, a defence of the modernist movement. He writes on architecture, urbanism and popular culture for *Building Design*, *Frieze*, the *Guardian* and *New Statesman*. He blogs on political aesthetics at nastybrutalistandshort.blogspot.com. He lives in London.

A GUIDE TO THE NEW RUINS OF GREAT BRITAIN

OWEN HATHERLEY

VERSO

London • New York

Trumpets around the walls of the Barbican. Trumpets turning into penny whistles and then, reflected in the new shining glass, suddenly and surprisingly accompanied by a respectful and celebratory choir.
—Raymond Williams

This paperback edition first published by Verso 2011
First published by Verso 2010
© Owen Hatherley 2010

1 3 5 7 9 10 8 6 4 2

Verso
UK: 6 Meard Street, London W1F 0EG
US: 20 Jay Street, Suite 1010, Brooklyn, NY 11201
www.versobooks.com

Verso is the imprint of New Left Books

ISBN-13: 978-1-84467-700-9

British Library Cataloguing in Publication Data
A catalogue record for this book is available from the British Library

Library of Congress Cataloging-in-Publication Data
A catalog record for this book is available from the Library of Congress

Typeset by MJ Gavan, Truro, Cornwall
Printed by ScandBook AB in Sweden

Contents

Introduction

The Change We See

In 2009, the dying Labour government came up with one of the more amusing of its political gambits. As urban regeneration and the new public buildings of the Private Finance Initiative were so prominent and so popular, how about a campaign focusing on them, presenting the buildings that resulted as proof positive that New Labour hadn't broken its promises, that it was the party of change, that it was rebuilding Britain, and that social programmes were at its heart? The campaign was christened 'The Change We See'. Go to the website and you find the explanation. 'Since 1997, we've changed this country—rebuilding the lives of children, older people and families. Make no mistake, this could not have happened without supporters like you. Now we face an opposition who wants to deny our successes and cut the public services we rescued. We must stand together and show how proud we are of these historic achievements.' So, it asks the public to submit photographs of PFI Hospitals, City Academies, Sure Start centres and the like to a Flickr group.

Sadly, it met with an immediate torrent of ridicule and subversion on a wide spectrum from political opponents to the editor of the *Architects' Journal*. The Change We See entailed barn-like buildings resembling those built in the eighties and nineties for the supermarket Asda, housing Sure Start children's centres; a surgery that resembled the cheap woolly designs used by the developer Barratt Homes; a Law Courts (sorry, 'Justice Centre') constructed in lumpily jolly 1986 postmodernist style that was, astonishingly, completed in 2005; a primary school that resembles 'Britain's Guantanamo', Belmarsh Prison; and much that is less immediately appalling, but all produced in the chillingly blank Private Finance Initiative (PFI) idiom of clean lines, bright colours, red bricks and wipe-clean surfaces, as if furnishing a children's ward. Soon, the Flickr group was being subverted by new 'luxury' tower blocks that looked like Soviet barracks; CCTV cameras; lampposts capped with spikes to deter vandals; stop and search cards; and images of poisoned brownfield land soon to be developed into housing ... all contributed by mischievous Flickr users with the tag 'Vote Labour'. This wasn't simply some architectural criticism of a real political advance that aesthetes and snobs just didn't appreciate. The functions are as awful as the forms: the omnipresent PFI schemes, or the bizarre notion that gentrification, as represented by the penthouses of Manchester's Beetham Tower, 'rebuilt the lives of children, older people and families', other than the children, elderly and families of the decidedly affluent, of course.

My own little contribution to The Change We See—which the administrators cheerfully added to the group when I put it forward—was Darent Valley Hospital in Dartford, on the edges

Darent Valley, Dartford, the first PFI hospital

of London, where I have had the privilege of being treated for a long-term condition over several years. It was the first major NHS hospital built as part of the Private Finance Initiative, with the entire complex built and owned by the construction company Carillion, who claim to offer 'end-to-end solutions' for public–private partnerships. Like all PFI hospitals it is very far from the town centre. For reasons probably connected to land values, PFI hospitals are always on the outer reaches, in the 'no there, there' places, quarantined away.

A landmark in the strange new landscape created by the loosening of planning controls in the 'Thames Gateway', Darent Valley Hospital is just adjacent to Bluewater, the ultimate out-of-town, out-of-this-world mall, which is bunkered down inside a chalk pit and impossible to reach on foot. So the bus takes you past the M25, through what is probably legally the green belt—that is, a landscape of 1930s speculative housing and minuscule farms where forlorn horses look upon power stations and business parks—before eventually dropping you off at the top of a hill, from which you can survey an extraordinary non-place. The Queen Elizabeth II Bridge, its ungainly, steep curve reaching to the hangars and containers of Thurrock, and an endless strip of sheds and cranes stretching out as far as the North Sea.

The hospital itself, designed by Paulley Architects in 1999, is done in the public–private style which is by now familiar from a thousand New Labour non-projects. No doubt constructed with a concrete or steel frame, it attempts to avoid looking 'institutional' via a series of plasticky wavy roofs (which, as a bonus, have also become the hospital's logo), tiny windows, some green glass, and a lot of yellow London stock brick. Inside the series of corridors and wards, into which natural light never seems to penetrate, there are dashes of jolly colour in the carpets and a peculiarly abstract colour-coding system. But the real design feature is the central atrium at the main Outpatients entrance, where a giant Carillion logo looks over a big branch of Upper Crust, a WH Smith, and a shop which sells a huge range of cuddly toys, amongst other concessions. The first time I went here I was quite alarmed by the rather early twentieth-century equipment in this 'twenty-first-century hospital', but one can purchase a wide variety of pastries here. In the Outpatients waiting room, large screens show—always grainy—footage of local appeals and health recommendations.

Don't get me wrong, I'm usually well treated here, bearing in mind the hours of waiting around, and I do what I'm told, placing all reasonable and unreasonable trust in the physicians, but sometimes the new landscape and the vagaries of hospital treatment can intersect in undignified ways. Behind the site is a new residential development, most likely built as part of the same property deals that created the hospital; the NHS is nowadays encouraged to maximize profit from its land. An estate of little spec-builder cottages spans out around a patch of wasteland, and their back windows look out into the strip windows of the wards. Some of the homeowners may have caught more than a glimpse of me undergoing a brief but rather invasive procedure, as the blinds wouldn't go all the way along the window. This was not, I presume, in the property brochure.

In the main Outpatients waiting room is a wall display on 'Heritage'. Everything in Britain, especially in the Home Counties, must involve Heritage somewhere. Obviously there isn't much to be found in a hospital which has only existed for ten years, but conveniently, it turns out that there was an Asylum for Imbeciles on the site in the nineteenth century. Sepia-toned pictures of this take up the space on the heritage wall. *This is England*, I always think when I'm here. I don't mean in the sense that Iain Sinclair did when he visited Darent Valley in his 2002 travelogue *London Orbital* and imagined it an apocalyptic bedlam of lumpen proletarian troglodytes wielding bull terriers. I know it well, and it isn't. It's more because it represents a horrible, unplanned new landscape, the embodiment of New Labour's attempt to transform the Welfare State into a giant business. It won't *admit* to its newness, instead remaining petty and provincial, simulating a nebulous heritage. With its sober stock brick and metallic surfaces (by now blackened by the hospital incinerator) it doesn't even have the pleasures of kitsch. Yet this dispiriting exurbia was not the whole story of Blairite Britain. The last fifteen years have also seen the attempted fulfilment—sometimes sincere, mostly cynical—of policies that purported to put urbanity and design at the centre of new building. In so doing, New Labour has fulfilled the wishes of some left-wing urbanists in a most unexpected fashion.

Be Careful What You Wish For

Perry Anderson recently wrote that Britain's history since Thatcher has been 'of little moment'.¹ Admirable as this statement is in pricking local pomposities and arguable though it may be in political terms, in architecture, as in art and music, the UK has retained a prominence that is out of all proportion to its geopolitical weight. British architectural schools (both in the stylistic sense and as educational institutions like the Architectural Association) have retained a massive importance. The High-Tech school of mechanistic style founded by former partners Norman Foster and Richard Rogers was successful in Paris and Hong Kong before London and Manchester, bringing prestige that was appropriately rewarded in the less than futuristic, if geographically

London's Financial District, as remade by Foster and Rogers

indeterminate titles the two men now carry, Baron Foster of Thames Bank and Baron Rogers of Riverside. The immediately succeeding generation of Will Alsop or David Chipperfield would have a similar fate, with successes in Berlin or Marseilles before the UK rewarded their firms with commissions; after them, students—seldom British—of the Architectural Association in London like Zaha Hadid, Rem Koolhaas and Steven Holl would achieve international prominence and domestic obscurity for their Deconstructivist warping of architecture into something barely functional but instantly 'iconic'; most recently, new ornamentalists like Fashion Architecture Taste (FAT) or Foreign Office Architects found employment in the Netherlands or Japan first and foremost.

This pattern isn't just at the level of architects-qua-architects, the famous Ayn Randian form-givers. The faceless megafirms for which British culture's unambiguous corporate fealty seems particularly rich soil, such as RMJM (who recently hired disgraced banker Sir Fred Goodwin as an 'adviser'), Building Design Partnership, Archial or Aedas, are especially prominent in the hyperactive building booms of China or the United Arab Emirates, producing watered-down versions of High-Tech and/or Deconstructivism for foreign export. Meanwhile, the brief televisual popularity of the Stirling Prize, the architectural Booker or BAFTA, showed both that there was an untapped public interest in architecture, and that British architects were as often to be found working abroad as in the UK, with the prize-winning entries in Germany or Spain more often than Wales or Northern Ireland. Why is it, then, that actual British architecture, The Change We Can See, is so very bad?

The answers to this question are usually tied up with New Labour's particularly baroque procurement methods and an ingrained preference for the cheap and unpretentious, causing a whole accidental school of PFI architecture to emerge—often constructed via 'design and build' contracts which removed any control over the result from the architects, with niceties like detailing and fidelity to any original idea usually abandoned. The

'New Home, New Life, New You'—CABEism in Holloway Road, London

forms this took were partly dictated by cost, but also by amateur-
ish parodies of exactly the kinds of high-art architecture
mentioned above, creating something which Rory Olcayto of the
Architects' Journal suggests calling 'CABEism',[2] after the Commission for Architecture and the Built Environment, the design
quango whose desperate attempts to salvage some possibility of
aesthetic pleasure from PFI architects and their developers led to a
set of stock recommendations. Their results can be seen everywhere—the aforementioned wavy roofs give variety, mixed
materials help avoid drabness, the windswept 'public realm' is a
concession to civic valour—but here I will call it Pseudomodernism, a style I regard as being every bit as appropriate
to Blairism as Postmodernism was to Thatcherism and well-
meaning technocratic Modernism to the postwar compromise.

The most impressive neoliberal sleight of hand, one pioneered
in Britain before being eagerly picked up everywhere else, has
been the creation of what Jonathan Meades neatly calls 'social
Thatcherism'. It has existed ever since the mid 1990s, and was not
begun by the Labour Party. From John Major's avowed intent to
create a 'classless society' to New Labour's dedication to fighting
'social exclusion', the dominant rhetoric has been neoliberalism

with a human face. The liberal misinterpretation of this has long been that it proves the existence of some kind of 'progressive consensus', a continuation of social democracy, albeit in a more realistic, less 'utopian' manner. In the built environment, the thesis of a social democratic continuum that connects, say, the Labour of Clement Attlee to New Labour has appeared to be supported by the resurgence of Modernist architecture after an eclectic postmodernist interregnum, and an apparent focus on the city rather than the suburbs. Lord Richard Rogers has proclaimed this to be the 'Urban Renaissance' in a series of books and white papers with titles that now sound deeply melancholic, not only because of the dyslexic architect's verbal infelicities: *A New London; Architecture—A Modern View; Cities for a Small Planet; Cities for a Small Country; Towards an Urban Renaissance; Towards a Strong Urban Renaissance* ...

This was enforced by bodies such as the Architecture and Urbanism department of the Greater London Authority locally, and the Urban Task Force and CABE nationally, with mixed success. It enshrined in policy things which leftish architects like Rogers had been demanding throughout the Thatcher years—building was to be dense, in flats if need be, on 'brownfield' i.e. ex-industrial land, to be 'mixed tenure', and to be informed by 'good design', whatever exactly that might be. The result—five or six-storey blocks of flats, with let or unlet retail units at ground floor level, the concrete frames clad in wood, aluminium and render—can be seen in every urban centre. Similarly, new public spaces and technologies were intended to create the possibility of a new public modernism. One of the most curious, and retrospectively deeply poignant expressions of this early New Labour urbanism dates from the point where it might have seemed a modernizing, Europeanizing movement rather than today's horrifying combination of Old Labourist chauvinist authoritarianism in social and foreign policy and relentless, uncompromising neoliberalism. This is Patrick Keiller's 1999 film *The Dilapidated Dwelling*, referred to by the director himself alternately as his 'New Labour film' or his 'naughty film', made for Channel 4 but unreleased on

DVD and seldom screened. Like his earlier, better known *London* and *Robinson In Space* it takes the form of an oblique travelogue, only this time with interviews and an ostensible overarching subject—rather than the earlier films' Problem of London or Problem of England, this is the Problem of Housing. Introducing it twelve years later, Keiller recalled that 'I thought in 1997 that we were going to rebuild Britain, after all the damage that had been done to it, like we did after 1945.' The film is a sharp pre-emptive analysis of why this would not happen.

Today, the message of the film is: be careful what you ask of capitalism, as it might just grant your wish. In short, *The Dilapidated Dwelling* asks the question: why does the production of housing never get modernized? (With the linked question, why is construction so backward?) It seems to derive from the search for 'new space' in the 1995 travelogue *Robinson in Space*, where the novel if unnerving spaces of containerization, big sheds, security, espionage and imprisonment almost entirely exclude housing, which is only seen in glimpses, usually of neo-Georgian executive estates. Housing, when this film was made in 1997–9, was not new space. It has become so since, however, especially in the cities.

There's a desperately sad yearning in Keiller's two 'Robinson' films for a true metropolitanism, a Baudelairean modernity worthy of the first country in history to urbanize itself. In *London*, the capital and its infrastructure are strangled by a 'suburban government'; and in *Robinson in Space*, ports like Southampton or Liverpool are weird, depopulated, the enormous turnover of imports and exports never leading to any attendant cosmopolitanism or glamour, the internationalism confined to the automated space of the container port. So it's interesting to consider these films after the Urban Task Force, after the palpable failure of the Urban Renaissance, the death of which was arguably heralded by the anti-congestion charge, anti-inner city 'Zone 5 strategy' that got Boris Johnson elected as Mayor of London.

The Urban Renaissance was the very definition of good ideas badly thought out and (mostly) appallingly applied. The expansion of public spaces and mixed uses led merely to pointless piazzas with attendant branches of Costa Coffee; the rise in city living has led to brownfield sites and any space next to a waterway, from the Thames's most majestic expanses to the slurry of Deptford Creek, sprouting the aforementioned Urban Task Force blocks. Meanwhile, the film's central suggestion—that new housing should not only be on brownfield or greenfield, but should moreover replace the much-loved but standardized and deeply dilapidated housing of 1870–1940 that dominates the country—was partially fulfilled in a disturbing manner. This is where the film is at its most controversial.

Britain, it argues, has the oldest housing stock in Europe, and the most dilapidated, and it is enormously expensive to retrofit—why not just knock it down and build something better? Chillingly for conservationists, Keiller takes for his model the modular, inexpensive, prefabricated construction of supermarkets, although introducing the film in 2009 he ruefully wonders 'why I thought we should all live in Tesco'. Nonetheless, why be sentimental about substandard housing from the era that coined the term 'jerrybuilt'?

The idea of destroying and replacing huge swathes of Victorian housing found fruit in the government's Pathfinder scheme. Designed to 'revitalize' the economies of a selection of post-industrial areas from Birmingham northwards, it entailed the compulsory purchase and demolition of (most frequently council-owned) housing not so much to replace it with something better, but for the purposes of, in Pathfinder's subtitle, 'Housing Market Renewal' in northern towns previously untouched by the south-eastern property boom. The results are inconclusive, to say the least, and reveal just how little the quality of a set of buildings has to do with its place in the property pecking order. As Heritage campaigners were keen to point out, the streets tinned-up ready for demolition under Pathfinder were just those which, in London, would have been long since the subject of fevered property speculation. In Liverpool especially, Pathfinder's demolition programmes encompassed some large bay-windowed nineteenth-century houses which would have gone for silly money further south—though they did not stop to ask exactly why their northern equivalents were less lucrative.[3] The infill that replaced the Victorian streets, where it appeared, followed the Urban Task Force rules impeccably, albeit that the 'good design' element is somewhat questionable.

The architectural argument misses the truly original element in Pathfinder, what differentiates it from the superficially similar slum clearance programmes of the 1890s through the 1960s. It is a programme of class cleansing. The new housing is not let to those who had been cleared, as was the case with most earlier clearance, especially after 1945, but is allocated for the 'aspirational' in an only partially successful attempt to lure the middle classes back to the inner-cities they deserted for the suburbs. This is in no way limited to Pathfinder itself, but forms part of the managed neoliberalism which has pervaded New Labour's approach to urban policy, as to so much else. Instruments brought in after 1945 in order to bypass the interests of slum landlords and landowners legally—Compulsory Purchase Orders, Development corporations —were now used to the opposite end.

In this New Labour were not pioneers. The first to use the instruments of social democracy against its social content was Westminster Council under Shirley Porter, in the 1980s. Concerned that the Council was at constant risk of falling to Labour, the local Conservative leadership found that council tenants, spread liberally across the area by earlier reformers, were more likely to vote Labour. The Council had the legal capabilities to get them out, rehousing them in inferior accommodation out of the borough and offering their—often very fine—flats for sale to upwardly mobile buyers. With an impressive prefiguring of New Labour nu-language, this programme was called Building Stable Communities. Of course, this was gerrymandering, and Porter herself is still essentially on the lam from justice because of it[4]— but New Labour would do something very similar, without even the rational excuse of ensuring electoral success. Under the banner of making communities more 'mixed', council estates such as the huge Heygate Estate in the Elephant and Castle or Holly Street in

Hackney were sold off and demolished, their tenants transferred elsewhere or heaped onto the waiting list, all in the name of what Deputy Prime Minister John Prescott would call Building Sustainable Communities.

The main semi-governmental organ of 'regeneration', English Partnerships, was designed to bring business and state together, the latter often sponsoring the former to such an extent that it would have been cheaper just to build on its own. It formed part of a weird grey area of almost entirely state-funded private companies—the Arm's Length Management Organizations to which much council housing was transferred, PFI and out-sourcing specialists like Capita and QinetiQ, both of which were formed out of government departments. They embody the phase of neoliberalism described by the cultural critic Mark Fisher among others as 'market Stalinism', where state *dirigisme* continues and grows, working this time in the service of property and land.[5] By 2009 English Partnerships had transmogrified into the Homes and Communities Agency (HCA), whose immediate task was to respond to the 2008 property crash with a house-building programme. Early on, there was some hope that this would lead to a new wave of council building, particularly given that waiting lists had spiralled after the crash, but instead private enterprise continued to be subsidized by the state, in the form of the Kickstart stimulus programme. This offered £1 billion of direct state funding to private developers and builders for 'high-quality mixed tenure housing developments', which would be assessed for said quality by the aforementioned aesthetics quango CABE.

After its first schemes were unveiled at the start of 2010, Kickstart was heavily criticized by CABE for extremely low scores on all their measurements—in terms of energy-efficiency, design quality, public space, access to facilities and public transport and much else. Both bodies refused to state who had designed the schemes that had been assessed or where they were, despite a Freedom of Information request by *Building Design*—the HCA's head Bob Kerslake claimed it would damage the house builders' 'commercial confidentiality'. At the very end of the New Labour project was a massive programme of public funding for substandard private housing. This was the change we couldn't see, as we weren't allowed to know where the schemes actually were— although some of those in this book are likely candidates.

Architecture Becomes Logo: The Rise of Pseudomodernism

In terms of policy, then, an attempt to reform the Thatcherite city has had extremely ambiguous results; but in terms of architecture, the postmodernist architecture that characterized the 1980s and 1990s is, in a superficial sense, very much on the defensive, and has been for most of the last decade. Although it persists as the dominant aesthetic for speculative house-building outside the large cities, it is by now almost wholly absent from the architectural magazines and the metropolitan centres. This decline could be dated to the late 1990s, when two huge postmodernist buildings in London—Terry Farrell's MI6 building and Michael Hopkins' Porticullis House in Westminster (although Hopkins absolved himself through the astonishing tube station designed in the building's undercroft)—were so aggressively statist and

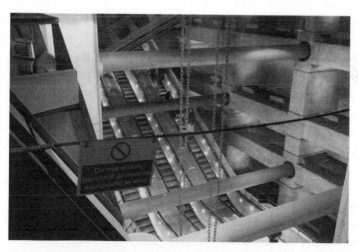

Michael Hopkins, Westminster Jubilee Line Station

weightily bureaucratic in form that the signifiers given out, always important in postmodernism's sign-fixated discourse, were deeply unattractive. On the contrary, the paradigmatic buildings constructed in London since the late 1990s have been those of Norman Foster, a once vaguely avant-garde technocrat notable for a seemingly Modernist lack of deliberate architectural-historical references and jokes, with an accompanying rhetoric of transparency and sustainability. This leads to what I call Pseudomodernism, which would be defined as Postmodernism's incorporation of a Modernist formal language. Pseudomodernism has several elements. The cramped speculative blocks marketed as 'luxury flats' or 'stunning developments', with their attenuated, vaguely Scandinavian aesthetic; the glass towers whose irregular panels, attempting to alleviate the standardized nature of such buildings, have been dubbed 'barcode façades'; and most of all, the architectural spectacles generated by 'signature' designers, most of whom were once branded 'deconstructivists' (Frank Gehry, Zaha Hadid, Rem Koolhaas, Daniel Libeskind, and a legion of lesser lights such as Make architects, who manage to combine formal spectacle and moralistic sobriety).

Norman Foster, Canary Wharf Jubilee Line Station

Terry Farrell with Liam Gillick, Home Office

Many former postmodernists are now pseudomodernists. The
most notable is Sir Terry Farrell, designer of a multitude of
quintessentially Thatcherite buildings in the 1980s, from Charing
Cross station to MI6. His most pseudomodernist work is the new
Home Office building, appropriately a PFI scheme, the first for a
government building. With its combination of Weimar Republic
curves and De Stijl patterns with eager-to-please colour—which
here is provided, as per the Blairite fetish for the 'creative industries', by the artist Liam Gillick—it provides a calm,
ostentatiously friendly face for the most illiberal administration in
the history of British democracy. Nonetheless, the Home Office is
merely an example of this idiom in its more domestically scaled
version. Unlike most of its contemporaries, it does not aim to be
that most essential of twenty-first-century architectural aspirations: an icon. The icon is now the dominant paradigm in
architecture to such an extent that at least four different buildings
erected in the last few years—one in Hull by Terry Farrell, one in
London at Canary Wharf, another in Glasgow, plus an 'Icona'
near the Olympic site in Stratford—have opted for some variant
on the very name 'Icon', although they range in use from nondescript blocks of flats to an aquarium.

A prospective image of London's 'Olympic Skyline' in 2012 released in the mid 2000s showed an entire skyline of competing icons. The skyscrapers announced under Ken Livingstone's tenure as mayor of London—named, in a manner Charles Jencks would appreciate, after gherkins, cheese-graters, walkie-talkies, helter-skelters, a shard—make none of the eclectic gestures and mashings together of different historical styles that characterized postmodernist architecture in developments like Broadgate and the original Canary Wharf. Stone has mostly been replaced by glass. Yet one thing that survives from Postmodernism is the conception of the building as a sign, and here as an easily understandable, instantly grasped sign, strongly opposed to the formal rigours and typological complexities of 'high' Modernism, especially its Brutalist variant. While it's possible that the original Gherkin received its nickname spontaneously, there's little doubt that the other towers, all announced around the same time, had a ready-made little moniker designed to immediately endear them to the general public, in order to present them as something other than the aesthetic tuning of stacked trading floors. Accordingly, by being instantly recognizable for their kinship with a household object, they would aim to become both logo and icon. Perhaps they might eventually become what Jencks describes as 'failed icons', more Millennium Dome than Frank Gehry's Bilbao Guggenheim; although always trying for the status of the latter, whose success in bringing well-heeled tourism to the Basque port has made it into a boosterist cliché, whereby the 'Bilbao effect' transforms a mundane city into a cultural capital, replacing unionized factory work or unemployment with insecure service industry jobs.

The other major change from the suburbanism of the Thatcher and Reagan version of neoliberalism is a new focus on the cities, something which is usually encapsulated by the under-investigated word 'regeneration'. Indeed, any form of building in an urban area is usually accompanied by this term. The vaguely religious air is appropriate, as it often accompanies a fundamentally theological conception of architecture, where by standing in

Daniel Libeskind, buildings for London Metropolitan University

proximity to an outstanding architectural work, the spirit is up-lifted, and the non-orthogonal geometry and hyperbolic paraboloids purport, for instance, to represent the experience of war through the disorientation they induce.

An appropriate English example is Salford Quays, where the Docks of Greater Manchester were transformed into a combina-tion of cultural centre and a development of luxury apartments, neatly combining both elements of Pseudomodernism. Two of the architects who most exemplify these ideas are represented there or nearby. There is Daniel Libeskind, whose tendency towards memorializing piety is so pronounced that he was described by Martin Filler as a 'human Yahrzeit candle'. His Imperial War Museum North, with its sloping ceilings and a form which apparently represents a world divided, is supposed to for-mally incarnate the experience of war. Meanwhile, not far away in central Salford is a bridge by Santiago Calatrava, who is the infrastructural embodiment of Pseudomodernism, his structures seemingly always placed in areas that are busy being transformed from proletarian spaces of work or habitation to 'regenerated' areas of bourgeois colonization. These transformations of space are, it should be remembered, fundamentally different in their social consequences to the superficially similar 'comprehensive redevelopment' of the postwar period. Once, a slum clearance scheme would involve the slum-dweller being rehoused by the state in something which was, more often than not, superior in terms of space, security of tenure, and hygiene, irrespective of the decades of criticism these schemes have been subjected to. Now that this sort of naïve paternalism is absent, the slums are cleared so that the middle classes can settle in them, something usually excused with a rhetoric of 'social mixing', dismantling what had become 'ghettoes'. The many schemes where sixties council towers have been replaced with PFI blocks are to urban planning what Pseudomodernism is to architecture.

That is, the Modernism of the icon, of the city academies where each fundamentally alike yet bespoke design embodies a vacuous aspirationalism; a Modernism without the politics, without the utopianism, or without any conception of the polis; a Modernism that conceals rather than reveals its functions; Modernism as a shell. This return of Modernist good taste in the New Labour version of neoliberalism has turned architectural Postmodernism, rather surprisingly, into a vanishing mediator. The keystones, references, in-jokes and alleged 'fun' of eighties and nineties corporate architecture now evoke neoliberalism's most naked phase, the period when it didn't dress itself up in social concern. In the passage from Norman Tebbit to Caroline Flint, the aesthetic of social Darwinism has become cooler, more tasteful, less ostentatiously crass and reactionary, matching the rhetoric.

Service Stations, Service Industry

However, it can be seen that the Pseudomodern takes many of its fundamental ideas, if not its stylistic tropes, from Postmodernism. At this point, we will take a historical detour. Postmodernist architecture was most intelligently formulated by Robert Venturi, Denise Scott-Brown and Steven Izenour in their 1972 book *Learning From Las Vegas*. This focused, via a critique of a caricatured

corporate Modernism, on the alleged inability of Modernist architecture to communicate adequately with its users. In response,
they privileged first of all, signage—the advertising signs of roadside architecture—and secondly, formal references to earlier,
most often classical styles of architecture as a means of providing
an architecture outside of the 'dumb box', as they described it.
Charles Jencks's *Language of Postmodern Architecture*, meanwhile,
turned to full-blown neoclassicism, with an accompanying narrative of Modernist hubris, where the dynamiting of one of the US's
rare forays into social housing in St Louis became the precise date
for the 'death' of Modernism. One element of Venturi's argument
was, regardless of their protestations, a Modernist one—a call for
an architectural montage of neon signs and jarring formal clashes.
Their praise for the chaos of signage that made up Vegas is,
in essence, not vastly different to the rhetoric of the Russian
Constructivists, whose work was motivated by what historian
Kestutis Paul Zygas calls a 'component fixation'; where designs
were always presented with affixed billboards, posters, slogans,
transmitters and tramlines, as if to plug them into the city's dynamism. Much of the architecture and signage they describe was
itself in a kind of Pulp Modernist idiom. Specifically, a 1950s style
usually called 'Googie' to distinguish it from the apparently more
rigorous Modernism of the International Style.

Googie was usually used to draw attention to burger bars, car
washes, coffee shops—the name comes from one such, designed
by John Lautner. It was an architecture that adapted itself to suburban sprawl and the sheer speed of the freeway by providing
dynamic forms which seemed to mimic speed in their formal dis-
tortions while attracting the attention of the prospective customer
travelling at eighty miles an hour via stretched angular forms and
lurid colours. In his book on the subject,[6] Alan Hess places the
style in direct opposition to the high-art Modernism of Mies van
der Rohe and his disciples, the classicist glass-skyscraper school
that became the spatial *lingua franca* of even the most conformist
parts of American capital. What's interesting here is that in the
American context, where Modernism was not as associated with

social democracy or state socialism as it was in Europe, the debate was purely aesthetic. While the opponents of 'Googie' accused it of being crass and commercial, Mies's Seagram Building was given tinted windows the colour of the client's brand of whisky. While its outrageous geometrical illusions and structural expressionism were being criticized as mere dressing-up, Mies's towers 'expressed' their structure by entirely decorative I-beams.

So in essence, the debate between classical and pulp Modernism in the US was one of taste. On the one hand there was the luxury aesthetic of the wing of the bourgeoisie that aspired to finer things: New York's successful attempt in the 1950s to wrest from Paris the accolade of world fine-art capital, with some CIA assistance. In order for this to occur it had to set itself against a more straightforward capitalist hucksterism. In fact, with their deliberate defiance of the rules of gravity and geometry, their brashness and lack of formal precedent, Googie buildings were more true to the original Modernist impulse—futurists or constructivists would have recognized themselves in commercial designers such as Armet & Davis, or in the architecture of McDonalds, Denny's and Big Boy, more than in Mies van der Rohe, Skidmore Owings & Merrill, Seagram or Lever. It's also a reminder that the idea of Modernism as 'paternalist' imposition on the benighted proletariat, upon which Postmodernism based much of its self-justification, makes sense only if we begin with an extremely limited definition of Modernism. Principally, one that was restricted to the International Style, itself a pernicious legacy of the Museum of Modern Art's dual depoliticization and classicization of Modernist architecture for American consumption. The Modernism that made it to New York was missing both the crass, neon-lit commercialism of the Berlin department stores and cinemas and the socialist fervour of the 'New Building', an anti-architecture for a new society.

It was not, of course, commercial Modernism which was critiqued by Postmodernists, but it can be seen in retrospect as the mediator between postmodernist theory and pseudomodernist practice. The work of Frank Gehry was, from the early 1980s, an adaptation of Googie's Pulp Modernism for the purposes of architecture as art. The style of which he was one of the leading lights, which was termed Deconstructivism by the mid 1980s (in reference to its grounding both in Jacques Derrida's philosophy and Russian Constructivist form) actually continued many of the formal strategies of the roadside architecture of the 1950s. These architects—Daniel Libeskind among them—were notable both for ignoring the postmodernist imperative to genuflect before neoclassicism, baroque and the traditional street, and for a vocabulary of the non-orthogonal, the exaggerated and the audaciously engineered that owed more to LA diners than it did to the Bauhaus. This style has been applied in the last decade principally for the purposes of museums, galleries and self-contained theme park-like environments such as Gehry's Experience Music Project in Seattle, or Nigel Coates's National Centre for Popular Music in Sheffield. Chin-Tao Wu's *Privatising Culture* lists a few of those that were erected in Britain around the turn of the millennium: 'you can experience ... a simulated journey into space at the National Space Science Centre in Leicester, find out about geological evolution at the Dynamic Earth in Edinburgh, have fun and learn about science at "@Bristol" in Bristol, or get hands-on experience of the steel industry at the "Making it! Discovery

St Paul's Visitor Centre, Make Architects

Centre" in Mansfield.'[7] In terms of their combined Disneyfication and intensification of the city's museum culture, these are deeply postmodernist buildings, regardless of their form.

The influence of Googie in contemporary urbanism is largely unacknowledged, but it is, I would argue, key to understanding exactly why the 'signature' wing of pseudomodernist architecture takes the form it does. Seemingly paradoxically, it aligns itself very closely with the heritage zones of the old capitals. Across the road from St Paul's Cathedral is a tourist information pavilion by Make architects, the group established by Ken Shuttleworth, job architect on Norman Foster's Gherkin. In its improbable geometry, its jagged zigzag showing zero interest in the expression of function or good taste, it could easily be selling donuts in 1950s Anaheim. There is by now a large amount of architecture like this, serving most often as a key component of urban regeneration strategies. Buildings for living in are more often done in a mild, asymmetrically patterned form of Scandinavian Modernism, while buildings for culture are allowed to make somewhat wilder gestures. This process can be seen in various buildings for the creative industries in Britain, with their logo-like names: Urbis in Manchester, The Public in West Bromwich, FACT in Liverpool. Its most extensive expression is not, however, in the UK, with its remaining vestiges of representative democracy, but in the oligarchies of Russia, China and the United Arab Emirates. Abu Dhabi, for instance, has set aside a district solely for 'iconic' cultural buildings by Gehry, Zaha Hadid, Norman Foster and Jean Nouvel (who has designed a branch of the Louvre). Barry Lord, the (English) 'cultural consultant' for this zone, notes that 'cultural tourists are older, wealthier, more educated, and they spend more. From an economic point of view, this makes sense'.[8] No doubt this applies equally well in theory to West Bromwich or Salford.

Much of this architecture has in common with Googie the reduction of the building to a logo, to an instantly memorable image: one that is appreciated in movement, as from a passing car, while quickly walking through an art gallery or museum on the way to the gift shop; or indeed while shopping, as with Future Systems and Rem Koolhaas's work for Selfridges and Prada in Birmingham and New York, respectively. Although it may accompany exhibitions of art or simulations of war, it is not an architecture of contemplation but of distraction and speed. Yet it also continues the moralistic rhetoric of postwar Modernism, without any of the actual social uses—local authority housing, comprehensive schools, general hospitals—to which it was originally put. The new Modernism, like the new social democratic parties, is one emptied of all intent to actually impr ve the living conditions of the majority. Instead, the social use of the pseudo-modernist building, forever groping for the Bilbao effect, appears in a rather Victorian manner to be the uplifting of the spirit via interactive exhibits and installations.

Nobody ever suggested that roadside diners had hyperbolic paraboloid roofs in order to make us better people or induce us to 'aspire', let alone to simulate the experience of war or the Holocaust. Nonetheless, the formal links between Googie and today's apparently radical architecture does suggest a truth at its heart—its forbears are in the aesthetics of consumption and advertising, in forms designed to be seen at great speed, not in serene contemplation. It should not surprise us that a style of consumption would return under neoliberalism, but the formal affinities of Pseudomodernism with this aesthetic offers an alternative explanation for what often seems an arbitrary play of forms. By drawing on the futurism of the McCarthy era, the architecture of the equally conformist neoliberal consensus establishes a link between two eras of political stagnation and technological acceleration. It also allows us to reinterpret what purports to be an aesthetic of edification as one of consumption. In the computer-aided creation of futuristic form, today's architects are producing enormous logos, and this is only appropriate. The architecture once described as deconstructivist owes less to Derrida than it does to McDonalds.

In (Partial) Praise of Urban Britain

The 'Urban Renaissance' is key to all this, and irrespective of its courting of suburbia, New Labour was very much an urban party. Its bases remained in ex-industrial cities, and its hierarchy was drawn from North London, Greater Manchester and Edinburgh. The Tories, irrespective of their capture of the Greater London Authority, are essentially an outer-suburban and rural party, so it will be instructive to find out what they plan to do with this major Blairite shibboleth. Coined in the late 1990s either by the sociologists Ricky Burdett and Anne Power or by Richard Rogers, under the auspices of the Urban Task Force set up by the de facto minister for architecture and planning John Prescott, this has become the optimistic term for a middle-class return to the cities, and an attendant redevelopment of previously demonized urban spaces. It is inextricably associated with the urban paraphernalia I define as Pseudomodern: in terms of architectural artefacts, the urban renaissance has meant lottery-funded centres, entertainment venues and shopping/eating complexes, clustered around disused riverfronts (Salford Quays, Cardiff Bay, the Tyneside ensemble of Baltic, Sage and Millennium Bridge); in housing, the aforementioned 'mixed' blocks of flats on brownfield sites, the privatization of council estates, the reuse of old mills or factories; extensive public art, whether cheerful or gesturing towards sculptor Antony Gormley's enigmatic figures (his 'Angel of the North', outstretched atop a former coal seam, is perhaps the most famous icon of regeneration), usually symbolizing an area's phoenix-like re-emergence; districts become branded 'quarters'; and, perhaps most curiously, piazzas (or, in the incongruously grandiose planning parlance, 'public realms') appear, with attendant coffee concessions, promising to bring European sophistication to Derby or Portsmouth.

The process is partial and unevenly scattered, but reaches its most spectacular extent in the miles of luxury flats in the former London Docks, the new high-rise skyline of Leeds, the privatized retail district of Liverpool One, and the repopulation of central

Manchester. Irrespective of the virtues or otherwise of these new spaces, this urban renaissance is widely considered to have ended in aforementioned city centre flats standing empty, as if the exodus from the suburbs to the cities was a confidence trick. Half-finished, empty or cheaply let towers in Glasgow, Stratford or Sheffield act as symbols both of the euphemistic 'credit crunch' and of the failure, as suburban boosterism might have it, of an attempt to cajole people into a form of living alien to British predilections—although the linked sub-prime crash in the US was a suburban rather than inner-city phenomenon.

So the suburbs—a fundamentally meaningless term, encompassing everything from Neasden to Bingley via Thamesmead and the entirety of Milton Keynes—are back, and with them a wave of criticism of the urban renaissance. It's exactly that renaissance that this book seeks to critique, albeit not for the same reasons. British cities deserve better than to be reduced to a systematic regeneration formula of 'stunning riverside developments' and post-industrial leisure in the urban core and outside it a sprawl of giant distribution sheds, retail parks and what Patrick Keiller described as 'reduced versions' of the houses of 150 years ago.

This book is an autopsy of the urban renaissance, but one driven by constant surprise and fascination at just how strange, individual and architecturally diverse British cities actually are. When researching the articles which eventually formed this book, mostly on foot, I was amazed by this richness, and at how widespread ignorance of it really was. I include my own ignorance in this. Apart from the opening and penultimate chapters, this book is almost exclusively about cities of which I had very little knowledge at the start of 2009, when on the strength of a long rant about my hometown on my weblog, I was commissioned by the architecture paper *Building Design* to write a series on British cities in the recession. The ensuing pieces appeared under the appropriately depressive, underwhelming title *Urban Trawl*. I took a friend, a theatre photographer and lecturer, along to take pictures, knowing that he would not resort to the clichés, sweeping perspectives and endless summers so beloved of architectural photographers. This—for better or worse—explains the ubiquitous signage, overcast skies and neck-craning angles you will find in the images in this book. And aside from a final, parenthetical visit to Liverpool, visited for other reasons, this follows the unplanned path we took across Britain for *Building Design*. Many, many cities are absent here, for no reason other than the vagaries of my particular architectural interests and convenience. Belfast, Cumbernauld, Birmingham, Harlow, Bristol, Plymouth, Edinburgh, Hull, Swansea, Coventry, Northampton, Aberdeen, Basildon, Barnsley, Sunderland, Middlesbrough, Preston, Barrow, Leicester and many others have my apologies for the implied but unintended slur on their character. I would have visited if I could.

Apart from quick trips as a child or adult to Newcastle, Glasgow, Liverpool and Manchester, these were places of which I had no prior experience, despite being obsessive about British architecture and politics (which may explain my occasionally Kaspar Hauser-like tone). This comes partly of being from the privileged south-east, albeit born and bred in one of its less privileged outposts. When I mentioned where I was going next to friends and relatives, there was often a certain amount of ridicule —*why* would you want to go to Leeds, or Milton Keynes, or Halifax? Why, when we all know that British cities are overpriced, ugly, thuggish and violent places built of concrete and glass, the 'Crap Towns' that *The Idler* compiled books about while its founder Tom Hodgkinson retired to the countryside to play at being a gentleman? The argument of this book, as well as the issue it takes with the pieties of Blairite regeneration, is that urban Britain is easily as interesting as the much mythologized piazzas of Italy. The problem is that after being given such a relentless kicking by successive governments and the invariably hostile press, by the 1990s local mettle and pride had broken, so *any* development was good, *anything* that 'brought jobs to the area' was permitted, and the towns strained to become something other than what they were, something distinctly less interesting—Florence in pine and glass, Los Angeles without the sunshine—when the mess and montage of these multiracial cities provided something which nowhere else in Europe can match. By far the bleakest and least welcoming city we visited for *Building Design* was Cambridge, which seems to suggest that there is an inverse correlation between national esteem for a place's qualities and the actual pleasure one can take walking through it.

The dominance of the south-east, i.e. of the increasingly vast London Metro Area, is threatened only very slightly by Greater Manchester—hence the horror of BBC workers on realizing their jobs were moving to Salford, a shocking two-hour train ride away from the capital—and by nowhere else in England (Scotland, as in so much else, is a different story). This is only partly because London's sheer size has such an overwhelming gravitational pull. In strict census terms, the nearest competitor is Birmingham, with less than one seventh of its population. If taken as conurbations, as continuous urban areas without rural interruption, then Birmingham, Manchester, Glasgow, Tyneside, Leeds, all suddenly become much larger—the populations of Nottingham and Newcastle more than double, while Manchester's leaps from around 400,000 to 2.5 million. Local government has not factored this in since the effective abolition of the Metropolitan Councils of the West Midlands, Greater Manchester, Merseyside, Tyne & Wear and West Yorkshire in the 1980s, along with the more notorious destruction of the Greater London Council. The capital partly recovered from this through the less powerful, more symbolic Greater London Authority, but the smaller metropolises never got theirs back in any way, shape or form. Accordingly, they tend to think of themselves as being far more provincial than they actually are. Cities like Sheffield or Liverpool too often play at being villages, with deleterious consequences for their true urban qualities; while the counter-movement to give them Urban Renaissance piazzas and towers ignores their actual features in a different but equally disastrous way, hence all those 'urban villages' bringing hermetic, provincial rural mores into the heart of the city.

Several books guided this guide, principal among them one

published in 1934, a travel book called *English Journey* by the Bradfordian writer J. B. Priestley.[9] In the following decade it was so widely read as to become one of those semi-mythical books that 'won the '45 election for Labour'—a sharp, populist, politely angry account of a deliberate attempt to look England in the face, from Southampton to Newcastle. This book is consciously written in Priestley's shadow, albeit extending it outside of the dubious centrality of England, and focused much more strictly on buildings rather than anecdote and general observation. A few others also cast a heavy shadow—the mid-century journeys of Ian Nairn, the 1990s *dérives* of Patrick Keiller—and what links all three, other than my (usually hidden) references to them here, is a disinterest in or critique of Heritage England, and the pervasive myth of either an overcrowded or a green and pleasant land.

By the mid nineteenth century, this was the only country in the world which had more urban than rural inhabitants. Even now, after a century of sentimentalism about the countryside, around 90 per cent of us live in essentially urban areas, and although around 70 per cent of the landmass is still agricultural land, only 300,000 people actually work it. This might be an urban island, but extra-ordinarily Penguin Books were able to release a set of twenty books in 2009 called *English Journeys*, in obvious reference to Priestley, every single one of which dealt with the countryside. The bulk of Priestley's account was urban, this being where the overwhelming majority of the English lived. At the end of this survey of a country torn between north and south, rich and poor, Priestley listed three Englands that he had found on this journey, all of them embodied in their man-made structures. The first was the countryside, an area of patchwork fields and local stone, one which has 'long since ceased to make its own living', pretty in its desuetude, if over-preserved. The second was that of the Indus-trial Revolution, of iron, brick, smokestacks and back-to-backs, more 'real' than the first but ruthlessly inhumane towards its inhabitants. Last was a third, commercial world of arterial roads, Tudorbethan suburbia, art deco factories and cinemas; cheap and ersatz, but without the brutality of the second.

Since Priestley, we could add a fourth and fifth England, or rather a fourth or fifth *Britain*, as this book attempts to avoid what Tom Nairn calls 'Englishry'. These are, respectively, the country of the postwar settlement, of council estates, Arndale centres and campus universities; and the post-1979 England of business parks, Barratt homes, riverside 'stunning developments', out-of-town shopping and distribution centres. This book is, at heart, an architectural guide to *this* country, to Britains four and five. It charts both the ambiguous remains of the fourth, and the fifth's frequent determination to wipe out any architectural trace of it, just as it tries to decimate the remnants of its collectivist politics—and here I attempt to treat Britain five with much the same retrospective contempt as it shows its predecessor, largely for the reason that I find its neoliberal politics every bit as repugnant as it does those of its socialist forbear. This is not, however, a ruminative book about urbanism that touches on architecture to illustrate an argument, but one where architecture itself is central, much as it is in New Labour's Change We See campaign. 'By these stones shall we be judged', said the leader of Vienna's City Council in his opening speech for the Karl-Marx-Hof, the gigantic council estate that Austrian Fascists would bombard a year later. This book uses architecture in an unashamedly subjective fashion to illustrate politics and vice versa, and aims most of all to awake in the reader an attention to their urban environment, in the hope that they will see it as something consciously made, something formed, rather than as a more-or-less irritating backdrop to the daily commute, a possible investment or a series of monuments and eyesores. Finally, if this book does that, it is in the hope that from there, people can think about how they can consciously make and consciously transform their environment.

I will begin, then, with the environment that did most to shape me.

Chapter One

Southampton: Terminus City

'I will begin, I said, where a man might first land, at Southampton.' This is how J. B. Priestley opens *English Journey*, and so begin the accounts of sundry other English travellers from the Edwardian era up to the 1970s. Until Heathrow replaced it, Southampton was where most visitors or returning travellers entered the country. Now, however, the main entities to land at and depart from Southampton are consumer goods, manufactured in China, unloaded at the city's Container Port, and freighted round the country by rail and lorry. What hasn't changed about the town is the way it appeared to Priestley as something indistinct, something that wasn't quite a place. 'It had no existence in my mind as a real town, where you could buy and sell and bring up children; it existed only as a muddle of railway sidings, level crossings, customs houses and dock sheds; something to be done with as soon as possible'. Well, children are born there, and they do grow up there. I was, and I did. And things are most certainly bought and sold in Southampton.

Although this book is written in great suspicion of the New Labour strategy of regeneration via the 'creative industries' and the clawing back of municipal pride from Thatcherite underdevelopment via sheds for sponsorship, relational aesthetics or 'interactivity', there is a hint—only a hint—of jealousy there. That is, jealousy that even though I may hate both the built result and its ideological legitimation, at least there is *some* kind of civic pride in places like Manchester or Gateshead, both on the part of their people and their architects and a sense that these cities are worth visiting for something above and beyond shopping. Southampton missed the meeting where the 'urban renaissance' was decided upon—perhaps because, despite being in the lower rungs of the twenty largest cities in Britain, it was never quite fully urban in the sense of being 'civic'. Too southern and too surrounded by the Tory heartland for the poor-but-sexy cool by association of northern industrial cities; too close to London to attain an identity and culture of its own.

Even Southampton's two Universities (one of which is a Russell Group research colossus) are so science-centric that the large student population doesn't lead to any attendant artiness. Culture is regarded with suspicion within the M27, the motorway which encloses it and connects it to Portsmouth. Southampton is a thousand-year-old nowheresville. Yet this, after all, might be what distinguishes it. I used to be annoyed by the way that whenever my home town was mentioned in a work of art—from Lennon's 'Ballad of John and Yoko' to Wyndham Lewis's travelogue *Snooty Baronet*—they never said anything about the town itself. It was only as a place to pass through. Off the boat, onto the train and into Waterloo in one hour fifteen. Southampton was Heathrow before Heathrow, and has never quite known what to do with itself since the ship was succeeded by the jet. I was missing the point though: Southampton is the city as terminus. One of the few to have described what he saw when he arrived was ex-colonial boy J. G. Ballard, who wrote in his memoir *Miracles of Life* of his shocked first vision of England in 1946.

> The *Arrawa* docked at Southampton, under a cold sky so grey and low that I could hardly believe this was the England I had read and heard so much about. Small, putty-faced people moved around, shabbily dressed and with a haunted air. Looking down from the rail, I noticed that the streets near the docks were lined with what seemed to be black perambulators, some sort of coal scuttle, I assumed, used for bunkering ships. Later I learned that these were British cars, a species I had never seen before.[10]

Then he's straight off to London, never looking back.

The secret story of Southampton's rise to (brief) prominence is deeply unnerving for those who like a city to be marked by the ambition of its architecture, or those who long for the South-East's grip on the country to be loosened. In the early twentieth century, Southampton overtook Liverpool as Britain's major passenger port. At exactly the point when Liverpool was erecting megacity monuments along the Pier Head, either to herald arrival at the centre of Empire or the grandeur of Liverpool itself, its business was being swiped by Southampton, with the White Star Line transferring there in 1907 and Cunard following in 1921. (Recently Liverpool has been threatening a belated revenge, with various cruise companies considering a move back to Merseyside, on the grounds that their passengers might want something to look at during their stop-off in England.) It is the misfortune of Southampton to have prospered most during the most uninspired period in British architectural history, the long slumber that lasted from 1914 to 1945. The shipping companies and Port Authorities built no Liver Building here, no 'Graces'. Southampton didn't make a distracting fuss about itself, and the provinces were not to get any more ideas above their station.

Southampton, like Coventry, Plymouth and east London, nearly became a non-place in a quite literal sense. In November 1940 the centre was flattened and thousands fled the city, many sleeping rough in the surrounding countryside to avoid returning to the inferno. Yet what happened when reconstruction came? Southampton is twinned with Le Havre, a French port that was similarly ruthlessly blitzed, yet Auguste Perret's reconstruction of that city as a series of neoclassical towers and boulevards was, while by no means fearlessly Modernist, confident, contemporary, urban, large-scaled, proud. Southampton got a one-storey Portland Stone shopping parade, now featuring the faded imprints of 1990s shop signs, since the shops have almost all moved into the city's newly-built covered malls. The planners of Le Havre might have cast covetous glances across the Atlantic at the US's skyscrapers and daylight factories, but those of 1940s

3

Holy Rood Church

Southampton recognized that the future lay somewhere else in the United States. In *The Buildings of England*, David Lloyd described the parade as being akin to 'an up-and-coming Mid-Western town with planning control and Portland stone'. While the gigantic ships, those ribbon-windowed beauties that inspired a million Modernist buildings, sailed to New York from just a few yards away, Southampton channelled the spirit of Iowa.

A ghost McDonalds, Above Bar

Shirley Towers

However, Southampton City Council took a thirty-year detour before realizing in the 1990s that Southampton's destiny was to be the most American city in Britain, in the least glamorous possible sense. In *Soft City*, an early psychogeographic study marked by a very early 1970s paranoia, Jonathan Raban accidentally found himself in a standard exemplar of the British transformation of Corbusian utopia into dystopia. A planned satellite suburb on the edges of Southampton, a 'vast, cheap storage unit for nearly 20,000 people', Millbrook seemed to be the perfect embodiment of well-meaning failure, producing an isolated and disturbing new landscape. Architecturally, Millbrook is not too bad—the towers, especially, by the Tyneside firm Ryder & Yates, are clever, patterned things—but in terms of planning it's as desolate now as it no doubt was in 1974, and the pitched roofs on the lower blocks don't lessen the effect; today they're as disconnected as ever. Millbrook Towers, the tallest building in the city placed bizarrely in its outer suburbs, may be an elegant building, but doubtless that was little consolation to its inhabitants when recently the lifts were out of action for eight months.[11] Raban concludes: 'were one to read Millbrook as a novel, one might say that the author had read and copied all the fashionable books without understanding them, and had produced a typical minor work in which all the passions

5

and prejudices of the current masterpieces were unconsciously and artlessly reflected.'[12]

Appropriately, the work of the city architect who planned Millbrook—Leon Berger, a Modernist trained in Liverpool and perhaps intent on applying some of its architectural ambition to its rival—is indeed a sort of amalgam of the period's motifs and clichés, applied with some wit, occasional panache and more occasionally, real talent. *Zeilenbau* ('line-building', a rationalist plan popularized at the Bauhaus in the 1920s) arrangements of disconnected blocks in open space at the estates on the eastern edges like Weston Shore or Thornhill; mixed development everywhere else, containing some or all of *béton brut*, rubble stone, weatherboarding, bare stock brick, slabs and points in varying quantities. Yet Millbrook's bleakness coincided with some extraordinary architecture.

Just outside the Central Station is Wyndham Court, designed in 1966 for the City Council by Lyons Israel Ellis, a firm that acted as finishing school for the more famous New Brutalist architects of the period like James Stirling, architect of the Leicester

Wyndham Court

6

Engineering Building among others. Listed in the 1990s against knee-jerk opposition from the local press, this is by far the finest twentieth-century building in the city. Without employing the easy formal references that mark the city's post-1979 shopping centres and flats, it immediately evokes the cruise behemoths that sailed from the nearby port. A glorious concrete Cunard, impossible to ignore, moored in a city otherwise intent that nobody should notice it—and it's still, as the satellite dishes imply, a functioning block of social housing, which would be unlikely now in London or Manchester. It clearly hasn't been cleaned in a very long time, and as Joel, gobsmacked, takes several photos, two youths shout over at us, in the fast Estuary/Yokel hybrid that is the Sotonian accent, '*Itwasn'tmyfaultmydaddidn'tknowjohnniesbroke!*' His urbane Bradfordian sensibilities offended, he asks 'Can you translate from the vernacular?', unable to imagine that they've been apologizing to us for their very existence. Adjacent is a small bomb site-cum-park, redbrick stumps of buildings, benches, rats and bristling vegetation.

Southampton had long been one of the best British candidates for a *Ville Radieuse*. Victorian planning created The Avenue, a tree-lined boulevard that ran all the way to the 'Gateway to Empire', a series of central parks, while the interwar years saw the building of the cohesive, verdant garden estates designed by the Quaker architect Herbert Collins. Collins's little Letchworths in the northern suburbs were inadequately emulated by the city council in the form of the inept Flower Estate adjacent to the university, its 'workers' cottages' and treeless streets the incongruous setting for perhaps the nastiest of its wide variety of nasty places. This is a place of which I have particularly bitter memories, having lived there as a teenager: most of what I remember is ubiquitous casual violence, something especially fearsome in 'Daisy Dip', the estate's little park, where a friend was baseball-batted for dyeing his hair.

Unlikely as it may seem for a town in Hampshire, Southampton is remarkably violent: Home Office statistics in 2008 listed it as Britain's third 'most dangerous city', with more violent acts per population than anywhere else other than Manchester and Sheffield, both far larger cities.[13] Much of this violence seems connected to a town vs gown divide in a city where the smug, affluent gown meets a chronically depressed town. Someone in Liverpool once impressed upon me that the difference between these two one-time transatlantic ports, the thing that makes the smaller of them the more brutal, is the lack of sentiment and civic pride. Liverpool has a whole mythology, however dewy-eyed, of its own importance and civic munificence; Southampton knows it fucking hates Portsmouth but proclaims very little else about itself. At a stretch, perhaps, it is proud of being the embarkation point of the 'world's biggest metaphor' in 1912, and the former home of Matthew Le Tissier, England's most underrated footballer.

It was not always so mediocre; sometimes the Southampton built in the 1950s and 1960s could be positively dramatic. Leon Berger's work took 'mixed development' to an occasionally preposterous extreme. A one-storey house next to a three-storey block of flats next to an eighteen-storey tower, Berger's Shirley Estate exemplifies what is striking about this architecture. I used to look at this place with some awe as a teenager, Bowie's 'Warszawa' running round in my head. This is appropriate, as Polish is now heard almost as often in Shirley as English, in a town which has always had a large Eastern European contingent—I propose a twinning of Służew and Thornhill. In winter, the tower is shrouded in mist, as if it were a mirage. None of the gardens are private, which we're now supposed to think is a bad thing, and the tower is simply enormous, nearly as wide as it is tall, infilled with panels of rubble as if to evoke the medieval town centre. There are three of these, in Shirley, Redbridge and St Mary's, and from an elevated point they become beacons in this sprawling, low-rise city, seeming to point to somewhere out of here.

The buildings the council didn't sponsor, those in the marvellously named central strip Above Bar and its environs, are in the style recently and amusingly described by Stephen Bayley as 'John Lewis Modernism', here at its most nondescript. When

East Street Shopping Centre

containerization and Heathrow destroyed Southampton's *raison d'être*, it gradually realized its future was to become Hampshire's Shopping Extravaganza, dragging the burghers of the New Forest, Romsey, Winchester *et al.* into the city to buy stuff. The city went through several drafts and false starts before it finally succeeded in its aims with the gigantic WestQuay in the twenty-first century. Draft One: East Street Shopping Centre, designed in the late 1960s. Nobody comes here. I can't remember anyone *ever* coming here. It adjoins a huge concrete office block, the Capital Tower, which is architecturally undistinguished but has a classic Brutalist escape staircase offsetting the mediocrity of the rest. Its apparatus of ramps and car parks cuts the centre off from the inner city and from St Mary's, the district that is Southampton's beating heart (currently more of a pacemaker). I recently found a copy of Le Corbusier's *The Modulor* in East Street Oxfam. It seemed apt.

East Street, actually placed in (or rather terminating) a street, and adjoining a tall, hard building, was clearly not sufficiently suburban. Draft Two, built in the early nineties: the post-modernist mall of the Bargate Centre sited next to the titular Bargate itself, an 'iconic' medieval remnant, and designed by the prolific and hopelessly mediocre local architects W. H. Saunders.

9

In Southampton even 'alternative' culture happens in shopping malls, and the Bargate found its niche in the late 1990s by catering to ravers, skaters, Goths and metallers rather than the original targets of tourists, children and their harassed parents. The medieval walls, and flats used by the council for emergency housing, sit at the Bargate Centre's edges.

The Bargate is one of four big malls in the city centre. On the outskirts Eastleigh, a former railway works with houses attached, adds another, the Swan Centre. It's now being redesigned in a metallic, vaguely deconstructivist manner, indicating that its bricky Postmodernism has been thoroughly superseded as the architecture of retail. I used to live right next to this mall, which swept away Victorian market streets, much to my joy. As a child I *loved* malls. We never used that Americanism (these were the more prosaic *Shopping Centres*), but I had a birthday in McDonalds with branded party hats and gifts, I ate Donuts and Deep Pan Pizza, and as adolescence hit I listlessly read magazines in WH Smith until I was thrown out. I was glad when I realized there was a word, loitering, for this pastime.

Upon moving into the city proper, my affections were transferred to the Marlands, Draft Three of the Sotonian Mall, which replaced a bus station (the city hasn't had this basic amenity in decades) and encased under fibreglass a fragment of the Victorian street it replaced, eating it up as a gesture of genuflection to complement the atrocious, grinning stone-clad façade. The Marlands nearly went bankrupt, but was transformed into the expressively named 'The Mall', where it now reaches a canopy out into some bland postwar blocks. Linked by a walkway at the back—traversing a site that dramatically slopes down to what was once the waterfront—to car parks and an Asda, the Marlands was the first strike in the transformation of a huge swathe of reclaimed land into the aforementioned up and coming (or by now, down and out) Mid-Western town, after Leon Berger's failed attempts at designing a coherent city. A huge site once occupied by a cable works and a power station was, in the late 1990s, turned into a series of strip malls and boxes. As it went up, curtain-walled office blocks went down, wrapped in plastic like Laura Palmer before being thrown into the sea. Then came the strip malls of Western Esplanade, then some rather functionalist car parks, then the vast WestQuay, the retail behemoth for which the others were merely unsuccessful drafts—and to which we will return later. Southampton today is an experiment, exurban America without the sun or the space.

In Search of Solent City

In 2008 the Liberal Democrat MP for Eastleigh and failed leadership candidate Chris Huhne condemned proposals for the building of thousands of new homes in his constituency.[14] This, he claimed, was merely the return after several decades of the 'Solent City', which would destroy the local identity of such distinctive, delightful places as Chandler's Ford, Havant, Paulsgrove and Locks Heath. In the local press this was reported as if everyone would know what the Solent City was, and why it was such a bad thing. Solent City was a mid-1960s proposal by the Harold Wilson government for a new metropolis. It would be made up of Southampton and Portsmouth with a Milton Keynes-style grid-planned linear city strung between the two towns, uniting them into one of the largest and most powerful cities in the country and creating for the first time in centuries a southern city which could resist the pull of London. The Solent City never came to pass, but perhaps its phantom persists in the myths the area tells about itself. The Southampton–Portsmouth war via football, which has caused full-scale riots at least twice in the past decade, says a surprising amount about politics and culture in this unglamorous bit of Southern England. As a Sotonian with family from Portsmouth and Fareham, I don't quite have the requisite visceral hatred for Pompey that is customary (although I should point out here I don't go as far as my Grandma, who always claimed to 'support both'). In any case, what is really interesting in the rivalry is that the alleged historical and political reasons for the intense mutual hatred have been imposed post-facto. For instance, Portsmouth supporters have always claimed that their chosen insult, 'scum', comes from 'Southampton Corporation Union Men', in reference to a dock strike allegedly broken by Southampton dockers in the 1930s. As Southampton is a commercial port and Portsmouth a military one, this is of course implausible, and I've never come across a reference to it in histories of either city outside of the abundant literature of the footballing rivalry itself.

The significance of the rivalry is that both of these cities, in relatively apolitical parts of the country, justify their sporting hatreds largely through reference to history (mutual enmity between military and civilian England) and left-wing politics (through imaginary breaches of working-class solidarity). The two cities like to vie for the roughest reputation via evident untruths. So Southampton is denigrated as posh and semi-rural because Winchester and the New Forest are nearby. A quick trip to St Mary's or Thornhill should rectify this misapprehension. Portsmouth is alleged to be an insular island, yet has played the Blairite iconic architecture/urban regeneration game far more effectively, with its Spinnaker observation tower and glass skyscrapers forming an incongruously slick enclave in amongst the two-up-two-downs. Southampton's 'urban renaissance' entailed nondescript retail and Barratt boxes. British cities' perceptions of each other, when refracted through the compulsory agonism of a sporting rivalry, tend to get very skewed. On close investigation, these rivalries are usually built on myth, and are very recent. The Southampton–Portsmouth football rivalry began in the late 1960s, at the exact point that Colin Buchanan was charged by the Wilson government with developing a plan for the 'Southampton–Portsmouth Supercity'. It could be argued that the Saints/Pompey hatred is what happened instead of this south coast megalopolis. Rather than a real modernity, we got dim-witted atavism—but one justified with recourse to the serious politics it effectively replaced.

There were two competing ideas about the Solent City: the grid proposed by Colin Buchanan, and the later proposals from a group of sociologists, architects and critics (Paul Barker, Reyner

Fawley Refinery

Banham, Peter Hall and Cedric Price, respectively) in *Non-Plan—Experiment in Freedom*, a once famous 1969 special in the magazine *New Society*, which advocated the removal of planning controls, using the Solent City as an exemplar. The enormous oil refinery at Fawley, which even now presents itself to the hillier parts of Southampton at night as a distant and beautiful neon-lit metropolis, was to be given extra *son et lumière* by the non-planners, while the space in between would be made up of festive spaces, caravans, instant cities springing up and then disappearing along the M27. Without any of the japery implied in the *New*

Eastleigh Station

Society writers' suggestions, a Non-Plan is essentially what happened when Buchanan's Solent City was abandoned. Appropriately, given Huhne's disdain, Eastleigh exemplifies the sort of indeterminate space which Solent City would have occupied, and is indicative of what happened instead. The area likes to think of itself as a semi-rural Hampshire Arcadia, but with the exception of the New Forest this is far from the truth. Along with Gosport, the largest part of the conurbation that isn't either Southampton or Portsmouth itself, Eastleigh is a small company town, planned as a complete entity in the late nineteenth century for the South-Western Railway. It was settled by workers transferred from the works at Nine Elms, meaning that it was for a while a south London enclave in Hampshire, and I swear the accent, at least, survived until the 1990s. On moving aged twelve to a council estate within the Southampton boundaries, not only did I find the semis and front gardens suspiciously posh-looking, but I also thought the estate kids' semi-yokel accent to be surprising and hilarious, which guaranteed me some perhaps slightly deserved kickings.

I suspect that by the 1950s Eastleigh had forgotten it was once a colony of London, and the gridiron plan was abandoned from the thirties onwards, so although incongruously dense at the centre it is mostly dispersed, exurban, straggling: the bleak reality of the libertarian promises of the Non-Plan which once aimed to turn the area into a discontinuous funfest. In walking distance from the centre is Southampton Airport, built on the site of an interwar camp for Jewish refugees midway from Eastern Europe to New York City—although this bit of history is seldom mentioned, lest it imply that Southampton was once not provincial, with a history based on transatlantic travel, migration and internationalism. Adjacent, The Lakes, an abandoned industrial site given its own railway and turned into a small pleasure park, carries perhaps a hint of Non-Plan in its conversion of brownfield into leisure. Eastleigh had its brief moment in the national news in the mid nineties when its Tory MP, Stephen Milligan, was found dead with orange in mouth, plastic bag on head and suspenders on legs.

Eastleigh Works

I recall BBC News visiting the town, an incredible, improbable breaking of telly into life.

The London–Southampton train, which I've taken hundreds of times in the last eleven years, goes through Eastleigh in its last stretch, and hence through an enormous cargoscape of rusting vintage carriages and freight trains carrying Chinese containers, Southampton's Ford Transit factory visible in the distance. So I remember seeing the bombed-out church, a place which to me always seemed incomparably ancient (I was so disappointed when I realized it was Victorian), restored in the late 1990s and early 2000s as a block of flats, improbably enough. It won an *Evening Standard* award for housing, and whether or not it was deconsecrated, the move from God to property seems highly symbolic. Some of what I remember is still there, but the inner streets—Cranbury Road, where I lived, Desborough, Chamberlayne, Derby Road, Factory Road—have a drinking ban in place to stop general ultraviolence from occurring in the residential area. It's not hard to see why this might occur, as the place looks traumatized. Everyone looks ill, half the shops are charity shops (not *wholly* a bad thing, but nor is it a sign of great economic health), and the first conversation I hear when I sit down with my drink in the Wagon Works, on my first visit to the town centre in over a decade, begins: 'Soon it'll be an Islamic

Republic ... Enoch was right ... still, there'll never be rivers of blood 'cos the English don't have the guts.' I remembered that when I grew up here most of my friends were second/third generation Asian, and I wondered, looking round town at all the white faces, whether they all escaped to the other side of the M27, or hopefully further than that.

It's a bizarre leap to blame immigration for Eastleigh's desuetude. I once came across someone describing Eastleigh as a Northern town lost in Hampshire, which is true in part (though certainly not at the super-affluent outskirts). It's a very thorough bit of planning, and its buildings are a residue of first, Victorian civic culture—the town hall, the two-up-two-downs, the churches, the red-brick Gothic school—and later, something else, something perhaps promising transformation: the garden city estates outside the grid; the 'Labour Party House'; The Comrades Club, which I'm amazed and pleased to see is still called The Comrades Club, though I suspect it's a karaoke and real ale fest rather than a hotbed of agitprop theatre. The town was once a Labour stronghold, but boundary changes and drift meant that by the 1970s it was a Tory seat. My Dad tells me that the town once had the second highest Labour membership in the south of England (after Woolwich), but only because anyone who was on the 'tote', buying a ticket for the party-run pools from the Labour canvassers, became an automatic 'member'. It's hard to imagine any active politics there now, corrupt or otherwise, as it's gone the way of most places of once-skilled labour—confused, lost, lumpen.

The place is planned for industry, very precisely. Railway Works at one end, Pirelli Cables factory at the other, with a grid of terraces in between and semis at the sides; more channelled and less 'adaptable' than any Modernist plan, although like all Victorian urbanism it's seen as some sort of force of nature, *the way things have always been*, rather than something directed and planned for industrial, pecuniary purposes. As it is, all the industries I remember being here even in the early 1990s are now gone: the Mr Kipling factory from whence we got slabs of chocolate and the revelation that Tesco cakes were exactly the same as the

Kipling cakes, the huge railway works, once one of the biggest in the country (as presumably there's no demand for new trains in the botched, privatized railway network). Most alarming is the disappearance of the Pirelli factory; I remember it always just in the near distance, at the end of Factory Road. In its place are new Heritage Flats, with street names taken from the handful of famous residents: Joe Meek's bleach blond boy, Heinz Burt from The Tornados, next to Benny Hill Close. Amusingly enough, there have been proposals to rename Factory Road because it gives the wrong impression of the place. At the centr. of Eastleigh is what can only be described as a Socialist Realist sculpture depicting a railwayman, erected around the time the railway works was being closed down. Eastleigh is the truth of the arcadia Chris Huhne wants to save from 'urban sprawl'. If Eastleigh has a history, it's made up of grids, planning, towns appearing out of nowhere, industrialization and infrastructure, closely linked to the metropolis to the point of originally being inhabited by Londoners—but with its renamings and pseudo-Victorian architecture it tries to rewrite itself into a quaint little town, which it never actually was. The Solent City is nearer to the historical reality of this place than the bizarre village fantasies of Benny Hill Close.

Eastern Dock

Like the abortive Solent City, Southampton itself has two centres, or a centre and an ex-centre. The ex-centre is where you could almost believe that you were in a great port city rather than a failed, dead yachting and shopping town. It is centred on two ex-places: the former Southampton Terminus, closed by infamous 1960s Conservative rationalizer Dr Richard Beeching, and the Eastern Docks, where the Titanic set sail in 1912. Heritage Southampton is entirely obsessed with the Titanic, not for any good reason, but because it's famous. The recently elected Tory Council had planned to sell off part of what is the City Art Gallery collection, one of the finest in non-metropolitan Britain, for the sake of creating a Titanic Museum in a 'cultural quarter' by the Civic Centre. Plans were laid to flog parts of a collection that features Picasso, Rodin, Blake, Flemish masters and Vorticists, Op Artists and Renaissance altarpieces, in favour of yet another attempt to drag tourists kicking and screaming to an increasingly provincial town. Thankfully, the council were (perhaps temporarily) deterred by a public campaign and a petition, which, while failing to sway the local press, found wide support outside of Southampton and among the city's usually quiet intelligentsia. The planned Titanic Museum will still go ahead, using what are darkly described as 'alternative sources' of funding.

There is in fact a permanent exhibition about the Titanic in the Maritime Museum by the Eastern Docks. However, that's in the ex-centre. The Civic Centre is far nearer to the WestQuay uber-mall and the Western Docks. The new Heritage Museum will include an Interactive Model of the Titanic, while the building entails a glass extension and remodelling of one wing of the 1930s Civic Centre, to be designed by award-winning regeneration engineers Wilkinson Eyre. It'll also be the first time—after a housing scheme by Richard Rogers was recently rejected—that an architect of any note has built in the city (as opposed to its University) since the 1960s. The 'cultural district', a belated sop to something other than mammon in a city that is otherwise cravenly devoted to it, is planned to include a 'mixed use' block by once famous 1980s postmodernists CZWG, but so far the only part of the area where building has actually taken place involves the replacement of an international style block of the 1960s with an international style block of the 2000s, in an act of astounding pointlessness. The redevelopment of the (listed) interwar Civic Centre has annoyed the traditionalist likes of *Private Eye*'s 'Nooks and Corners' column, but as this stripped classical complex is already functionally little more than a roundabout flanked by offices and malls worthy of a business park in Fareham, the damage was done a long time ago. The suspicion that Wilkinson Eyre were hired because the councillors had seen their Mary Rose Museum in Portsmouth, rather than for the work they had produced elsewhere, is inescapable. No other towns really exist.

South Western Hotel

But get someone to drop you off at the old Terminus blind-folded, take off the blindfold, look around, and you could believe you were Somewhere. There's a lush square ringed by stylish bow-windowed terraces, some Gin Palace-like Art Nouveau hotels, the handsome former station and, oddest of all, the South Western Hotel. Now—obviously—luxury flats, this was The Hotel Where The Titanic's Passengers Stayed, a wonderfully ridiculous high-Victorian confection that would look at home in South Kensington. More interesting is the block adjacent, a 1920s extension of the hotel. It's a freakish anomaly in the city, an example of hard *Grosstadtarchitektur*, eight storeys, minimal clas-sical ornament: perhaps inspiration was taken from the thousands of New Yorkers who must have stayed here.

According entirely with the 'Manhattanism' described by the Dutch architect Rem Koolhaas in his book *Delirious New York*, the South Western Hotel is an example of the 'culture of conges-tion', irrespective of its serene 1920s façade. Its skyline is never quite clean or precise, due to a series of accretions—first the 1870s hotel given its dramatic 1920s extension, then some more utilitar-ian extra storeys added during its successive uses as the local BBC headquarters between the 1960s and the 1990s, and its subsequent use as luxury flats, all creating an illegible jumble. Even on the Portland stone front of the 1920s extension, one corner abandons the classical symmetry, going off in its own utilitarian direction, leading to the seedy stock brick of the sides facing the train shed. It's as if the metropolitan skyline the city otherwise lacked were incarnated solely in this building, dominating everything around it, especially from the raised vantage point of the 1970s Itchen Bridge. The South Western Hotel introduces into Southampton a robust urban scale that is replicated nowhere else in the town, with nothing taller (bar the Civic Centre clock tower) built for half a century. Its environs are one of the few places where you can get some idea of what the first skyscrapers might have been like, in that the two-storey surroundings are dominated by something four times their height, and nothing has really attempted to follow it in the immediate area, so it still suggests an imminent departure for somewhere more exciting, frozen in time. If the Terminus Station were reopened, then the city's centre of gravity would be shifted from a gigantic retail park to a disparate, complex city, near to the depressed council estates of Northam, St Mary's and Holy Rood, the (small but quite lovely) walled town, and some attempts at civic architecture courtesy of Cunard, White Star and the South-Western Railway. The station is now a casino.

The Titanic ought to be a bitter, painful memory for Southampton, because most of the crew—those who weren't allowed into the lifeboats—were from the town, and most of them were from the slums of Northam. Their pay was cancelled immediately, and White Star gave no benefits or compensation, giving a clue as to why this Hampshire town became stridently red after World War One: a sudden shocking realization that, regardless of all that King and Country nonsense, the ruling class *doesn't care about you*, a shock which has since dissipated into aiming to join the ruling class (think of the way early 2000s slick soulboy Craig David, hailing from the Holy Rood council estate, used to refer to himself in the third person, talking about himself as 'Craig David the Brand'). Instead, this mass death is something we revel in, because it reminds us of Kate Winslet posing nude for Leonardo DiCaprio, or our heroes embracing atop the ship's stern while Céline Dion warbles in the background. The Isle of Wight ferries depart from here, and were the focus of solidarity actions with the Vestas wind turbine factory occupation on the Island in 2009, a reminder that the city is not as defeated as it may first appear. The wonderfully silly Edwardian dock building adjacent is now Maxim's Casino.

The area around the former eastern docks and the former Terminus is where most new residential development is concentrated. New Southampton looks much the same as New Everywhere Else, with the proviso that it took them a little while longer to cotton onto the pseudomodernist turn, so pitched roofs and 'decorative' banded brickwork continued here for longer than in other cities. It includes the 'French Quarter' (Southampton is lucky enough to have only one 'Quarter', aside from the aforementioned and as yet unbuilt Cultural Quarter), which contains a 'Property Café'. Near to all this is a fifty-year-old attempt to design a new city district, the Holy Rood estate, designed to replace a slum bombed during World War Two. Designed by Lyons Israel Ellis, it has always seemed the poor relation to their later masterpiece, Wyndham Court.

By comparison, Holy Rood is a much more straightforward scattering of low and medium-rise Modernist blocks, using the soft-Brutalist vernacular of stock-brick and concrete. The interesting things about it come from the layout rather than the

Holy Rood Estate

aesthetic, which is robust but not tectonically exciting. You pass under buildings, through courtyards and gardens. (You can't drink there, as signs point out.) At one end, a piece of public art, an abstracted steel seaman carrying a ship, manages to be surprisingly good, providing a signpost for the place which doesn't make it look institutional without going for the usual alternative of being brightly patronizing. The effects of aerial bombardment are visible on practically every corner round here, if you look hard enough, but Holy Rood Church is the most eloquent statement of it, a bombed-out church which was left in its ruined state as a memorial to the Merchant Navy. It has become a generalized memorial space, so there is a plaque dedicated to the dead of the Falklands War (rather grotesquely putting this dirty little war on the same level as the fight against Nazi Germany) as well as an earlier memorial to the Titanic.

Near here is the original Eastern Dock, the one from which the Titanic (and all the other ships that didn't sink) sailed, the place to where Cunard and White Star moved their offices from Liverpool. In the 1980s the dock was transformed into 'Ocean Village', a combined marina, business park and leisure complex. The name itself implies what was supposed to happen to this area of the city. I tend to think that a place which builds something like the South Western Hotel, or Wyndham Court, or even the 1930s Civic Centre, is not a village, nor even a town, but a city. Evidently the City Council disagreed. The Art Deco Ocean Terminal was flattened to build Ocean Village, and the most recent building here is a car park in neo-deco style, as if in some kind of act of repentance. Surrounding it are the local bank HQs, all designed in a business-park style that is a fine reminder of why the period between the late 1970s and the 1990s is currently as much loathed by architectural fashion as the 1940s to 1960s period was previously, aside from mere knee-jerk reaction. What is so depressing about this place is the way that the formal return of decoration, and the use of traditional materials and pitched roofs that was then called 'vernacular', is paralleled by an alienating, anti-pedestrian approach to planning inherited from Modernism's worst aspects. It is basically a series of surface car parks with buildings in between, rather than vice versa. All the jollity, the stained glass, the patterns and the pediments appear as pathetic attempts to distract the driver or pedestrian from the alienating newness of the landscape. I do have some good memories of this place in its form as a leisure complex, I'll admit, and I find the Postmodernism of spectacle and geegaws somewhat preferable to that of vernacular, of Poundbury and woolly recreations of an imagined past—the Trocadero over New Urbanism.

The sole surviving dock building here used to lead into 'Canute's Pavilion', a tacky mirror-glass mall which featured such joys as a humorous T-shirt shop, Edwardian arcade games and ice cream parlours. It also had a shop which sold nautical tat of various sorts, including a piece of coral onto which I fell as a child, gashing my arm and bleeding all over the ornaments for sale. Later, in the mid 1990s, the city council sponsored the building of an art house cinema, the Harbour Lights. It was a visual triumph, a dynamic little building that is quite possibly the only thing of any architectural worth built here between 1969 and 2009, and which made life here as a teenager much better than it would otherwise have been. After only around fifteen years of existence, Canute's Pavilion was demolished. In its place is one of the few attempts here at the Urban Renaissance manner: two blocks, restaurants on the ground floor, three more shelved by the recession but masked by the ads, big meaningless bit of Public Art (a stern! Who knew?) in the middle, and preservation of the disused public transport tracks as ornaments.

The pornography of property is plastered across the building site. What sort of luxury is this, which seems predicated on the occupants of the flats being so permanently exhausted by their work that they need be infantilized, that they need to relax and be *indulged* in these secluded, ostentatiously calm places? Not to mention the question of what sort of luxury involves such minuscule proportions and such mean materials. Yet compared with the woeful vernacular architecture of the rest of the marina, I have to confess to feeling thankful that this at least resembles city

Property propaganda, Ocean Village

architecture, and admit to preferring that central Southampton resemble aspirational, yuppified Leeds or Manchester than upper-crust Havant or Bursledon. This is one of the few ways in which Blairism is marginally, if almost imperceptibly preferable to its more straightforward precursor, Thatcherism. There is, however, no sense here of the freedoms of a city, while the marketing, based on exclusivity and seclusion, implies that these are suburbs in the guise of inner cities, as Jonathan Meades claims. That even the Urban Renaissance redesign of Ocean Village won't stick in somewhere as doggedly suburban as south-east England is indicated by the unfinished nature of this already cheap project. But Southampton's hold on urbanity is light, indefinite. It is liable to crumble at a touch.

Western Dock

The port is divided into leisure and utility. On the one hand you have the cruise ships, on the other containers, with nothing much (save the Isle of Wight ferry) between luxury and automation. I flick through the local *Daily Echo* and find that soon Southampton will briefly be home to the gargantuan Celebrity Eclipse, 'a twenty-first century, 122,000-ton engineering marvel'—built of course in Germany rather than the defunct Soton shipyards and boasting, among other features, a golf course on its roof. Another cruise ship, in port on the day we took some of these pictures, apparently features a dining room where the tables and chairs are made from ice—you are recommended to wear warm clothing. These floating Dubais, placeless and opulent, transport the cruiser through (literally) nowhere. The other sort of ship is attended to largely by the 'robots', colossal semi-automated cranes, with their additional skeleton crew of bored humans.

You can see the cranes in the distance from Mayflower Park, a windswept public space laid out in the 1960s by the City Architects' Department that is (officially) the only publicly accessible stretch of the harbour. Pre-financial crisis, it was the mooted location for Avery Associates' Spitfire Wing, an observation tower intended to mimic the aerodynamic form of the plane designed in the city, the only proposal for the waterfront to conjure the 'Bilbao Effect'—or as the *Echo* calls it, 'the wow factor'—though it seemed a fairly transparent attempt at one-upmanship with Portsmouth's Spinnaker Tower. An article in the same paper in October 2008 claimed that it had been replaced by the 'woe factor', as almost all the new projects that had been announced or had received planning permission were cancelled or shelved. Since then, a couple have limped their way to completion, presumably representing 'green shoots'. In response to all this, Tory

Mayflower Park

council leader Royston Smith commented that 'Southampton's golden age will just have to be put back a couple of years'.[15] In Mayflower Park, the wait for the golden age entails the no doubt temporary survival of some strange and beautiful artefacts—two shelters by Leon Berger in rubble stone with jagged concrete roofs, a tribute to Frank Lloyd Wright, which seem an efficient shelter for the cider-drinking youth that gather there.

My dad often took me, my brother and sister to Mayflower Park, to enjoy its now demolished playground, which included a concrete maze, aptly enough. Being a child of the eighties I was fairly obsessed with robots, specifically *Transformers*. Mum likes to tell the story about me coming home from nursery school claiming we'd been told about 'this robot called God' (well, how else to explain it?), and on Mayflower Park I would dream of robots in disguise. I was missing a trick, as they were a few yards from the park, in the containerized Western Dock. This vast dock complex was built in the 1930s on reclaimed land, to take the ever-more ginormous cruise ships of the era such as the Queen Mary. In the 1980s its vastness meant that, unlike Liverpool or London, it could accommodate containerization with ease. It's also damn hard to see, at least from the Southampton side of the River Test, because you're not *meant* to see it. It's an incredible sight, but it's never going to be on Southampton City Council's Heritage

Ships seen from Mayflower Park

itinerary—and unless you have a pass, you won't ever see it up close. The cranes induce the morbid thrill of seeing our replacements.

The difficulty in seeing the port should not surprise overmuch, as for all the drastic changes in port cities over the last few decades, docks were always heavily guarded places. The London Docks used to have a gigantic wall to keep out those not on business, a barrier which now exists in a less tangible form in the financial district of Docklands. In Southampton the exclusion is yet more subtle in that although the docks seem to have little effect on the town, they still exist, and are (or rather were until the crash) thriving. I went to the city's main comprehensive school, and *nobody* I knew had parents who worked on the docks. More often, their parents' jobs derived from the service industry in the centre, or from the Russell Group university in the suburban north. Yet beginning at the centre of town and straggling its way along the inner-city district of Freemantle, past Millbrook and ending at the edge of the New Forest, is the major cruise port and the second largest container port in Britain. Its success, size and centrality are matched only by its invisibility.

There are few places where you can gain any sense of it, let alone at its full scale, unless you're lucky enough to have a tower block flat in Millbrook, Shirley or Redbridge. You could look from the other side of Southampton Water (I've never done so—there be dragons) or, more interestingly, there is a bridge and a pathway which begins at Millbrook Railway Station. This is itself a strange remnant, one of those stations which receive about one train an hour that miraculously survived the Beeching Axe. Were you walking from my Mum's house in Freemantle, you could see the container port start to rise above the terraces and flats, its arcing cranes softened by the winter light. The cruel scale and drama of the cranes make everything around seem petty.

As you walk through Freemantle towards the docks, past the recently closed British American Tobacco Factory, they loom incongruously above the terraces, steel arms hovering derisively over Salt & Battery Fish & Chips. The disassociation of industry and architecture after Modernism is spectacularly visible along the Western Docks, as most of the architecture built after the container port was established in 1969 is in the vernacular. Looking out onto the industrial cyber-architecture of the port, the flats and houses are utterly absurd, architecture placing its hands over its ears and eyes. Nothing has even attempted to exploit the drama of this place, which is again unsurprising, I suppose, as container ports are not seen as part of the city itself. Mostly they stand in out-of-the-way places like Felixstowe or Tilbury, rather than near the centre of medieval cities. So, there is only one way. You climb up the frighteningly unstable-seeming motorway bridge which leads to Millbrook station, and from here, equipped with zoom lens and/or binoculars, the port reveals itself at nearly its full extent. The neglect of the place is clear enough from the foliage that has draped itself around the concrete and steel of the station bridges, a mutant nature which is particularly virulent round here.

Walter Benjamin differentiated Communist Constructivist aesthetics from Fascist Futurist aestheticism by pointing out that the latter were merely interested in the *look* of technology, and had little interest in finding out how it worked, in mastering and applying it—it was instead a subject for a kind of technological nature painting. I don't know how this port complex works, but I find it almost convulsively beautiful. Although my intent here is to

DP World Southampton, from Millbrook Station

examine what happens to a place when something like this is in its midst, it is important to work out how the port functions, to explain the networks of trade and power that keep it going. Here I can offer some minimal information, but not much else. Southampton Container Port is officially known as 'DP World Southampton'. It is 51 per cent owned by DP World, which is itself owned by Dubai World, the insolvent state-run conglomerate. The other 49 per cent is owned by Associated British Ports, denationalized in the early 1980s and now largely owned by Goldman Sachs. That these institutions would have little interest in Southampton itself is again deeply unsurprising. Dubai World rationalized the port still further throughout the 2000s, introducing more automation and decimating the already tiny workforce. Their unimportance to the operation can be gleaned from the several industrial accidents at the container port over the last couple of years. In July 2009 one worker's legs were crushed by a crane, and in March 2010 a 200ft crane collapsed, narrowly avoiding claiming any further victims.[16]

Rather than being introduced in one confrontational Thatcherite stroke, containerization and the destruction of Southampton dock labour was gradual, until after a few decades robots practically outnumbered dockers. How to respond to these cranes, then— these complex, almost autonomous creatures, operated (or not) by something fleshy in their interior? How could we possibly have fought them? They promise a true liberation from work, one of the most visible pieces of evidence for the genuine possibility of an automated labour replacing us and letting us fish in the afternoon, philosophize in the evening and so forth. Yet instead servile service industry work replicated—needlessly, pointlessly—the old structure of forty hours (plus) a week and a pay cheque, this time with fewer rights, less bargaining power. How could *we* have used the robots?

We might at least have done something more interesting with them than this. The port transports cars, it transports consumer goods manufactured in the Special Economic Zones of the People's Republic of China, and it piles up waste and scrap;

the literal embodiment of an overwhelming sense of waste, both political and actual. The port is one of the main importers of cars into the UK, and it transports some of the few made here out of the country—the Ford Transit, made in the north of the city in a factory threatened with closure throughout 2009, and whose workers took industrial action in sympathy with the Visteon–Ford occupiers in Enfield and Ireland. These views of the car port half empty may be a portent of the obsolescence of that particular form of locomotion, which looks rather antiquated when seen as a component part of this triumph of blank, rectilinear automation—the freight trains seem to slot into it far more neatly. But we cheated here by taking photographs soon after Christmas 2009, in what was no doubt a fallow period even by the standards of the deepest recession in British history. Assembled together according to type, they looked surreal, Lilliputian: three red cars all in a line, waiting to be transported around the country.

Walking down the steps of Millbrook Station's railway bridge brings you to the passageway. It's incredibly thin and overgrown, and it continues for around a mile to the Central Station. This pathway has at one side the motorway which runs alongside the port, on the other the railway line, so it is bordered on each side by metal fences, topped with barbed wire on the port side. The view of the cruise ship Oriana, through the barbed wire or otherwise,

The Oriana

Cars at the container port

exemplifies how Southampton works rather neatly, with hidden, untouchable luxury amidst general meanness. The Oriana was built in Germany by P&O in the mid 1990s. Apparently, the original intention was to build it in the UK but no shipyard capable of such a feat survives … There's something rather comic about the contrast between the sleek Corbusian melodrama of a cruise ship and the self-effacing container ships. In the former, superfluous luxury is massive and bombastic; in the latter, a vast amount of consumer cargo is contained in a seemingly small, undramatic space. The path is not blocked off, so in principle this is a public

Modern warfare

right of way, and I've seen other people walking it—but there are pylons in its midst, which you could touch, were you to throw caution to the wind. Like everything else here, greenery takes over as much as it possibly can, creeping up the pylons themselves. Nearby, crows and robins are irritated to have their calm disturbed. *Call of Duty – Modern Warfare 2* is advertised across the road, and modern warriors depart for Iraq and Afghanistan from Marchwood, over Southampton Water.

In fact, this path used to be parkland, a green hinterland created between the 1930s docks and the Victorian housing, which implies that once this was considered a spectacle worth seeing. Halfway along the path the passageway is traversed by the motorway, in the form of a tight, oblique-angled overpass, leaving a triangular sheltered space. This space has some kind of lake inside it, a puddle deep enough to make it enormously unpleasant if one is not wearing wellingtons, as the mud and vague, indeterminate pollution coalesce into a viscous, soupy gloop. But here there is evidence that this passageway is enormously prized, at least by some—a series of planks have been laid across it, forming a precarious but usable bridge, as tentative and partial as the concrete bridge above it is solid and certain.

Outlaws Cru

Messages of some sort or another

The reason for all of this soon becomes clear. It has become a canvas for Southampton's graffiti artists. Tagging usually seems a drab micro-egotism, cliquey territorial pissing never aimed at the buildings that really deserve it—but here they've done something spectacular. Not by recourse to Banksy-style 'subversion', but seemingly from being in a secluded (though for the passing trains, extremely prominent) space, obscure enough and far enough from surveillance to be able to work on tags long enough to render them as lurid, jagged works of temporary art, blaring purples, greens and oranges. Dazzle painting.

It's magnificent, exhilarating, and the only aesthetic response of any sort to the area's extreme modernity—but like the cranes and containers it can't be enjoyed unambiguously. Each is a weird combination of glaringly visible and hermetic, neither really wants to communicate anything much, and both are expressions of disconnection, of adjacent places appearing to be in different worlds. It's a chaos of illegibility (which is no doubt dense with reference to the thirty or so people in the know), shout-outs to places in Lithuania and obscure portraits—and caveats aside, it's wonderful. At the head of it all are the words, clear this time, 'THE OUTLAWS CRU'. Big up The Outlaws Cru, whoever you are.

Boxes on boxes

Then another bridge, this time a rickety 1930s construction which once led from Freemantle to the docks, but now takes the lost pedestrian back to civilization of a sort. Around here you find bits of discarded clothing, and on the steps of the bridge, the single word 'HELP'. The signs of life are horribly unnerving. A pair of women's trousers, impaled on the spiked fences. A pair of unmatching shoes. They look like fragments from a rape, clues to a murder, something only accentuated by the sight of the containers just behind the trees. It can't get much more sinister than this, and accordingly the passageway opens out and begins to resemble somewhere you could walk a dog without being dumped in the bushes, or without worrying about encountering strange temporal phenomena. Here, the container port's cranes are no longer so visible, and the containers themselves take over—pile after pile after pile of them. Through the undergrowth a sign says 'City', and then the familiar city I know and love/hate comes into view— the ribbed-concrete tower of HSBC, the Brutalist stern of Wyndham Court, the clock tower of the Civic Centre on one side, and on the other the postmodernist horror show of the 'Pirelli site'.

Shedscape

Southampton presents itself as a puzzle. Every time I go back I ask myself, 'How did this happen?' How did this city, by all accounts once the undisputed regional capital, get to the point where an entire stretch of its centre, as large as a small town, was given over to a gigantic retail park? How is it that this, the sixteenth largest city in the country, has the third highest level of violent crime and the third worst exam results, despite being at the centre of one of the country's most affluent counties? And does any of this have anything to do with the fact that the city contains what was, when built, the largest urban mall in Britain?

In simple policy terms, these questions are easy enough to answer, and were extensively discussed by George Monbiot in *Captive State*. A large industrial site on reclaimed land became 'open for development' in the 1990s. The Labour council decided to designate it as a retail area at the same time as the rival inner-city retail centre of St Mary's was 'regenerated' out of recognition, its shops demolished and its covered market torn down, leaving little more than a scattering of introverted student flats (in the vernacular, naturally). As this site was already easily accessed from the M27, the result is that the extremely affluent surrounding areas can get into the shopping malls easily and quickly, where they will

Mountbatten Retail Park

find abundant parking space. Jobs For Local People are no doubt the stated aim, and the alibi for extremely profitable land deals. The result is a city devoid of any palpable civic pride, with a series of chain pubs where shops used to be, competing to sell the cheapest pints. I know how and why this all happened, but there's more to this city, elements to it which suggest different things could have happened and indeed could still do so.

Leaving the deeply unprepossessing Southampton Central Station on its southern entrance, you can see the containers already, next to the grimy sheds of the Mountbatten Retail Park. The most immediately noticeable urban artefacts are the hotels. Hotels are, in my experience, the most reliably awful examples of British architecture built in the last thirty years, closely followed by the similar typology of Halls of Residence. Is this to do with some kind of national aversion to the concept of hospitality? Do their developers worry that architecture might deter custom? Or are they just unbelievably tight-fisted? This particular cluster of hotels was lucky enough to receive a specific denunciation from the hilarious, depressing weblog *Bad British Architecture*—a Novotel and an Ibis, similarly lumpen and blocky, aptly described by the blog's writer the 'Ghost of Nairn' as 'simply incompetent building, let alone design'. Its astounding crapness makes you wonder if there is a deliberate policy of discouraging cruise passengers from actually staying in the city. Across the road from them a Police Operational Command Unit is being erected to designs by multinational giants of shit Broadway Malyan. The site currently consists of a concrete frame and some brickwork, presumably to be In Keeping with something or other. There's an onsite Christmas tree. This seasonal jollity is not continued by the police advertisements outside the station itself, which are all, rather staggeringly, about knives and knife crime, presenting those driving in from the M27 with another reason to avoid venturing any further than the malls.

The major dockside building is the Solent Flour Mills, which, remarkably enough, is still working. Equally remarkably, there have to my knowledge been no proposals to turn it into a lottery-

Solent Flour Mills

funded art gallery. It's absolutely huge, and of course inaccessible to the public. The dock gates were built around the same time in the early 1930s. The clocks have all had their hands removed. The most salient thing about industrial architecture after Fordism, the old form of industrial organization based on centralization, high wages, collective bargaining and intensive, linear mass production, is the changeover from an architecture of light to an architecture of windowless enclosure. The Solent Mills are a fine example of a Fordist 'daylight factory', notable as much for expanses of glass as for expanses of brick. Conversely, post-

Ford showrooms, Shirley

Fordist industry (there *is* such a thing—the presumption that post-Fordist automatically equals post-industrial is seldom correct) is marked by sheds without glass, where the ideology of transparency is transferred to financial capital and its shiny office blocks. Even Ford's own Transit works in the suburbs are windowless, a 1990s steel box looming over the top-lit earlier factory buildings. The de-industrialization of Southampton (which happened in train with the intensified automation of the container port) means that there are few windowless industrial sheds in the centre of town. There are, however, windowless leisure sheds.

The biggest of these is Leisure World, an 'adaptive reuse' of a former automated warehouse that in the late 1990s was transformed into a gigantic shed of entertainment: nightclubs, chain restaurants, and a multiplex, with lots and lots of car parking. The entrance is framed on one side by a casino, one of several in the centre, presumably intended for the cruise passengers; and on the other by 'Quayside', a simulacrum Victorian pub for an area which was under water in the Victorian era. The car park of Leisure World is one of the few places where certain of the dock's architectural features reveal themselves—the cyclopean scale of the Flour Mills, for one, and for another, the pathetic tin canopy of the City Cruise Terminal. I spent much time walking round

Leisure World

Quayside Pub

said car park with a camera, where I saw among other things that the nightclubs—formerly Ikon and Diva—are now called 'Reykjavik Icehouse' and 'New York Disco', perhaps in some partial memory of the thousands of New Yorkers who passed through this city in the first half of the last century. You will note the lack of photographs of any of these things. As I take a picture of the wavy roof of Ikea from behind the Leisure Container, a voice from behind me says 'What do you think you're doing?' I get out my NUJ Press Pass, which says on the back that the Police

Castle House vs the De Vere

39

Federation recognizes me as a 'bona fide news gatherer'. 'That's nice,' he says when I get out the card. 'But have you got permission?' 'What, to take photos in a car park?' 'This is private property. You have to have permission.' He then makes me delete the photographs I took in the car park from the digital camera, one by one, before I am allowed out onto the 'street'.

Except there is no street here. This whole gigantic site is designed solely for the car, so my being a pedestrian is already suspicious, impeccably white and well-spoken though I may be. There are two recent buildings as part of this spreading mass of shed: one for Ikea, which includes some public art on the wooden spirals of its car park; and another for cruise operator Carnival, which, with its high-tech cribbings, is almost a work of architecture, although not a work of *urban* architecture—it's another business park building that is, somehow, literally yards from a medieval walled town. Similarly un-shed-like is the 1994 De Vere Grand Harbour Hotel ('a shit-brown postmodern Brunswick Centre with a big glass pyramid fucked into it', says *Bad British Architecture*, marvellously[17]). I've long thought this a risible, ridiculous building, but somehow in the context of blank, deathly sheds it seems to have at least some ambition, some statement of place and clumsy grandeur—and surely better a failed, ridiculous grandiosity than the utterly grim utilitarianism of the other city hotels. Behind the De Vere is a different conception of civic grandiosity, Eric Lyons's Castle House. Better known for his private housing, Lyons designed here a powerful council tower block, detailed precisely in stone, concrete and wood. On the last of the walks where these photos were taken, it was being reclad with green glass and UPVC, a material which housing expert Sam Webb claimed had proven to be lethal in tower blocks at the Lakanal House fire in Camberwell.[18] Regardless, it's the cheapest and easiest way to dress a tower, whether a former president of the RIBA designed it or not. The assumption seems to be that its original fabric is automatically worthless, irrespective of it being considered 'the finest tower in the south' as late as the 1980s.[19]

WestQuay hinterland

But this is all really just leading up to Building Design Partnership's enormous WestQuay mega-mall, the main occupant of the former Pirelli site. I've often avoided it gingerly, taken routes that circumvent it. I don't like it, obviously, but the language that is used to attack it is remarkably similar to that which is used to attack some of the architecture I love. It's out of scale, it's too monumental, it's fortress-like, it's Not In Keeping, it leads to abrupt and shocking contrasts, it's too clean and too shiny ... well, yes. At one point it bridges the street, next to a line of Regency Terraces, and is full of arch contempt for that which precedes it, irrespective of an attempt to 'respond' to the terrace's scale through an industrial, lightly brick-clad wall, with storage ever so slightly legible as its function. The shopping mall has a suppressed dreamlife, from the socialist politics of its 'inventor', the Viennese architect Victor Gruen, to Walter Benjamin's conception of the shopping arcade as the house of the dreaming collective. BDP, the architects of this and many, many other recent British buildings, have their own socialist past. They began as a co-operative founded by George Grenfell Baines, an architect of Lancastrian working-class extraction, to unite architects, engineers, sociologists, in a non-hierarchical Partnership which could sidestep the hoary old myth of the autonomous architect (that they became a normal private company in 1997, of all years, seems apt). The mall derives from an attempt to recreate social spaces, to become a socialist-inflected social condenser in the context of consumer capitalism. If we condemn the malls without being very careful about how we go about it, we line up with the likes of Paul Kingsnorth, those who care more for the destruction of village shops than the collapse of industrial civilization.

I still hate it. Some of my friends helped build it, you know. Indulging in a bit of manual labour to save up money for their gap years. The first time I ever went to WestQuay I was shocked by it, not least because of the fact it coincided with the destruction of St Mary's Street—and in their Waterstone's I found a copy of the Monbiot book which has a chapter on this very topic. I read the entire chapter in there as a minor, piffling protest. Before WestQuay there was Colonel Seifert's Arundel Towers—two office blocks surmounting a car park, a slide of which I have been known to use as illustration in discussion of the destruction of modernism in Britain. I remember it faintly; the strangeness and intrigue of its multiple levels and the Dog and Duck pub more than the twin towers. The break with Arundel Towers' approach to urbanism was hardly total.

In terms of how it interacts with the landscape, WestQuay is as aggressive and forthright as any 1960s public building. It incorporates a deep slope, multiple levels and entry points, and two major walkways bridging the roads that the developers couldn't obliterate. Unlike some of its postwar precursors, such as Castle Market in Sheffield (of which more later), there's no pleasure for the walker in traversing all these different ways of getting from A to B. This isn't merely because the earlier building is picturesquely lived-in and dilapidated, but because it's not seamless: you feel the movement from one place to another, you are able to enjoy it in some manner, and the spaces contain places where you could stop and think rather than be induced to consume at every possible moment. But it is a remarkably complex building, including within itself a deceptively small street façade to Above Bar, the high street it destroyed, a glazed viewing area as part of the food court, and a John Lewis store reached via (internal, hardly

WestQuay car parks

palpable) walkways. Inside is what the mall's website describes as a 'focal point', a descendant of Gruen's 'social' spaces, where the lifts and escalators are all clustered, giving a frictionless impression of constant movement. The gestures at contextualism are present, correct and pathetic. At the end which faces the Medieval Walls, the architects have given it a complimentary and functionless watchtower, and the shiny, plasticky cladding is infilled with rubble to be In Keeping (something which was also employed by Leon Berger in his tower blocks at St Mary's and Shirley). This rubble is mostly at ground-floor level, where it is part of sloping

WestQuay's social condenser

walls, thick enough to withstand a blast or a ram-raid. It has a symbolic function quite aside from the pomo 'reference' to the medieval wall: to deter anyone who ought not to be here.

What makes it particularly malign is what happens at the back. Behind the walls and behind Above Bar is a large patch of wasteland[20] and WestQuay's service areas, which take up a massive amount of urban space. They are made up mostly of multi-storey car parks, but also of the series of retail parks that accompanied the main mall—three of them, all themselves with attendant massive car parks. Needless to say, this is not a nice place to walk around. The entire area, a mile or more, is simply not for pedestrians. Although this might be expected on the Kentish hinterland of the M25, it bears repeating that this is right in the centre of a city, in an era when government white papers have endlessly rambled on about the walkable city. This centrality is part of its justification: it keeps people in the city. But the economy is exactly that of an out-of-town mall: reached by car, actively discouraging leaving the malls and venturing into the city around, uninterested in the possibilities of the city itself, and leaving the other side of town, the side that is not shopping mall, to rot. One upshot of this is the weekend violence along Above Bar, another is the continuing disintegration of St Mary's. But service industry jobs were indeed duly created.

WestQuay does *make an effort* in certain respects, and this effort makes it all the more tragic. You can promenade around it, as you can along the city walls. Yet there's a spectacular incoherence to it all. Each part seems disconnected to the other, aside from the wipe-clean white cladding, and it's never pulled together through any design idea of any sort because it's simply impossible to do so. You simply can't make a building like this into something legible unless the architects are exceptionally talented and/or conscientious (apologies to all at BDP for the implication that they may be neither). We can see here how over the last decade a Modernism of a sort has continued, not as a coherent ideology, an aesthetic or a formal language which embraces and intensifies the experience of modernity, but via the element of it lamented by

Marchwood Incinerator

urbanists and sentimentalists since the 1920s. This is a landscape where the car is dominant, where the idea of streets, walking, any element of surprise, are comprehensively designed out. Conversely, the only way to rediscover some kind of element of excitement in these spaces is to walk around (not inside) them, precisely because the planning itself does not want you to. You see things. You don't see people, but you see intriguing *things*, some sort of autonomous logic of commerce almost without leavening or prettification. (I say almost because some of the car parks are faced in brick, the vernacular of some language or other.) Like the Western docks, WestQuay is an inhuman space where capital no longer needs to present a human face, where it thinks nobody is looking.

What is appropriate about WestQuay, though, is the way in which it joins onto the container port almost imperceptibly. The roads in the Western Docks are called First, Second and Third Avenue. Follow them and you might reach the Millbrook Superbowl, where you can play that most American and blue-collar of sports, ten-pin bowling. Go back the other way along the approach to the M27, and the containers become an organizing principle. Stacks of containers full of goods on one side, stacks of containers full of people buying goods on the other, each in the form of coloured or corrugated boxes. The elegance of the principle is perfect and some enterprising post-Fordist is bound to combine the two sooner or later, completing the circle by transporting people in those boxes too, using them for transportation, shopping and living all at once. Sure, there are no windows in these things, but put in a few branches of Costa and nobody will complain. Then, untouched by human hands, the containers could be dropped in Dubai or Shenzen, the cruise ships of the twenty-first century. Just across the water from this container city is a gigantic incinerator, designed by Jean-Robert Mazaud. A perfect dome, not Rogers's deflated tent, silvery steel, not Teflon. It turns rubbish into electricity, and it shines with sinister optimism.

Chapter Two

Milton Keynes:
Buckinghamshire Alphaville

Milton. Keynes. Surely it's partly the name that explains why this
is the most famous and/or notorious of the several New Towns
designated and built by the Labour governments of Clement
Attlee and Harold Wilson. Combining John Milton, poet of the
English Revolution and of Paradises Lost and Regained, with
John Maynard Keynes, the reformist economist who helped prevent a second revolution, it marries epic national poetry with
careful reformism: the perfect Old Labour combination. Alterna-
tively, it conflates Keynes and Milton Friedman, respectively the
economists of the postwar consensus and of the post-1979 apothe-
osis of capitalism now collapsing around our ears. This seems
highly appropriate given that Milton Keynes, a pet project of
the Harold Wilson administration, was largely realized under
Margaret Thatcher and hence became known as Britain's token
'successful' new town, its charms (principally, its shopping mall)
advertised on television right through the 1980s. It's a crushing
disappointment to learn that the name just comes from one of the
villages incorporated into this town—or rather this 'non-place
urban realm', being the term (borrowed from the American soci-
ologist Melvin J. Webber) that the planners used to describe the
dispersed, indeterminate motorcity they were creating. In its
privileging of the car and relative lack of council housing, with the
government eventually laying out little more than the intricate,
almost traffic-light-free roads, Milton Keynes is Non-Plan

Milton Keynes Central Station

actualized, managing to keep elements both of its utopian promises and its bland, kitsch Thatcherite reality.

A New Career in a New Town

In 2007, perhaps not coincidentally the year that Milton Keynes celebrated its fortieth anniversary, Gordon Brown's government announced that ten 'eco-towns' would be built on various sites across Britain. These towns were to have been sponsored by state largesse, but developed by institutions ranging from the Co-Operative Society to Tesco—PFI cities, if you will. Settlements of around 50,000 people, apparently designed to be self-sufficient and 'carbon neutral'—nowhere near as ambitious as a Milton Keynes, but nonetheless a resurrection of an Old Labour idea that English middle-class common sense had dumped in the 'failed' category. Protests ensued almost immediately in practically all of the areas that were slated to have an eco-town next door, fronted by a motley selection of local celebrity leaders ranging from Judi Dench to Tim Henman's dad. There's little doubt that eco-towns were more about property speculation than they were a product of ecological enthusiasm, and there was much justified criticism that these were disguised commuter suburbs, with no infrastructure and no industry—just as Basildon or East Kilbride eventually were. Yet the opposition seemed driven more by hatred of the idea of city-dwellers ruining what Clive Aslet, ex-editor of *Country Life*, recently called (on the subject of Milton Keynes) '22,000 acres of formerly good hunting land'." As if on cue, at a protest in front of Parliament some held up placards declaring that these eco-towns were mere 'New Towns'. Apparently, we all know what that means—towns full of 'eyesores', concrete cows and unsightly proletarians, bereft of the 'heritage' that so obsesses the British psyche. It became clear that these people hated the very *idea* of new towns, of any dispersal of people across what is, in terms of space, if not population, still an overwhelmingly green country.

A couple of years and a property crash combined with the part-nationalization of the banking system later, it's all rather beside the point, as new housing that would have sold for absurd sums only six months ago now sits empty—and under the coalition government, it's unlikely any of the eco-towns will be built. Even given the justifiable reasons for hostility to the eco-towns, there's something rather sad about the opposition to them. In essence, the conviction is that any new town which stressed its 'newness' would necessarily be 'soulless', or 'ugly'. It's notable that the only major new town begun since the late 1960s is Prince Charles's pet project, Poundbury, while the stealth new town of Cambourne in Cambridge's 'Silicon Fen' is similarly *retardataire*. Poundbury's planner, Leon Krier, is an apologist for the Nazi architect and politician Albert Speer, whose pompous classical edifices would, if Hitler had won the war, have transformed Berlin from a modern metropolis into the neoclassical showpiece 'Germania'. Speer wanted to design new buildings that somehow didn't look new, with their eventual ruinous state centuries hence factored into the design—a 'theory of ruin value' that has been embraced in Prince Charles's new town, where buildings are apparently pre-distressed to give them an old, distinguished appearance, and where any technological innovation post-1780 is (at least officially) *verboten*.

There's a long history of these places, of course. The eigh-teenth century produced model towns as diverse as Tunbridge Wells and Bath, all based on vistas, clean lines and an urban repre-sentation of scientific and mathematical concepts. Yet most were new towns for the rich, those who could afford the new spaces' light, air and openness. The late nineteenth century saw contrite industrialists plan ideal settlements like Saltaire or Bourneville; and between the 1900s and the 1920s Ebenezer Howard, a very late-Victorian combination of crank and pragmatist, pioneered the garden cities of Letchworth and Welwyn. Yet when people talk about New Towns they don't mean the garden cities, which, like precursors to Poundbury, used antiquated materials and winding street patterns in order to simulate historical accident. Rather, they mean the postwar new towns. They mean concrete precincts and cows, glass shopping centres, flat-roofed houses and roundabouts. They mean Cumbernauld, with its central shopping centre that was an architectural *cause célèbre* for a few years and an 'eyesore' for decades more; they mean Crawley or Stevenage, towns which were intended to be self-sufficient but became just another part of the commuter belt.

With regard to the years since 1997, however, Milton Keynes has taken on some new meanings. This 'suburban city' that has yet to receive city status (when it applied, it was absurdly passed over in favour of Brighton and Hove, a place with no meaningful inde-pendence from London) is on the one hand, the opposite of professed urban policy. Unashamedly diffuse, the original plan for a non-place urban realm is implacably alien to the ideas of urban renaissance. The idea that social life would occur in piazzas and on the street was anathema—Milton Keynes doesn't have streets. Unlike the new areas of Southampton, there are real social spaces slotted into its relentless motorized grid. Yet with its acres of speculative housing and its economy of business, leisure and retail, Milton Keynes exemplifies the unspoken urban policy of expanding the suburbia of South-East England as whole acres of streets lie derelict further north. Plans for the town's expansion and urbanization have, though, faced major opposition. Things which are pejorative outside of 'MK'—suburbia, minimalism, underpasses, grids, motorways—are here defended trenchantly by various local campaign groups.

The first thing we (adoptive) Londoners noticed in Milton Keynes was space. Sheer, vast, windswept open space, which one could call desolate if that desolation wasn't evidently so popular with its users. This is helped by the striking planned vista that hits you when leaving the train. The 1982 station square designed by the architects of the Milton Keynes Development Corporation (Stuart Mosscrop, Derek Walker and Christopher Woodward[22]) is one of the most remarkable Modernist set-pieces in Britain, a bracing landscaped plaza flanked by three perfectly detailed Miesian blocks, with the old British Rail logo prominent. This is *Alphaville* in Buckinghamshire, and it's like a bucket of cold, fresh water in the face, initially shocking but sharply refreshing. Like the same architects' nearby mall, the relentless grids plugged into another grid suggest the mock-utopian Continuous Monument of the leftist Italian architects Superstudio, the grid behind all planned towns elevated into an advancing object that consumes the whole world. If it does follow in Superstudio's footsteps then it does it quietly, with skateboarding teenagers in the middle of it.

After passing through the plaza we have to learn, as in London's Barbican Centre, a new way of walking, using the black steel

Portes Cochères

portes cochères and the remarkably well-kept 'redway' underpasses rather than instinctively walking into the fast roads. Hailing as we do from cities with an exceedingly badly kept 1960s infrastructure (me from Southampton, Joel from Bradford) we're almost amazed to see *clean underpasses*, a little glimpse of what our home towns could have been like had anyone cared enough.

Quite soon after passing under the first redway, we are in the new hotel district, with most of the glass/wood/render blocks, such as Barratt Homes' characteristically named 'Vizion' (flats atop a Sainsbury's), displaying what will no doubt soon be known as 'early twenty-first century irregular windows'; but although the architecture is familiar, the landscape is not. The new buildings provide only a slight contrast to the Californian Postmodernism across the majestically named Midsummer Boulevard. Both forms would be at home in other 'enterprise zones' at the Americanized edge places, like Heathrow or the Great West Road. Here, though, they make more sense than does their rude irruption into historic cities like Southampton, leading to the feeling—which sticks with us throughout—that Milton Keynes is the only city in Britain to have made post-Fordism look pleasant. This is partly because of the remnants of the earlier era—when blandness threatens, the sci-fi side of the old new town reappears, as when

The new urban Milton Keynes 'Vizion'

The Point—the space age abides

the wonderfully clunky 1980s neo-Constructivism of the Point stares down the new blocks.

The End of the Space Age

In order to create these new hotels and blocks of flats, the unique spaces of this Social Democratic version of Los Angeles had to be vandalized first, with underpasses infilled and buildings built up to the road line that once backed away from it, leaving space that was unforgivably commercially unexploited. Those achingly elegant *portes cochères* are now under threat in the attempt to 'normalize' the city through density. The streets are still largely deserted and the 'vibrancy' has yet to arrive—the lack of it makes this non-city feel rather civilized. Even that gobsmacking Central Station square has been slated for filling in with more 'urban' blocks in the vein of those which have sprouted up everywhere from Portsmouth to Edinburgh during the boom, at the hands of drab International Style revivalists Allies & Morrison.

Meanwhile, in Stuart Mosscrop and Christopher Woodward's justly celebrated (although not by its owners, who are campaigning against a proposal to list it) Miesian mall, the spaciousness and ease of the city creates a weird serenity that feels a million miles from the rat-runs of the Arndales and Westfields. It was once a public right of way, this mall, open at all hours so that residents could walk through it at night, something clamped down upon in the allegedly 'libertarian' Thatcher-era (apt, though, in that she opened the building in the first place). This still doesn't feel like a mall, though—the public art isn't crass enough, the second-hand shops not sufficiently glitzy. It feels like a town centre, but a town centre in a mid-1970s science fiction film. Next to John Lewis, an enormous bouncy castle in the shape of a hen presides over the glass geometries, its cute atavism feeling oddly appropriate; a gigantic plastic fertility symbol under glass.

A walk to the newer shopping areas next door, such as GMW Architects' Midsummer Place, brings you to a more familiar space of wavy roofs and cramped circulation. Grim normality seems momentarily to have won out, but walking from there to the new 'Theatre District', the quiet spaciousness reasserts itself—an art gallery and a theatre, a Californian cube and a crisp piece of mild Modernism respectively, both designed by Blonski Heard, and both of which have a markedly more interesting programme than one might expect in a town of this size (no Jim Davidson tours in evidence). Their new spaces are used, and the gaping openness at the front of the theatre and the tiny, elegant box of the gallery are

The Hen presides over the Shopping Centre

Milton Keynes Theatre

apparently the setting for impressive *schmutter* on a weekend. This ability to utilize negative space is what makes Milton Keynes so incomprehensible to the planners of the urban renaissance—the possibility that emptiness, underpasses and windswept plazas might actually be used and enjoyed far more than the piously romanticized 'streets'.

It's a great irony that the coiner of the term 'urban renaissance', Richard Rogers, has been deeply involved in one of the new ultra-

'Eco-hats' at RSHP's Oxley Woods

suburban outposts of the non-city: Oxley Park, a greenfield site built on after much opposition, an example of a dual strategy of expansion at the edges and densification at the centre. There are two salient things here: the traditionalist truth of the place, and 'Oxley Woods', the enclave produced by Rogers Stirk Harbour. This is a typical spec estate, Wimpey at its most drab, the aesthetic form of the first rung on the recently kicked-away 'property ladder', the dominant form of residential building for the last thirty years. It is a reduced version of the Victorian house, where terraces are replaced by closes and cul-de-sacs (named, curiously enough, after actors), lacking either the cheerfully vulgar bay-windowed display of the 1930s semi or the dour cohesion of the nineteenth-century rows. It's dispiriting housing.

Where the original districts of Milton Keynes, planned within the grids, all had an attendant community centre to counter new-town boredom and isolation, Oxley Park has a Tesco Express. As our cab (there's practically no other way here for the pedestrian) winds through these tiny mock cottages, it comes to the place in the magazines. These are the famous 60k eco-homes, and a pile of their angular red 'eco-hats' lies on the building site, where we can see a fair few more in progress. They're atypical for Rogers, but they fit perfectly in Milton Keynes—colourful, sharp, and perhaps more conformist than they look at first glance. With their

Oxley Woods

The rest of Oxley Park

lack of the tweedy pine and brick which signifies Eco, the Oxley houses prove brilliantly that an 'eco-home' doesn't have to mimic nature, although this is moot given the preponderance of private transport; the cars all belch into the atmosphere, no matter how green the houses they're parked in front of. This is still an enclosed corner of a volume estate, and the fences and gates are all in Wimpey's in-house style. Oxley Park is the meeting point between two aesthetically different but structurally similar approaches to architecture. Ever since the 1960s Richard Rogers has advocated clip-together prefabricated homes as a solution to a housing crisis, as, irrespective of style, they are apparently easier and cheaper. In terms of ease, cheapness and mass production, however, it's difficult to match Bovis, Barratt or Wimpey, who construct thousands upon thousands of standardized homes, albeit in a manner which reassures buyers of the houses' traditional nature. At Oxley, the two torn halves of something which does not add up meet each other, and the result is peculiar indeed.

We visit a minuscule show home in a half-terrace (these are, after all, buildings which Ivan Harbour, architect at RSH, referred to as 'rabbit hutches'[23]), where the estate agent immediately assumes we're a couple (why else would we be here?), but are told to go to the semi instead. Here we find a tiny little wooden shed in the back, wonderfully incongruous with the brightness and geometry of Rogers's houses. This is an odd, but rather charming place. As we wind round Oxley Park's cul-de-sacs, we find two men and a dog sitting outside their house and catch the pungent whiff of illegal substances, as if to emphasize the gently psychedelic nature of these futuristic houses caught in the most mundane of settings. Like the rest of Milton Keynes, Oxley Woods is both an exemplar of the shabbiness and greed that got us into the current mess—the property ladder, speculation and the fetish of house as castle/investment—and of what might get us out of it. As planning, this is the same as everywhere else, but the form is different, which is not insignificant. If employed by a local council, these peculiar but elegant eco-houses and their ingenious construction techniques could be the basis for a major wave of public housing that looks new and genuinely Modernist without retro reference, while their cheapness and energy efficiency seem, at least so far, enormously impressive. But here at Oxley, it's clear that they were only ever a progressive sop to get planning permission to build on virgin land.

From there we set off to Bletchley, an older town eaten up and redeveloped as part of the New Town, a place where hulking concrete bridges and cottages glare at each other. Milton Keynes as a Bennite dream of a scientific Albion encompasses within it the headquarters of the Open University and Bletchley Park, where

Wimpey Shed at Oxley Woods

Brunel Centre, reclad

the code-breakers are commemorated. The snobbery which the new towns invariably face is not wholly analogous to the persecution of Alan Turing, but both exemplify a similar small-mindedness. In the 1970s talented architects designed various buildings that are now treated with ostentatious disrespect. A pyramidal swimming pool by Faulkner Browns, declined listing, was demolished in 2010 in favour of a PFI scheme so awful that the Commission for Architecture and the Built Environment urged that it be declined planning permission. The Bletchley Pyramid was one of the remaining residues of the science fiction nature of early Milton Keynes, space-age architecture to go alongside the yawning open spaces. Here, the *Boys' Own* futurists Archigram built their only completed structure, an adventure playground. It was demolished soon enough. There's also a mini-version of the main mall—the black glass Brunel Centre, by the Development Corporation's architects. Part of it is still in use, its chic original stylings just about perceptible, a sleek arcade that is notably less affluent than its central equivalent—but the nearby office block has been façaded by Lloyd Thomas Architects, its rigour effaced with *de rigueur* off-centre windows and weak patterning.

Travelling from Bletchley back to the centre, the divisions within Milton Keynes become more and more apparent. Most recent housing has been done in the spec-builder manner once

derided by Stuart Mosscrop as 'pixie shit', but you can still see
the estates of the development corporation—Dixon Jones's
Netherfield, Norman Foster's Bean Hill. Despite the fame—the
extreme fame, in the latter case—of the architects, these are not
places that ever feature in their career retrospectives. They were
knocked up quickly with inferior materials, as the Development
Corporation ran out of money in the 1970s, and were heavily
altered for functional as much as aesthetic reasons. Foster's corrugated metal-clad houses were eventually given pitched roofs,
while Dixon Jones's stern Modernist terraces are painted a variety
of colours—some falling apart, some well looked after, all bat-
tling with the original cohesion. Today, the ultramodernity of the
non-city's central grid and smoothly maintained infrastructure
doesn't extend to most of the housing; given that the earlier areas
were more often council-owned, the more Modernist an area in
the grid, the poorer it is likely to be. The Centre on the hill looks
odd at a distance, like a service station seen a few miles off on the
M60, with the Xscape indoor ski-slope, MK's tallest building,
turning from a mildly amusing urban object into a *Stadtkrone*.

On the bus back to the centre, we start to see the limitations of
this autopia in the tedium of its retail parks and distribution
centres, no matter how smoothly they run. While the motorcity

Back to normality at Midsummer Place

The edgy Hub

manages to encompass both the car and a huge amount of public space, for an established city to follow it would necessitate an impossible level of redevelopment—and the idea of a 'sustainable' or 'green' Milton Keynes, is, for all its verdancy, surely a contradiction in terms. Milton Keynes works, but it is the only place in Britain where the fossil fuel economy really does work, because everything else has been subordinated to it. What is more, it's the only place where it can work, so as a model it is worse than useless—worse, because its example has been emulated elsewhere without the amenities and networks that the original planners left behind here.

Aesthetically, though, the non-city is fascinating, haunting, a truly beautiful illusion, an oasis. Even the new 'dense' areas are overtaken by its limpid quietude. So The Hub, a series of towers around a square which attempts to introduce an 'edgy' (as its architect Glenn Howells puts it[24]) urban grain into the city, is cold and serene. The new areas of Milton Keynes, the new spec flats and hotels, recreate in a more dense form the same Ballardian voids as the original 1970s city, although if the trend goes further it could face becoming Reading or Basingstoke with more efficient roads and a couple of unusually elegant buildings. Today, however, Milton Keynes is still the non-place it was planned to be.

And why not? The idea that a city should exist for youth and 'vibrancy' is a tired combination of baby-boomer nostalgia and romantic guff about the virtues of poverty's dirt and noise, a superannuated idea that is as amenable to knock-it-up-cheap developers as are the developers' cul-de-sacs. Perhaps after the unseemly noise and blather of the boom, the non-city's calm, serenity and order could offer us a way out. Today, Milton Keynes feels as though it is in a weird state of suspension—the beautifully managed car economy obsolete and environmentally destructive, its retail and finance-based economy doomed. Perhaps one solution could be for it to embrace the destiny of all planned towns and become an administrative city—the capital of a sane new England, modern and rational. That is, if the diplomats don't mind living in Barratt homes.

Chapter Three

Nottingham: The Banality of Aspiration

The branding of cities as capitals of this or that has a tragicomic nature—any Glaswegian reminded of the 'Glasgow's Miles Better' campaign that preceded its spell as European City of Culture will tend to be upset—but this doesn't stop cities appealing for them, and the subsidies they just might have attached. As we set off for the East Midlands, whispers have it that Nottingham will imminently be the British entry for one of the less famous of these, 'World Capital of Design'. Whether or not this means Forest and County will elicit the same derisive chants that were directed at Liverpool FC fans from rival terraces—'Capital of Culture, *you're having a laugh*'—remains to be seen. The real story with these capitals of art, culture or design is always one of triumphing against the loss of industry, urban transformations from production to consumption. So the question with Nottingham must be: has it replaced the industries—consumer manufacturing, mainly, which died a lot more recently than other parts of industrial Britain—which have gradually been erased? If so, with what? Whether this replacement counts as 'culture' we will leave to the judges, but in terms of design, we can make a few judgements of our own.

Despite its role in national myth (through that strange socialist monarchist, Robin Hood) and its medieval street plan, Nottingham's built environment is overwhelmingly of the last two centuries. This is a big city, one of Britain's largest, but the refusal of many of its suburbs, in a depressing act of egotism, to admit to being part of it means that its true population is significantly larger than the number of people the city council can tax. It's immediately recognizable as a (former) industrial town, with some massive mills and warehouses in the centre. Architecturally, it is dominated by two styles. These are, from the nineteenth century, a dramatically decorative commercial red-brick Northern Renaissance, Bastardized Bruges, Gradgrindian Gothic; and from the twentieth, a commercial Brutalism, where the earnest urban theories and philosophically argued forms of Alison and Peter Smithson are less important than the profit margins of Arthur Swift and Arndale. These buildings rampage over ancient streets, skywalks and car parks brashly breaking and entering the rows of gables. Both styles can be thrilling and mediocre in roughly equal measure, and in one great moment—where A. E. Lambert's 1898 Victoria Station clock tower plugs itself into the melodramatic stepped high rise of Peter Winchester's 1965–72 Victoria Centre —the two styles are part of the same structure.

The monuments to industrial power and civic pride are now more often housing bars, shops, 'Number 1 Eighties Nights' and

The Victoria Centre

The Ibis 'Pod'

seventies theme pubs. In one example of sheer historical farce, a Pitcher and Piano inhabits a former Unitarian church. The Midland Gothic, the earlier of the city's two main styles, already based on dreams of a bygone England, is ripe for heritage sightseeing. This brings us to the first in our list of things to do with a post-industrial city: tourism. Nottingham has not, to its credit, opted for simulated Victoriana to fill in the gaps, notwithstanding the tame attempts of 1980s and '90s vernacular architects. Recent infill is usually modern, as are its new hotels, contemporary buildings billeting those in search of castles and caves. Some are nondescript (Holiday Inn), others are dreadful (Jurys Inn), but one of them is excellent, in fact the only interestingly designed hotel we will find over the next nine months.

The Ibis 'Pod' is designed by veteran Modernists Benson & Forsyth, whose work has long had the air of followers of the old-time religion. In a sense, their Ibis is just as much of a retro gesture as the nineties bank offices, but while they simulated a past that never occurred, Benson and Forsyth draw on a future that never arrived. In plan, this is a postmodernist building, slotted into the street and determined by aesthetics rather than function, but in every other way it's Modernist in the 'heroic' 1920s sense. Clinging to the street line, the lower floors of the building are given over to the glass walls of Tesco Express. Above and askew, the hotel floors are detailed in Suprematist manner, El Lissitzky for business class. The primary colours are from the De Stijl book of do's and don'ts, yet the angles culminate in a glazed point in an alleyway which would not pass any functionalist exam. It's a building that one at first enjoys almost guiltily, its imaginative angles and views compensating for the reduction of idealism to style, but after a while in Nottingham it seems a towering achievement, an uncompromising, fearless thing; one of two new buildings which actually do suggest a city with serious design ambitions.

Bespoke Containers

So much for tourism. Second thing to do with a post-industrial city: hand it over to the culture industry, or more politely the 'creative industries'. Here, also, Nottingham has the usual—a boutique here, a vintage clothes shop there—and another building which impressively avoids contemporary clichés, in the process starting a whole new cliché. Still unfinished when we first visited, it was hard to come to some sort of judgement about Caruso St John's Centre for Contemporary Art (or 'Nottingham Contemporary'), but we did at least guess at the likely local jibes or nicknames when this doily-covered shed, this lace shipping container, is finally completed. In fact, within a few weeks of opening its roof had sprung a leak, adding a bucket to the gallery exhibits. What we have here is a series of curtly corrugated boxes stepping down a hill, whose green and gold concrete cladding is, now famously, dressed in lace patterns. Initially, this seems like one of those ubiquitous, shallow gestures at contextualism (here with the former lace mills nearby). After its completion, several proposals for 'doily' façades by lesser architects would follow, standard blocks overlaid by repeated images of some local talisman. A building proposed by Bond Bryan for Sheffield Hallam University would reduce it to farce, featuring a pattern of cutlery on its curtain walls.

The concrete doilies of Nottingham Contemporary

This is one of a handful of genuinely unique buildings designed in this decade of competing, egotistical icons, and Caruso St John, usually purveyors of a sober minimalism, seem almost ashamed of their own daring, of the possibility they'd veered into kitsch here. Even critic Ellis Woodman commented, in an otherwise rapturous *Building Design* review, that he thought the lace pattern was 'a little naff',[25] although Caruso St John's appeals to the precedent of the proto-Modernist Chicago School and Louis Sullivan brought them back onto firm scholarly ground. The rippling colours and patterns of the façade are intriguing enough not to need a direct excuse, but in terms of its 'meaning', Nottingham Contemporary actually seems to signify something unexpected, and something pointed: a visual amalgam of nineteenth-century industry—intricate patterns, made by underpaid workers on the inhuman machines of the nearby mills—and the twenty-first century's semi-automated out of town industries, the non-aesthetic of containerization and its windowless warehouses.

On returning to Nottingham nearly a year later to see the completed building at last, it appeared that others had had the same idea. Taking a route to Nottingham Contemporary which traverses the smooth concrete Tram bridge by Nottingham Station, you descend onto the pavement to find two actual shipping containers, one painted green, the other yellow, the same colours as the gallery itself. This is surely someone's little joke. From then on, however, my initial hesitancy about the building seems like mere bet-hedging. This is a terrific piece of work, fearless and subtle, with a refreshingly intelligent programme (shows are about 'The Future under Communism' or 'Combined and Uneven Geographies' rather than the customary sensationalist and/or patronizing fluff), which has, at least early on, attracted large crowds. The doilied-up concrete is especially tactile and puzzling up close, but the ornamental display coexists with a raw physicality. The building steadfastly refuses the obvious, even in its means of entry, which is not from the street, but from either a corner entrance by the Lace Market, or up a series of angled stairs from the bottom of the slope. Yet this avoidance of current urbanist common sense doesn't seem to have put anyone off, given the amount of people milling around when we visit. Walking in, around and through the place's concrete surfaces, its patterns, colours and angles, I wonder if this might, irrespective of its leaky roof, be the first masterpiece of British architecture of the twenty-first century.

Shipping containers near Nottingham Contemporary

The completed Nottingham Contemporary

It's especially apposite that Nottingham Contemporary gestures, consciously or otherwise, at the shedscapes of post-Fordist
industry. We pass several of these sheds, all quite central, albeit
not on a Sotonian scale, on our way to the third thing to do with a
post-industrial city: 'new industries', the built embodiment, and
currently the ruins of, the 'Anglo-Saxon model' of financialized
capitalism. The roads are ceremonially named. At the junction of
Enterprise Way and Experian Way is ng2 (note the modish lower

Experian—Spam Architecture

case), a business park, fairly central but set back from the railway in an obvious attempt to move this exurban typology back into the city. The most prominent and most interesting building here is the headquarters of Experian. That it even exists is strange enough in itself. I had always considered Experian to be a sort of spam company, existing only to ask, unbidden, whether you want to see your credit rating (and I know I don't, nor do most people in Britain right now). To find it has a corporeal presence is surprising, although this 2004 building by Sheppard Robson does everything it can to deny its corporeality, as per the curiously enduring myth that glass makes a structure ethereal and transparent rather than opaque and puzzling. Experian's central feature is a cantilevered drawer, picked out in an irregular bright blue pattern, overlooking a dangerously deep pond (we know, because a sign tells us so, although it seems so tiny we almost consider testing the idea). Architecturally, it's the only remotely notable part of ng2, a ring of wasteland and don't-look-at-me offices for sundry banks, including the deceased HBOS, all of which eschew the dotcom display of Experian for a blank, stolid brick Pseudomodernism, curving over those bits of blasted ground architects call 'public realm' in their planning submissions. The pathetically material form of the once so dynamic immaterial finance. A billboard for ng2 declares 'We're here, why aren't you?' in front of fenced-off wasteland, reserved optimistically for future development, but which may lie empty for years.

'An evangelical college without God'

The melancholic atmosphere of this failed business park is rather similar to that of Nottingham University's new Jubilee Campus, opened in 1999. Things to do with a post-industrial city number four: education. Here this was to be housed in buildings by Make, the practice formed by Ken Shuttleworth, a former partner of Norman Foster, who left the firm in a flurry of controversy over 'authorship' of the City of London Gherkin. Very quickly, Make amassed a huge quantity of commissions, for everything from

Gateway and 'Aspire', Jubilee Campus

massive redevelopment schemes to skyscrapers and an astound-ingly anti-contextual pavilion next to St Paul's Cathedral. Unexpectedly, given the hype, this, Make's first large-scale work, was on completion the subject of a chorus of critical derision (at least in the handful of architectural avenues where critique still exists). It's easy to see why. In its combination of jollity, bathos, vacancy and authoritarianism, it sums up the Blairite era in three dimensions.

The site is a former bicycle works, and concrete mills still mark a gateway. The prefab tower blocks filmed in Anton Corbijn's *Control* to replicate pre-gentrification Manchester loom nearby. This is in fact where Arthur Seaton works in Alan Sillitoe's *Saturday Night and Sunday Morning*, where 'generators whined all night, and during the day giant milling machines working away on cranks and pedals in the tunnery gave to the terrace the sensation of living within breathing distance of some monstrous being that suffered from a disease of the stomach.'[26] It sits on a ground zero for kitchen-sink England, and next to it is the set for a pastiche post-punk rehash of the same genre. So, this seemingly random assemblage of deconstructivist-lite tat, with its apparently contextual pinkish tiles (a bit like brick!) and its giant sculpture (a bit like some spokes in a wind sock), is placed in an area so rich in

71

pop myth that it's surprising this too wasn't 'referenced'. Near the entrance are some earlier buildings by Michael Hopkins, designed in the late nineties. They're very different—relatively warm, akin to Ralph Erskine's Greenwich Millennium Village and the Scandinavian style, all wood and water features, with an amusing and possibly inadvertent hint of intimidation in their symmetries and turrets, as is so common with these kinds of buildings. Even given the drama of some of this, presumably it wasn't 'iconic' enough, as the extension is, from the risible central sculpture 'Aspire' on down, all about the flash.

'Aspire' is a horrendously shrill title for this ridiculous structure, and in the context—the overwriting of former spaces of work, overlooked by the former spaces of working-class housing —it sounds like a gross interpellation. Aspire, god damn you! Aim high, recalcitrant proles! Aspirational bling in architectural form is particularly evident in the metallic Gateway Building which forms an alternative processional entrance to the campus, while the pink-banded International House and Amenity Building are prime examples of Make's unconscious po-faced spin on 1950s Googie, suggesting both 1970s sci-fi dystopias (*Logan's Run*, perhaps) and a desperate eagerness to please. It begs the viewer (and this is *viewing* architecture, not something physical) to applaud its

Jubilee Campus

Hopkins's Phase One of the Jubilee Campus

vaulting geometries, bids us be dazzled by its colour scheme, to the point where a violent reaction is all but inevitable. This is, in function as much as in form, the ideal neoliberal university, made up of 'business incubator units' and 'fitness suites'; our rueful guide to the Jubilee Campus, a lecturer who shall remain anonymous, describes its atmosphere as being like 'an evangelical college without God'. While one might expect students to be Nottingham's avant-garde, involved in the artiness and politics which denote a 'cultured' city, he tells us that Nottingham University is quietist and deeply conservative. Nottingham's management has been notorious for its role in the detention without trial of a staff member, Hicham Yezza, whose 'crime' was downloading an Al-Qaeda training manual for a student's research project. Nottingham was the only university that refused to negotiate with the recent Gaza solidarity occupations, eventually hiring muscle to evict the protesters by force. All very appropriate for this university as business park. A poster declares: 'Your future's right here'.

The presence of the two Universities in Nottingham is prominent indeed, with a large amount of new student accommodation. The worst we see is Haskoll's awful mixed-use block in Trinity Square, a pompous red-brick box with a ridiculous cod-

Trinity Square

deconstructivist titanium outgrowth at the back, the architectural equivalent of a stockbroker wearing a bumptious tie. This structure is so bad that both the city council and the developer disowned it on completion in late 2009.[27] An adjacent block promises 'plasma screens in every flat' to its prospective undergraduate tenants. Others cast shadows over council estates and derelict terraces, as if to invite burglaries. Much of the city is clearly very poor, its gun crime statistics oft-quoted, and the gap between haves and have-nots is nonchalantly displayed in its architecture.

Yet the most worrying things we see in Nottingham are the Police Pledge posters. Based on 'Keep Calm and Carry On', the rediscovered, unproduced WWII propaganda poster which became 'iconic' as the recession deepened, they're a bizarre double bind of a design. They share Keep Calm's minimal layout and its humanist sans serifs, replacing the crown with the police badge. The written content, which we follow around central Nottingham, at first assuming these are local posters for the Nottinghamshire Constabulary in an oblique anti-gun campaign, consists of three slogans, all based on particular clichés used by the police in the popular imagination, albeit in one case with a decidedly sinister twist; 'WE'D LIKE TO GIVE YOU A GOOD TALKING TO', 'ANYTHING YOU SAY MAY BE TAKEN

DOWN AND USED AS EVIDENCE', and, remarkably, 'YOU HAVE THE RIGHT NOT TO REMAIN SILENT'. Underneath, in an extremely small, easily missed print, is the 'official' message, based on 'the Policing Pledge', a managerial initiative intended to 'restore confidence' and 'enable choice'. For instance, the 'talking to' poster 'pledges' to listen to the consumer of policing, while the 'right not to remain silent' suggests you make complaints against the police should they inconvenience you. In their split between an authoritarian exclamation and a liberal, caring small print which supposedly gives an amusing gloss to the large print, these are spectacular examples of disavowal and the use of irony to say appalling things unchallenged. The sleight of hand is thus: the pun, the pay-off, is in small print, reminding us that really the police force are all about helping old ladies across the road: 'the police now pledge to listen ...'; the truth, of course, is in large print. Given the recent suspension of Habeas Corpus, you genuinely do not have the right to remain silent. So while this 'witty' gesture claims to play with the brutally state-protecting image of the police, it also says, very loudly, that the rules no longer apply, something made all too obvious at the G20 protests in London on 1 April 2009.

The Policing Pledge

Green leatherette at Hollies' Caff

Given Nottingham's aspiration to become a chic 'Design Capital', and the shrill commands of its new architecture, this use of design for political ends sits rather well. This seems a slippery city, hard to encompass, a city of contradictions and tensions, juxtapositions which initially appear accidental, but acquire a certain perverse logic. Before leaving I enjoy a fried breakfast in Hollies, a greasy spoon café. Inside is the 1970s in aspic, green leather, brown formica and untouched signage, begging to be used as a film set. On my way out, I do a double-take, noticing the café is part of a garishly façaded redevelopment which has somehow left the interior untouched. But no matter how much Nottingham gestures at modish brightness, it seems a dingy but fascinatingly weird industrial city in essence. Yet it might be running out of ways to fill this post-industrial shell, irrespective of the variable quality of its design.

Chapter Four

Sheffield: The Former Socialist
Republic of South Yorkshire

Sheffield was once an extremely architecturally important place. Any book published on modern architecture between 1960 and 1980, whether by an Aldo Rossi or a Kenneth Frampton, will contain a discussion of its municipal housing schemes. In the early 1960s it even got a special issue of *Architectural Design* devoted to its new architecture. This is partly because Sheffield was both a boom town in the postwar era and a particularly left-wing one, with a series of entrenched labour councils, but after the 'decline' of the steel industry the city disappeared from the itineraries of architectural tourists, and was seldom subjected to radical architecture. Aside from the occasional mention in the music press, it seemed replaced by Leeds as Yorkshire's main centre, with the West Riding's other metropolis overtaking it in population and certainly in influence as it embraced the economy of finance and property. But in 2009 Sheffield accidentally seemed important again, largely because the ghosts of its recent past have returned to haunt the rest of the country. The recent twenty-fifth anniversary of the Miners' Strike has had an unexpected resonance in recession-hit Britain. Sheffield was home to both the headquarters of the National Union of Mineworkers and Orgreave coking plant, site of the notorious 'battle' (or police riot). While I'm there, local news is full of the Hillsborough disaster anniversary, commemorating the day that ninety-six Liverpool fans were crushed to death in Sheffield Wednesday's stadium. Mass unemployment, meanwhile, is something Sheffield experienced barely two decades ago.

It claims to be 'England's biggest village', but Sheffield is not only historically important; aesthetically much of it is hardly provincial. It just doesn't seem to know how good it actually is. Sheffield's futuristic pop music, from the post-punk of the late seventies, the bleep techno of the early nineties and the bassline of recent years, was always more original than Manchester's increasingly dull vainglories, irrespective of Branson Coates's one-liner, the defunct National Centre for Popular Music. Sheffield's postwar architecture is often better than London's, let alone that of any provincial competitor. Gollins Melvin Ward's Arts Tower is sleeker and sharper than their similar attempts at slick Miesian Americana in the capital; Park Hill is a far more impressive, imaginative and inspiring streets-in-the-sky structure than its London cousin, Robin Hood Gardens; the Modernist picturesque of the Gleadless Valley council estate definitively surpasses its forbear, the Alton East estate in Roehampton; while Castle Market is a shopping centre with a weirdness and individuality that put all the Arndales to shame.

All of the above buildings make great use of the thing that makes Sheffield truly special—its landscape. Practically any view

The skeleton of Park Hill

here provides you with a photogenic picture of either the cityscape or the Peak District, so you're always conscious of being in the presence of both a big city and an abundant countryside. Sadly, this political, aesthetic and natural uniqueness has been decidedly underused in recent architecture. The Blair-era boom brought a rash of new building, of which only a very small proportion was of any great worth; an abortive attempt to completely replan the city centre which was similarly banal; and recession has hit hard. When we first visited in spring 2009, Sheffield was dominated by two overwhelming skeletal concrete frames, both housing almost identically scaled flats—that of Park Hill, of which more later; and of Conran's St Paul's Tower. The latter, a thirty-two storey glass block, faced first the collapse of its sponsor, City Lofts Inc, who went into administration in 2008; subsequently, there was a controversy over a change in cladding, whereby a cheaper glass was proposed by the administrators and rejected by the council, stalling the project. Over the course of the year, we watch an impressively elegant concrete frame morph into a desperately tacky high-rise: the panels that can be seen on the lower floors suggest a rather unexpected revival of seventies corporate architecture.

Adjacent is one of the handful of interesting new buildings, the Q Park, a car park by Allies and Morrison. Its faceted steel panels look viciously razor-sharp, as if you could cut yourself on the façade—fitting in the once-futuristic Steel City, although it's notable that the new car parks designed to bring shoppers back into the centre seem unwilling to articulate their hardly 'sustainable' function, with architects preferring to create illegible but occasionally beautiful objects. The cars are entirely hidden, the ramps invisible. Sadly, the inventiveness of the parking floors doesn't extend to a street level as nondescript as the nearby hotels and offices, but from the station it announces Sheffield a damn sight better than the hopeless Conran Tower.

Just off the Wicker, where the submerged river Sheaf meets the River Don, near the small, long-disused docks, is a cluster of recent spec offices and flats, most of which seem empty. These are

Allies & Morrison's Q Park

a compendium of neo-modern clichés—'aspirational' mixed-use redevelopment in the form of Cartwright Pickard's moronically named iQuarter, its tacky curtain wall haughtily ignoring its context of picturesque red-brick industrial dereliction; a return of all the worst features of the International Style in its sheer ignorance of the urban grain and its pseudo-executive sheen. There are also two office buildings full of borrowings from Will Alsop's jolly

The Sheffield 'iQuarter'

The Digital Campus

pop architecture, in the form of Aedas's Wicker Riverside and BDP's North Bank, with their obligatory wonky pilotis, angular shapes and 'friendly' colour. The latter was an entry in Yorkshire RIBA's recent Sheffield Design Awards—half of which was made up of refurbishments rather than new buildings, for obvious reasons.

Walking from here towards the ever present shadow of Park Hill, across a great, accidentally Piranesian system of elevated tramways and pedestrian bridges, you can survey an almost successful attempt to wipe out anything that might be architecturally striking. This takes the form of a continuous strip of pseudomodern Blairboxes, stretching from the iQuarter via blocks of drab flats by the Park Square roundabout, to Carey Jones's icy Digital Campus. The latter at least uses the topography to produce raised levels rather than merely plonking down a box. The best-known feature, an impressive example of business infantilism, is a slide which takes young entrepreneurs down from the upper floors to the reception (or it would do, if the place was occupied). They're pockmarked by the equally Modern, but deeply strange architecture of an earlier era: the cantilevered shelf of Jefferson Sheard's Epic Building, and a sculpted concrete column announcing the Castle Market.

Complexity and Contradiction in Sheffield Modernism,
Part 1: Castle Market

If these buildings take their cue from Modernism's least attractive side, its deafness to its surroundings and Platonic blandness, then Park Hill and Castle Market, Sheffield's most fascinating sixties buildings, are reminders that there was always another Modernism, one which has not continued into the present day to anything like the same extent: Modernism as montage, messiness, and the drama of multiple levels and scales. Just as Park Hill famously tried to replicate slum bustle in the sky, Castle Market recreates the teeming strangeness of an old market in a fearlessly Modernist form. Nearby is the Co-Operative's 1964 Castle House, by G. S. Hay, recently listed. The granite elegance of Castle House contrasts with Castle Market's gaunt angularity—yet the latter seems a more urgent candidate for listing, a unique structure under threat of demolition. Its several levels are built into the sloping landscape, from a raised gallery outside to a fish market in the basement. Inside is a joyous mess of vintage sixties signage, sights, smells and visual chaos, soundtracked by a stall playing easy listening, full of old cafés where net curtains and Mondrian geometries make richly perverse bedfellows. The market was planned under J. Lewis Womersley, the City architect hired in 1952 who within a decade commissioned 50,000 homes ranging from Park Hill to the extraordinary Modernist suburbia of Gleadless Valley, designing on the side a multitude of schools and local centres, of which the finest surviving is our subject here. Now that Park Hill is undergoing stripping and gentrification and Gleadless languishes in obscure poverty, Womersley's socialist, Modernist Sheffield is best seen in this remarkable shopping centre, of all things. Built in 1960–5, Castle Market is now slated for demolition.

The job architect here, Andrew Derbyshire, designed what could be described as a megastructure before the fact, although never as domineering and 'iconic' as that would suggest. Rather than plonking down a hangar or a slab from on high as is customary, Derbyshire fitted a multitude of interconnected structures into a small, sloping site: an office block with a distinctive angular profile; a raised walkway system with shops; and the markets themselves, three floors all with access to the street on different levels of the hill and a wildly curving entrance ramp at the back. Inside is a panoply of strange and fascinating things.

Like Park Hill, what is clever and unusual in Castle Market is that it's a Modernist design which specifically tries to engineer bustle and individuality, so that you notice both the ingenious design of the labyrinthine structure and the competing design ambitions of the many stalls and built-in shops. Much of Castle Market, both the building itself and its individual units, retains original 1960s signage, making it a particular goldmine for classic caff enthusiasts. There's The Soda Fountain, in elegant, continental sans serifs seemingly absconding from a Blue Note record cover; and the competing signs of Sharon's, where more recent promises of greasy excellence sit alongside a mid-century modern sign declaring it to be a 'Snack Bar'. On the outside walkway is the deep red vitrolite box housing Café Internationale, its name appropriately reflecting the former Socialist Republic of South Yorkshire; the formica tables and oddly Victorian chairs at Tennant's, and the aspirationally named Riviera Snack Bar, replete with palm tree motifs and the promise (or threat) 'Watch out for our specials'. Best of all is the excellent Roof-Top Café, which boasts a fantastically ambitious space-age suspended ceiling hanging over formica tables, a patterned floor and net curtains. That's just what's open on a Thursday morning.

This state of design delirium is maintained as you gradually descend from the Roof-Top Café to the food market in the basement, either on foot down the elegantly cantilevered stairs or via the exposed lift that sweeps up and down the space. There's a sweet shop using the same font as *The Prisoner*; original signs at Castle News; the intriguingly named Grocock's; and N. Smith & Sons, which sells an array of things from Toys to Baskets to Travel Goods. This visual richness is more than matched in Derbyshire's own design embellishments. Mosaic all over the

The Roof-Top Cafe, Castle Market

place, including a cantilevered Castle mosaic at one entrance; seemingly random outbreaks of sixties geometric patterning; abstract, multicoloured tile designs; fine sans-serif signs, usually missing a letter or several; and in the catacombs of the food market, a grid-patterned ceiling to leaven the dungeon-like effect.

There's more on the outside galleries, where Lew Burgin's Ladies' Salon (closed) and New County Hair Stylist (open) look untouched since 1965. Florid, hardly Modernist metal signs were installed on the walkways in the eighties, although they fit quite well with the general organized chaos. Along one of the walkways is a shop selling old postcards, and on one visit I come out with a handful of demolished Sheffield buildings and Edwardian post-cards from Switzerland. The ageing owner is a little amused by my liking for postwar Sheffield, looking quizzically at the card of the 'egg box' Town Hall, built in the 1970s and demolished only twenty-five years later. 'It's just like hole in road', he says, assum-ing that I'll know what Hole In Road was. When I look it up, it turns out to have been a shopping centre with an aquarium, reached by escalators from the street through a hole in the road. In Sheffield's postwar self-portraits it appears proudly as a bizarre, unique urban object, sleekly modern; but this was apparently far from the reality. 'They never looked after it—even the aquarium

got smashed up.' Local architect and historian Steve Parnell later
gave me a few more details on Hole in Road:

the hole was quite famous—you could navigate by it, which
makes it a genuine landmark. Really, a kind of inverted icon in
every way. It wasn't a shopping centre itself, though, just a through-
way, under the inner ring road. You could access the shops on
each corner, I seem to remember, from basement level, and there
were tabac-type kiosks in there and ad-hoc opportunist street
traders. It was open to the elements and formed the centre of a
traffic roundabout above. I used to love it. I remember standing,
staring for ages at one of those pictures that you had to lose yourself in to get a 3D effect. And there were the giant fish tanks in the
walls (not quite aquaria) with living, swimming, breathing fish in
(which rivers Don or Rother couldn't boast at the time!). It did
stink a bit, though, as the tramps used to congregate there and
sleep on the benches, as is their wont. But in the same way that
Brutalism extended their walkways above ground, this was the
kind of opposite, burrowing down. As if Sheffield didn't have
enough topology to play with, it invented another level. Ulti-
mately, it was deemed dangerous and smelly and so got filled in
unfortunately. I think many Sheffielders are nostalgic about this
hole, more so than any building, strangely. It was taken for
granted and I don't think they realized how unusual and special it
was until it got concreted.

North Gallery, Castle Market

The description of its state of preservation and the relatively anti-quated nature of the shop signs and its going concerns might all imply that Castle Market is a rotting, abandoned time capsule. Owners Sheffield City Council would argue so, and certainly its time-out-of-joint nature is what makes it so fascinating. Even on the overcast morning that these photos were taken, the place was clearly well used, and the Market has in fact been turning a healthy profit, especially since the recession hit. Yet whether young second-generation Asian women or elderly men who still say 'thee' and 'thou', the thing that unites Castle Market's visitors is that they are working class, which does not sit well with Sheffield's intent to make itself as yuppie-friendly as Leeds or central Manchester. The market and almost everything around it—including, if the council gets its way, the listed Castle House, whose preservation they fiercely opposed—will go to make way for a combination of the two things cities are now supposed to exist for: regeneration and heritage.

The market sits on the site of Sheffield Castle, and though the ruins are open to the public, the exciting promise of small stone walls open to the air is being used as an excuse to sweep away an entire area, with a character lacking from the more gentrified areas

Steps, Castle Market

of central Sheffield, in favour of a new financial district. You can see the beginnings of this from the upper levels of the market; the spec flats and offices of the iQuarter, their barcode façades and empty units glaring at the unfashionable multiformity and civic ambition of Castle Market. The whole place will be relocated to the other end of the town centre, to the gigantic outdoor mall being planned by the developers Hammerson—a glass hall as bland and flashy in appearance as Derbyshire's market is complex and rewarding. Unlike the emblems of regeneration, this is a place that rewards more on close inspection than from icon-spotting distance.

The New Sheffield now under construction is a mere reprise of the Modernism of interchangeable blocks and egotistical towers, rather than the city's own, far more original approach to modern design. Interestingly, this decline was prefigured by the architects themselves. Womersley himself would later design Castle Market's antithesis, the ignorant bulk of the Manchester Arndale; while Derbyshire would pioneer woolly, vernacular postmodernism with his Hillingdon Civic Centre. Neither would repeat this combination of modernity, sensitivity to place and architectural permissiveness. Regardless of its pockets of desolation, Castle Market is still very much open and, though hardly upkept by a council eager to knock it down, the recession has given it a stay of execution likely to last a couple of years. Get there while you can: nothing like it will be built again.

Complexity and Contradiction in Sheffield Modernism, Part 2—Park Hill

Brutalist architecture was Modernism's angry underside, and was never, much as some would rather it were, a mere aesthetic style. It was a political aesthetic, an attitude, a weapon, dedicated to the precept that nothing was too good for ordinary people. Now, after decades of neglect, it's divided between 'eyesores' and 'icons'; fine for the Barbican's stockbrokers but unacceptable for the ordinary people who were always its intended clients. When the heritage industry lays its hands on Brutalism, it unsurprisingly gets its fingers burnt—as it has in its attempted restoration of what continues to be Sheffield's most famous building, with the somewhat clumsy participation of English Heritage, the body which monitors those parts of the built environment considered worthy of preservation, who have listed several postwar buildings over the last decade, often in the face of trenchant opposition.

English Heritage itself was formed in 1983 as a quango split off from the Department of the Environment, at the height of the reaction against the new face grafted on to England by Old Labour's technological 'white heat'. Brutalism's aesthetic and the heritage ethic would seem to be inherently opposed. *Romancing the Stone*, the second episode of *English Heritage*, a grimly funny BBC2 series on the quango's activities which ran through summer 2009, profiled the 'regeneration' of Park Hill, Grade II* listed in 1998. Here, preservation experts worry over 'historic fabric' while Urban Splash, the property developers who are transforming it, threaten to paint the whole thing pink. Stereotypes are rife: the English Heritage contingent speak in RP, the developers are flash Mancunians, the restoration's architect is a middle-aged Frenchman who dresses in lime green, and locals are presented as bluff Yorkshiremen who don't know much about architecture, but know what they like.

Park Hill

Enjoyable as these tensions are, they obscure a deeply complex story, one which perfectly exemplifies Britain's tortured relationship with its recent past. We would never know from the anathemas on a monolithic Modernism that Park Hill was an early response to what were considered, even in the 1950s, to be Modern architecture's failures. Empty spaces, isolation, a lack of street life, a middle-class 'this is good for you' ethos—all were fiercely critiqued by its planners and architects. Unfortunately for its advocates, the style of these buildings—reliant on *béton brut*, unpainted concrete—was christened 'the New Br..talism'. The New Brutalism's chief propagandist, Reyner Banham, pondered in a 1966 book whether the idiom was an 'Ethic or Aesthetic', so firmly marked was it by social concerns. He claimed that the Brutalists were the architectural equivalent of the angry young men of the fifties, of Arnold Wesker or Alan Sillitoe. Banham wrote that these architects were of 'red-brick extraction'; products of postwar class mobility, usually Northerners, like its main theorists and occasional practitioners, the fiercely self-promoting Stockton-on-Tees and Sheffield-born intellectual couple Alison and Peter Smithson, whose Golden Lane scheme for a deck-access block of council housing defined Brutalism.

'In our zeal to erase the evils arising out of lack of proper water supply, sanitation and ventilation, we had torn down streets of houses which despite their sanitary shortcomings harboured a social structure of friendliness and mutual aid. We had thrown out the baby with the bathwater', claimed Jack Lynn, co-designer of Park Hill, in 1962.[28] Reading the above quote, you have to remind yourself that Lynn is not talking about the building he designed at all, but the orthodox slum clearance Modernism he and his colleagues were setting themselves against. Park Hill was, alongside London's slightly larger but contrastingly affluent Barbican estate, the largest-scale application of Brutalism's ethic and aesthetic. It cleared a notoriously violent slum by Sheffield's Midland Station nicknamed 'little Chicago', but rather than rehousing the residents in isolated towers, the architects—Jack Lynn and Ivor Smith with Frederick Nicklin, selected by Lewis Womersley—

attempted to replicate the tightly packed street life of the area in the air. Associates of the Smithsons, Lynn and Smith were enthusiasts for the close-knit working-class life supposedly being broken up by the new estates and new towns. As in the Smithsons's mythical unbuilt Golden Lane scheme, claustrophobic walk-ups or corridors were rejected in favour of 12ft wide 'streets in the sky'. These 'streets' were almost all connected with the ground, on steeply sloping land. Street corners were included where the winding building twisted around, with the spaces around the blocks filled with shops, schools and playgrounds. Park Hill was closely monitored to see if it succeeded in its aims, and had its own tenants' magazine, the laconically named *Flat*.

Meanwhile, the architectural aesthetic was shaped by a rejection of the clean geometries of mainstream Modernism in favour of roughness and irregularity. The marks of concrete shuttering were left, in the fashion of Le Corbusier's Unité d'Habitation. Yet the use of multicoloured bricks, gradated from scarlet to yellow, in abstract patterns aided by artist John Forrester, connected it with a specifically Northern English idiom. The blocks rose from four storeys at the highest point of the hill to thirteen at the lowest,

A street in the sky

giving a continuous roof line visible from much of the city: at the highest point they look out over the expanse of the city centre and the post-industrial Don Valley, and at the lowest they mingled unassumingly with Victorian terraces. Despite—or because of— Park Hill's aesthetic extremism, early responses to the blocks were very positive indeed. *Romancing the Stone* features much footage of children and OAPs praising the place's modernity and community. Over old footage of the playgrounds, a South York-shire voice intones: 'There's no stopping this collective thinking. It's the future.' Encouraged by these responses, the architects designed a Park Hill Mark Two built just behind the site—Hyde Park, which rose to an eighteen-storey 'castle keep'. Later, a mark three, Kelvin Flats, was designed by other architects west of the city centre.

In 1962, the book *Ten Years of Housing in Sheffield*, document-ing Lewis Womersley's tenure as City architect, was published in English, French and, rather extraordinarily, Russian. It's a curi-ously sad book, an object from what now seems a completely alien culture, which makes clear just how tentative the planners and architects actually were—no grandiose declarations of success here. Park Hill was presented as an experiment, albeit one about which the writers were cautiously optimistic. Noting that there was a huge risk in such a development of 'creating a vast inhuman building block', Womersley was at pains to point out how much they had attempted to lessen this effect, from the public park cre-ated between the estate and the street to the way the courtyards opened out further as the storeys rose—though he noted that 'it must be left ... to the occupants to judge to what extent the archi-tects have been successful.'[29] Meanwhile, along with the expected shops and schools, Park Hill and its sister scheme Hyde Park were unpretentious enough to include no less than four pubs.

Streets in the sky were only one facet of Sheffield's housing programme. The less futuristic but equally remarkable suburban counterpart to Park Hill's urbanity was Gleadless Valley, a collec-tion of houses and flats making breathtaking use of the hilly landscape, resembling a strange socialist South Yorkshire version of fifties Southern California. Park Hill makes sense best when seen as part of a larger project in total city planning, aligned with other estates also placed on prominent hilltop sites, such as the more straightforward tower block and maisonette Modernism of Woodside and Netherthorpe. As the head of the city's Labour council, Howard Lambert, noted in *Ten Years*, all of these projects had a topographical specificity that, incidentally, was also at the heart of Brutalist preoccupations. In the process, he made an Italian comparison which has since become a commonplace for regeneration in northern England:

> most of our projects feature as important additions to the total environment—the more so because the topographical character-istics of the city allow many of them, such as Park Hill, Woodside and Netherthorpe, to be topographically related to each other. The careful exploitation of this topography—the building up of hill-top architectural compositions—is gradually producing something of the fascination of Italian Hill-towns. It is stimulat-ing, exciting!

By the end of the 1970s, over half of Sheffield's housing was council-owned, and they were still building Brutalist deck-access housing, albeit on a warmer, smaller scale that can still be seen in Gleadless, which we will come to presently. This is a reminder that council housing was never intended to be the emergency measure it is now, but something which was genuinely 'mixed'.

Early criticism of Park Hill was positive. One of the most pene-trating articles on it was by Ian Nairn, who visited in 1961 and again six years later. His account of these visits notes something which is still apparent on visiting the building. Its sublime scale is initially overwhelming—the blocks 'might not frighten the inhabitants, but they certainly frighten me'[30]—yet up close, the human scale and intense sense of place is far more apparent. Few who don't live there ever venture that close. Nairn's account was featured in *Britain's Changing Towns*, a book which attempted to weigh up the results of sixties Britain's version of regeneration. On the whole, Nairn was deeply unimpressed by what he saw as the flashy, meretricious and loveless results of redevelopment. Sheffield, however, received unremitting praise from this most unsentimental of critics. He noted that 'an enlightened housing exchange system'[31] (and the huge amount of council housing) meant that the young could freely choose flats while the old or families choose the lush suburbia of Gleadless and the like. Swapping accommodation as many as three or four times was considered normal; while Park Hill itself, first seen in a slightly ambiguous light, was by 1967 viewed as an incontrovertible success. 'The surfaces are weathering well, and the multicoloured brick is achieving its purpose, as it disappears under the grime, of providing a gradual lightening of tone from bottom to top.'[32] Meanwhile, Reyner Banham, a critic who could be expected to praise Park Hill, wrote that it was the nearest attempt to create a genuinely 'other' architecture, unconcerned with conventional notions of elevations, design or elegance, but instead creating 'a building more concerned with life than architecture'. It was the definitive monument of Brutalism, its finest moment: 'the moral crusade of Brutalism for a better habitat through built environment probably reaches its culmination at Park Hill.'[33] Even so, this embodiment of the Bevanite Brutalists' bloody-mindedness was partly devised by the future Labour 'modernizer' Roy Hattersley, opened by the exemplary compromiser Hugh Gaitskell, and praised by Harold Macmillan.

Park Hill was not utopia, nor was it intended to be. It had too few lifts, and the concrete on the taller sections was spalling by the eighties. More arguably, it might have been excessively successful at recreating the space of the old rookeries—like them, it was full of escape routes and shadowy spots. The notion that it could have single-handedly preserved a working-class communal life being obliterated everywhere else is unsurprisingly unconvincing. However, there is little evidence that it ever became a 'sink' until at least the mid nineties. Some of the critiques of Park Hill are barely worth taking seriously—the most famous, Nicholas Taylor's diatribe in the *Architectural Review* of 1967, appears to have been based on entirely imaginary statistics, and surveys right into the

1980s showed a high level of satisfaction with the flats.[34] The documentary *Romancing the Stone* mentions that the 'dream turned sour in the early 1980s', but not why that might be the case: the transformation of the steel industry into a low-workforce automated process. The mass unemployment this created turned Sheffield rapidly from a prospective City of the Future into a remnant of the past; while the Right to Buy council housing would turn unpopular estates into refuges of last resort. In an optimistic period Park Hill looked confident; as that world collapsed, it looked intimidating.

In the 1990s Hyde Park was partly demolished, and its remnants became part of a wider project influenced by the work of the conservative geographer Alice Coleman and her once-famous book *Utopia On Trial*, in inexplicable aid of the World Student Games held in Sheffield in 1991. Coleman, a sort of urbanist Gillian McKeith with charts of the preponderance of faeces on public housing estates, argued that the aesthetic form rather than the conditions of council housing caused its poverty—pseudo-scientific graphs demonstrated that the building type most likely to inculcate crime was tall, deck-access, and made of concrete, so Park Hill fit the bill very precisely (as did the Barbican, but unsurprisingly it didn't feature in the survey). Meanwhile she argued that a 'natural' form of housing, the 1930s semi, clearly

Hyde Park

'owned' with ease of surveillance and set back from the street, was the peak of architectural achievement; something from which paternalist postwar planners deviated out of aesthetic prissiness. So the 1960s terraces that were part of Hyde Park and the 1930s flats that preceded Park Hill were both reclad with new elevations that made them resemble the 1980s speculative suburban housing of the likes of Wimpey or Barratt. Hyde Park's decks were filled in, creating exactly the kind of desolate, soulless, depopulated space that they were designed to combat. Its taller segments were demolished and the whole thing was clad in brick and plastic, while Kelvin flats were levelled completely.[35] At night, the surviving Hyde Park blocks still look astounding, at a peak above the city, and the planned Sheffield of the 1960s becomes briefly palpable.

While conventional architectural opinion was turning against the streets in the sky, popular music told a different story. The Human League were keen to point out that their shimmering proto-techno instrumental 'Dancevision', described by Simon Reynolds in terms which describe contemporary Sheffield rather well as an 'ambiguous alloy of euphoria and grief', was recorded in front of Kelvin Flats, and the group staged a deck-access romance in the video to 'Love Action'. Pulp recorded two conflicting accounts of these places: 'Deep Fried in Kelvin', a desperately bleak indictment of a place 'where pigeons go to die'; and 'Sheffield: Sex City', where it is transfigured into the culmination of a metropolis infused with utopian carnality—'everyone on Park Hill came in unison at 4.13 a.m., and the whole block fell down'. In fact, it could be argued that when Sheffield City Council was no longer prepared to create an image of the future and a new way of life, Sheffield's techno producers did so instead. At the same time that Hyde Park was being transformed into its current retrograde form, Warp Records and Sheffield producers like Richard H. Kirk or Rob Gordon were creating an art form that formed a continuation of the streets in the sky's vertiginous sense of new space and their Brutalist low-end rumble. Nonetheless, it's almost certain that Park Hill would have suffered the same fate as Kelvin and

Hyde Park had it not been listed in 1998. Practically inescapable in Sheffield, it is an overwhelming reminder of what it once wanted to be—the capital of the Socialist Republic of South Yorkshire— rather than what it wants to be now, a local service and cultural industries centre. Yet like all British cities, it spent the following decade undergoing the dubious ministrations of regeneration.

On the first of my visits to Sheffield, in spring 2009, I interviewed two interested parties: first Ben Morris, a local Defend Council Housing campaigner; and then Simon Gawthorpe, of the property developer Urban Splash, charged with the regeneration of Park Hill. Morris wasn't all that interested in Park Hill: although he liked the building, he had a wider story to tell. Critics of Park Hill have always demanded 'homes with gardens' instead—well, to artificially stimulate (sorry, 'renew') the housing market, Sheffield City Council spent a decade indiscriminately demolishing council housing, whether it was Modernist, in the form of Womersley's obliterated Woodside Estate, or traditional, in the form of arts and crafts semis at Shirecliffe. Morris took me to Woodside, now almost completely demolished; and to traditionalist interwar garden suburbs like Parson Cross, now pockmarked with demolition sites that are intended to be filled eventually by 'aspirational' new housing developments, for sale.

Under the administration of Bob Kerslake, Sheffield's New Labour Council was proud of its policy of demolishing council housing to create 'Housing Market Renewal Pathfinders', i.e. to stimulate a property boom. Whether tower blocks or houses with gardens, nowhere was safe from Kerslake's wrecking ball. The policy, intended to invite 'mixed communities' through new buildings that seldom arrived, created a huge council waiting list—between 2001 and 2007 it quadrupled from 14,301 to 58,706, and Morris estimates that the recession may have pushed it as high as 90,000.[36] If you don't want council estates to become emergency refuges inhabited mainly by the desperate, this is a weird way of going about it. Accordingly, Park Hill went from the product of a policy of slum clearance to one of slum creation, as its inhabitants are decamped to the already heaving waiting list. Park

Hill will lose around nine hundred council flats, with roughly three hundred being run by a Housing Association, sixty of which will be for shared ownership. Six hundred will be sold on the open market. Yet this incredible destruction of public assets is only a fraction of the thousands of dwellings lost under Kerslake.

On the basis of his 'success' in Sheffield, in 2009 Sir Bob Kerslake was appointed chair of the Homes and Communities Agency (HCA), a super-quango merging the Public–Private Partnership sponsors English Partnerships with the Housing Corporation. This proud demolisher of council housing is now head of the agency that intends to sponsor new social housing to help people through the property crash, although in its first few months its only activities appeared to be a vast £2.8 billion bail-out of the country's property developers, something missed by the press in the face of the even larger bail-outs of the banks. Of this, Urban Splash received £3.8 million, despite being the only developer on the list not to be providing flats for rent.[37] Moreover, the HCA has 'frontloaded' its £16 million sponsorship of Park Hill's redevelopment, with the developers contributing a speculative £88 million.[38]

The estate was transferred—for free, not sold—to Urban Splash, the Manchester-based property developer best known for turning derelict mills, office blocks and factories into city-centre lofts. It grew out of a pop poster stall run by founder Tom Bloxham, a former Labour Party Young Socialist, and is an interesting amalgam of two New Labour fixations—the 'creative industries' and property speculation, as opposed to Old Labour's heavy industries and social housing. Urban Splash has always stressed a link between its work and the Manchester of post-punk and acid house, and its brochure for Park Hill was elegantly rendered by Warp Records' and Pulp's sleeve designers, the Designers Republic, themselves a recent casualty of the recession. Full of quotations from Sheffield bands like the Human League and ABC, the whole document is written in infantile music press clichés that contrast tellingly with the popular but non-patronizing language of *Ten Years of Housing in Sheffield*. 'Don't you want me baby?' it asks, and proceeding through numerous factual errors, it promises to restore 'the love' to Park Hill. 'Make it a place', it says. 'Make it a special place. Make it an EXTRA special place.' At least they're honest enough to admit that 'we're in this to make a profit.'[39]

Walking around Park Hill today is a surreal experience. At one end it's still inhabited, and on various trips through 2009 I've seen children playing, tenants chatting in the streets in the sky, and front doors left open. At the other end is a monolithic, empty frame. I asked Simon Gawthorpe why Urban Splash took so drastic an approach, and he replied that the intention was to transform the place from a 'sink estate' into 'a place where people would want to live and invest'. Some of their ideas are reasonably thoughtful, such as opening a four-storey entrance to relieve the block's wall-like appearance, and some much-needed repairs to the spalling concrete; others seem designed to make Park Hill as brightly tacky as any other piece of regeneration architecture.

In a move decided upon before market failure made money scarce, Urban Splash stripped the entire North Block at great expense, when this structurally sound building could have been refurbished simply enough. This is something the developer had done elsewhere, as in the transformation of Birmingham's Rotunda office block into flats—but that was on a far smaller

Park Hill, inhabited sector

scale, and with an obvious rationale through the change of function. To take the same approach to transforming flats into flats seemed perverse. So I had assumed it was space standards that dictated the stripping, the desire to carve out larger spaces for the new middle-class buyers, but Gawthorpe tells me they will mostly keep its internal proportions. What they are doing is removing all the bricks, to be replaced by anodized aluminium panels, replicating the colour scheme while entirely abandoning truth to materials. Astoundingly, this was done with the permission—and monetary sponsorship—of English Heritage. This removal might be a direct repudiation of Brutalism's rough aesthetic, but neither developers nor conservationists mind the other removals that destroy its ethic. Urban Splash certainly finds the 'utopian' rhetoric of 'heroic' Modernism attractive, and Gawthorpe proudly talks about a woman who had lived there since the sixties telling them, 'People think we live in a slum. They don't realize that I live in a penthouse looking out over the city'. He couldn't tell me where the council had moved her. Already three hundred (roughly half) of the two thirds of residents who have been cleared so far have specifically registered an interest in returning, indicating that the building is still held in high esteem by those it was designed for— but only two hundred flats will be available for social rent, and that from one of the philanthropic institutions reviled by Brutalists and Bevanites. Meanwhile, and perhaps most telling of all, in the new scheme the streets in the sky will be gated off where they meet the real streets of the surrounding area, finally settling the question about whether they were ever 'real' streets at all, in the negative.

You get the inescapable feeling that a whole claque of publicly funded bodies have become subject to a property developer's whims, with 'private enterprise', as Aneurin Bevan put it when Minister of Housing, 'sucking on the teats of the state'.[40] Perhaps the only sympathetic figure in *Romancing the Stone*'s fly on the wall farrago was the estate's caretaker, who drives along the streets in the sky in a golf buggy, picking up refuse bags and drug paraphernalia. In the face of this astonishing structure, patronized by heritage and property, he comments: 'I love the old girl. She's an old lady who's fallen on hard times.' Here at least, Park Hill has inspired the sense of belonging its architects tried to create. Park Hill is a battered remnant of a very different country, one which briefly turned housing for ordinary people into futuristic monuments rather than shamefaced little hutches. Although it's unclear what Park Hill will become in the next few years (the regeneration project is scheduled to be finished in 2017, so will take considerably longer than the actual construction of the place; and given the pace of change and Urban Splash's current 'troubles', strange things could happen), it's abundantly clear that here, the ideologies of Regeneration and Heritage, when applied to the very different ethical aesthetic of the old New Brutalism, can only destroy the thing they claim to love.

Replanning Sheffield—Hung, Drawn and Quartered

The destruction of the planned hilltop Sheffield of the 1960s, which proceeded incrementally from the 1980s onwards—first Hyde Park, then the recladding and part-demolition of Netherthorpe, then Kelvin, and finally Woodside—marked the end of one experiment in seeing the city as a totality. But as ever, this does not mean the end of urban *dirigisme*, nor that Sheffield has ceased to be divided up into discrete parcels. The planning efforts of the last ten years focus not so much on the social housing of earlier years—after all, nobody wants to court the 'core vote'—but on the centre, which has been replanned as a series of thematic Quarters, of which there are a mathematically improbable eleven. They include the 'Heart of the City Quarter' (the area around the town hall), the 'Devonshire Quarter' (the student district) and the 'Cultural Industries Quarter', of which more later. One of these sectors was designated before actually being built— the 'New Retail Quarter', recently renamed 'Sevenstone'. An entire area bought up by Hammerson, the shopping mall developers responsible for Southampton's WestQuay, among others, it is explicitly modelled on Liverpool One—a multitude of architects designing contrasting buildings as part of a wider plan, the area

Site of the New Retail Quarter

patrolled by private security as a 'mall without walls', explicitly designed to compete with the out-of-town shopping hangar of Meadowhall. Before the crash, a couple of moderately good buildings—a patterned car park, a decent, unspectacular red-brick fire station by BDP, which for no perceptible reason replaced a decent, unspectacular red-brick fire station built twenty years ago—were finished, but by the start of 2009 the New Retail Quarter was credit-crunched, leaving a quiet, derelict area in the city centre, one which, unable to make a profit, acquired a certain dreaminess, with the space to let the imagination wander.

It was always doubtful that the total retail experience of Hammerson's New Retail Quarter would be anything like as interesting as Castle Market, but its designated area is pervaded by weird and brilliant postwar architecture. This includes out-breaks of fierce originality amidst the compromised Portland stone modern-ish of The Moor, a parade in a similar vague vein to Above Bar in Southampton, without the vigour of a real Modern-ism or the bombast of proper classicism. But totally dominating all of this is the thrillingly paranoid Cold War megastructure of the 1978 Manpower Services building, designed for the DHSS by some unusually addled committee at the Property Services Agency as a complex, inscrutable ziggurat, its multiple levels

The Manpower Services Ziggurat

adding an imaginary topography to Sheffield's already complex layers and outcrops. Generations of Sheffielders will have had the dubious pleasure of signing on in this massive complex, and there is what proper architecture critics might call a 'processional route' here: the wings of the ziggurat shelter a plaza housing an abstract, Hepworth-esque sculpture leading to what was once a public walkway, now closed off because of the alleged terrorist threat to depressed Yorkshire towns of little economic or strategic significance. This turns Manpower Services into a wall, closing it off from the south of the city; a convenient excuse for demolition, as is the grime which creeps up the Grosvenor Hotel. Another Modernist showcase, the hotel is a squat, patterned tower that is cutely clunky, facing off against the full-on technological white heat of Oxley & Bussey's Telephone House, a rough-hewn slab of bureaucratic sublime. There's no such excuse with another fine building now on borrowed time, Yorke Rosenberg and Mardall's elegant John Lewis store, clad in white tiles which, while now fairly filthy, could probably be cleaned in an afternoon.

An even more inscrutable gesture is made by Jefferson Sheard's 1968 Electricity Substation, a shocking paroxysm of a building, an explosion in reinforced concrete, a bunker built with an aesthete's attention to detail, a building which is genuinely Brutalist in both

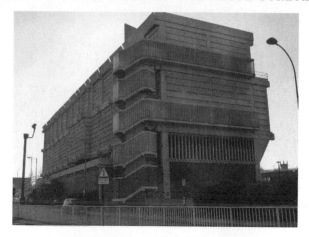

The Electricity Substation

Velocity Tower

senses of the term. Around it, derelict steelworks and patches of wasteland sit next to absurd outcrops of regeneration, such as Broadway Malyan's Velocity Tower, another glass block with absolutely nothing to do with its surroundings—aptly, as it was originally designed for another site entirely. It's adjacent to some of Womersley's red-brick tower blocks, which, in a similar act of

Steelworks, near Velocity Tower

wilful blindness, are being clad in grey panels. Velocity is the name of the developer, which is building a 'Velocity Village' elsewhere in the city. Its website has a semi-literate description which makes clear how much it appeals to a particular notion of high-style Modernism, albeit one which has little interest in the actual Modernism of Sheffield: 'built of acid washed concrete but mostly faced in steel and glass—think sparkling white "Le Corbusier" style, shining in the sun brightening up the landscape in an area due a little aesthetic value—this is one of the largest mixed use developments in Yorkshire.'

This at least seems preferable to the Pythonesque veneration of the Victorian, an era during which Sheffield was by all accounts a suburb of Hell, that marked the 1980s and '90s in the city—but not all its postmodernist gestures were as banal as this. At Barker's Pool, opposite the stripped classical City Hall, is a small but tautly powerful office block, in surprisingly good nick considering its evident dereliction. This is Malcolm Lister's NUM headquarters, designed in the early 1980s, commissioned by Arthur Scargill in an effort to move the union from its offices in London to the more amenable territory of the Socialist Republic of South Yorkshire. Its yellowing Yorkshire stone and columns are a clear attempt to blend in with the City Hall, albeit without the pat gestures of

The NUM

mainstream Postmodernism. Developers have proposed numerous abortive schemes for the site on which it sits, so far without success. Nobody, however, advocates keeping the building, one of the few examples of architecture specifically commissioned by the 'Hard Left' of the 1980s—which in a neat irony is far more sympathetic to the historical city than anything built by New Labour, despite their occasional genuflection towards Heritage.

Aside from retail, Sheffield has dedicated its post-industrial shell to students and the creative industries, which make up the rest of the new area. The Creatives are housed in some rather decent structures, like the conservative Modernist firm Fielden Clegg Bradley's Persistence Works, a complex concrete building which marks perhaps the only engagement with Brutalism in the post-1979 city; the student population is represented in new architecture by some aggressive jollity, in the form of RMJM's lime-green Information Commons, a library with tube-station-style automated access doors. We do not gain access to it, but we see enough to note how spectacularly cheap and tinny the detailing is. This is not the case with Sauerbruch Hutton's similarly blaring Jessop West, where strips of overbearingly loud coloured glass sheath an environmentally and visually inventive interior, performing all manner of energy-saving feats in an organic style that is more weird and intriguing than tweedy and worthy. The shape of the building is decidedly reminiscent of the only Sheffield building its Anglo-German architects are likely to care for, the inescapable Park Hill. There are still high-density housing developments in Sheffield, but they are designed for students rather than working-class families—and they're still huge, dominant things. They don't exploit their hugeness, however, are not interested in elevating it into a virtue.

Take the West One development, where Leeds pseudo-modernists Carey Jones designed a series of hulking blocks around a courtyard, where the ground floor houses chain restaurants and offices for PFI corp Capita Symonds and the upper storeys contain flats which would have been considered far too cramped for 1950s steelworkers. Yet the bright colours and arbitrary 'features' attempt to soften these lumpen blocks. It could almost serve as a guide to what Urban Splash wants Park Hill to become, and its raised four-storey entrance is the evident inspiration for the new ceremonial gateway they plan to carve into the building.

For all this, Sheffield is still a unique city, with a sense of possibility about it that is wholly absent from its sewn-up rivals. If it is to remain unique, it could do with spending less money trying to make itself like everywhere else and more time on the neglected

Gleadless Valley

Holy Cross Church

places that make it so. Places like the Gleadless Valley, planned under Womersley at the same time as Park Hill; a bizarre and beautiful landscape, Bruno Taut's Berlin via Neutra's Los Angeles, refracted through the English Picturesque. After 1945 many British architects and thinkers appropriated the idea of the Picturesque for Modernist purposes, under the influence of Nikolaus Pevsner's ideas about the 'Englishness of English Art'. Schemes like the Lansbury neighbourhood or the Alton East estate in London are the best known of this attempt to create a specifically English integration of architecture and landscape, but Gleadless shows this aesthetic at its most stunning, set in a dramatic natural landscape and with an equally dramatic abundance of parkland, which is lush and planted rather than bleak and scrubby.

Built into a steep valley, the buildings make remarkably similar use of the contours and contrasts of the landscape to Park Hill, only in low-rise, low-density form. The estate has a variety of different building types adapted to the site: terraces with monopitch roofs paralleling the steep inclines; 'patio houses' divided into two levels with entrances from different parts of the hill; more straightforward low-rise blocks of flats with deck access from the slopes; and two enclaves of towers to provide an urban drama that might otherwise be lacking, with the gentle expressionism

The Arcadian landscape of Gleadless

of Braddock & Martin-Smith's Holy Cross Church forming a diminutive *Stadtkrone*. Two of the towers have been cheaply clad, and the more fastidious might be offended by residents' replacement doors and windows, but in general the poverty of the area has ensured the survival of its architectural integrity. A mixed blessing.

New additions to the estate were made up until the late 1970s, the most idyllic being a set of timber-framed flats, designed by Peter Jackson and John Taylor at the City Architects Department

Deck-Access Blocks, Gleadless Valley

National Centre for Popular Music (former)

as part of a series, with others in Heeley and Netherthorpe. They're far from monumental, but otherwise they seem like miniature versions of Park Hill, stepped with deck access from the street and planting on the balconies, collectivizing the sunbelt dream for a significantly less climatically blessed city. When we're photographing these late flats, some of their shirtless tenants, enjoying the spring sunshine, shout over: 'You don't want to take pictures of us, we're just chavs.' Since the seventies, the estate has been neglected, and despite the extraordinary architecture and planning, the area is one of Sheffield's poorest. Though this is for reasons—employment, education—which have little to do with the architecture, it has evidently rubbed off on perceptions of it, as even the tweediest anti-Modernist would have to apply industrial strength blinkers to see this place as harsh or inhuman. As we walked round Gleadless we were genuinely amazed by it, without the caveats we'd apply to the Brutalism of the centre. We talk about how fantastic, and how unlikely, it would be for something with this much green space, with this much architectural intelligence, to be built now. Except nobody notices it, because it's a 'sink estate'. As we walk around the curving roads in awe, a woman, incredulous for different reasons, asks us: 'You're taking pictures of Gleadless? That's sad.' Indeed it is.

Culture Industry/Steel Industry

At the centre of Steel City is something called the Cultural Industries Quarter. This contains the former National Centre for Popular Music, four steel blobs designed by Nigel Coates, a somewhat faded 'Millennium Project' which closed within a couple of years of its completion. Now used by Sheffield Hallam University for offices, its Blairite nature is still stressed through the list of lower-case verbs that decorates the entrance: 'empowering. enriching. celebrating. involving. entertaining.' Then there's the long-standing Leadmill Club, the Site Gallery and for some reason a branch of Spearmint Rhino. More to the point, the quarter contains a faïence-tiled 1930s moderne building housing the Showroom cinema and Workstation, home of Warp Films, the only part of Warp Records' media empire that is still based in the city. The very name 'Cultural Industries Quarter' is New Labour nu-language that seems a bad joke amidst the recession's foreboding harshness. The notion that an economy can run itself through the 'creative industries', financial services and tourism has taken an extremely heavy knock. It's particularly symbolic that these 'industries' sit next to the rail station of a once-proud heavy industrial metropolis that has never quite worked out what to do with itself since the steel industry's 'restructuring' in the 1980s. (Unlike South Yorkshire's coal mining, steel never ceased production, and through the 2000s the city made as much from it as it ever did—only with a tiny fraction of the workforce.) What Sheffield *has* had since the late 1970s is perhaps the most consistently brilliant popular music of any city outside of London.

The city's electronic music, from The Human League and Cabaret Voltaire to early Warp artists Forgemasters and Sweet Exorcist, took palpable inspiration from the cyclopean factories of the Don Valley and the fearless, grandly scaled 1960s architecture built for their workers. It's no surprise, then, that Warp Records' twentieth anniversary celebrations in the city the label left in 2000 take place in the disputed remnants of a council estate and a steelworks, with film screenings in the former and a rave in the latter.

Magna Science Adventure Centre

The proceedings are assisted by the local regeneration quango, which bears the instructive name 'Creative Sheffield'.

That this is not entirely benign is obvious as soon as we arrive at the first of the two events, a Warp Films showcase in Park Hill itself. It's this boarded-up portion of the estate, not the skeleton or (unsurprisingly) the inhabited part, which Warp is using for this showcase of its film production arm, and given the sheer quantity of public space that defines Park Hill, we initially assume that as pedestrians we could just walk in. Instead, metal fencing marks off the film event from the inhabited section of the estate, with police watching from the walkways. Even the playground is fenced off. As a preview of the 'mixed class' estate promised by Urban Splash and its public sponsors, it is not encouraging.

Nonetheless, once inside the films (mostly) fit the space well. A film on the All Tomorrow's Parties music festival is about as interesting as someone else's home movies, but Warp's music videos remain playful, ambitious and intriguing. These videos, from Jarvis Cocker and Martin Wallace's early efforts for Sweet Exorcist and Tricky Disco to more extravagant works like Alex Rutterford's 'Gantz Graf' for Autechre, or Chris Cunningham's bling absurdist film for Aphex Twin's 'Windowlicker', are mini-masterpieces of the form. Certainly the futurist melancholia of the latter record feels appropriate for this tragic, sublime building.

The main event takes place in—again, note the already dated nomenclature—the Magna Science Adventure Centre, a winner of the Stirling Prize in 2001. Again we have a perfect meeting of place and sound, and again an overwhelming reminder of the area's class conflicts and disputed transformations. Magna was once the Steel, Peech and Tozer steelworks, part of the industrial zone that stretches between Sheffield and Rotherham. The road out from the centre goes seedy first, the strange sexualized landscape of Attercliffe, until it becomes fully post-industrial, arriving at the surviving steelworks and a zone which has for decades been subject to several regeneration attempts. Most have been on the same long, low scale as the plants they replaced, repurposed for leisure and shopping—'iceSheffield', the Don Valley Stadium, and the enormous Meadowhall shopping mall, a postmodernist megastructure of glass domes and fibreglass Victorian details abutting the M1. This in turn was for decades overlooked by the Tinsley Cooling Towers, concrete hyperbolic paraboloids that once marked the 'gateway to the north'. The city's 'creatives' banded together to try to save the towers from their mooted demolition, proposing to turn them into enormous works of public art. In this instance at least, the culture industry did not supplant the truly industrial: a new power station, which may or may not turn out to be considerably less iconic, is being built on site. Next to business parks, retail parks and still functioning (if recession-threatened) steel plants, Magna attempts to unite the two 'industries' by offering steel up as a spectacle—and it's an awe-inspiring one, a superhuman process whose eventual lack of need for human workers seems entirely unsurprising. Inside a cold, physically arresting hangar-like space, reached through views of the overwhelming machinery, are the hilariously tiny DJs.

Warp Records is now a decidedly international operation, lacking the regional sentimentality of, say, Factory Records, which has spared Sheffield the tedious myth-making of the Mancunian music scene: the label very seldom signs local acts. Nonetheless,

Yorkshire producers created Warp's most enduring, powerful music in the early nineties: the precise, compulsive techno of Sweet Exorcist's 'Testone', LFO's 'Frequencies', Nightmares on Wax's 'Aftermath', or Rob Gordon's Forgemasters, named after another Sheffield steelworks. Nightmares on Wax feature at Magna, billed as a reformation of their original lineup. After one album of Yorkshire techno in 1991, Nightmares on Wax split, leaving one member to pursue a rather less interesting trip-hop direction under the same name. At Magna their DJ set starts worryingly with a couple of tracks from these later albums, but after interspersing Nitro Deluxe's 'Let's Get Brutal' it becomes a techno set, concentrating on the cavernous, concussively physical, spacious sound they pioneered twenty years ago. It's awe-inspiring to hear it in a space like this, although the irony that it would have once occurred in disused warehouses and factories illegally, but is now doing so with local government assistance, is doubtless not lost on some of the older participants. Alongside this controlled ferocity, the juxtaposition with the whimsical, wistful electro-jazz of Chris Clark or Squarepusher is not kind to later Warp, their prettiness woefully inappropriate to the context.

Sheffield does not lack for new electronic music. Yet it's a very different kind, the sort I heard teenagers play off their phones that day on the Rotherham–Sheffield train—bassline house, Yorkshire's Brutalist version of two-step garage, which owes much to the tinny synthetic stabs and enveloping bass rumbles of early Warp, splicing it with a far from minimal commercial crassness. It's an expression of the city as it is, a living, messy thing, which is very seldom 'tasteful'. Yet rather than being quango-funded, Niche, the club where it started, was closed by South Yorkshire Police in 2005, in the tactfully named 'Operation Repatriation'. It exists now as a high-security superclub, but nonetheless there was nary a hint of bassline at Magna. 'Creative Sheffield' remains a divided place.

Chapter Five

Manchester: So Much to Answer For

Greater Manchester, Cottonopolis, was once the world's most futuristic city. In the early decades of the nineteenth century, architectural visitors like Karl Friedrich Schinkel saw in the repetition, inhuman scale and industrial materials of its mills a prophecy of the architecture of the future. We now live in that future. The unplanned industrial convulsions in China's Pearl River Delta have their antecedents here. Nonetheless, Manchester offers a rather different aesthetic to the architectural traveller than that of toil and material production. More than any other city in Britain, Manchester has become a flagship for urban regeneration and immaterial capitalism. What other cities have dabbled in with piecemeal ineptitude, Manchester has implemented with total efficiency. If the regeneration that has taken place since the mid 1990s has a success story, it is surely here; and if we are to judge regeneration in its purest, least botched form, we have to turn to Manchester, a city which has neatly repositioned itself as a cold, rain-soaked Barcelona. Sit by Tadao Ando's stained concrete furnishings at Piccadilly Gardens, squint at the strolling and coffee sipping, and you could almost believe it.

An impressive thing about Manchester's new buildings is just how *popular* they are. In the newsagents, you can buy postcards of the Beetham Tower, Urbis or the Lowry, all sure signs that they have entered popular affection in a way relatively few modern buildings have since the 1960s—so to knock Manchester's pride in its architecture could easily seem churlish, and the finer buildings here genuinely are superior to their equivalents in Liverpool, Leeds, Sheffield or Glasgow, albeit within rather limited parameters. The populism of the new Manc Modernism should not be a surprise. Manchester's regeneration industry draws extensively on the city's legacy of extraordinary popular art, an area in which it has been markedly unimpressive since the early nineties, when the regeneration game began, although this doesn't seem to have put anyone off. Regenerated cities produce no more great pop music, great films or great art than they do industrial product, although they may produce notable art galleries or museums. What they *do* produce is property developers—most famously Urban Splash, which has spread its 'creative' approach from here to as far as Plymouth; signature architects, such as Ian Simpson, subsequently much in demand elsewhere; and regeneration experts such as the unelected council leader Howard Bernstein, who is now busy transforming Blackpool, where he already finds a city devoted to leisure rather than having to transform a city of production into one of consumption.

Manchester City Centre has been repopulated over the last two decades to an undeniably impressive extent, at least in statistical terms: in 1987 its population was 300; now it's over 11,000. As

The Hulme Arch, entrance to the New Manchester

Ancoats, History–Prosperity–Technology

someone who has only the vaguest memories of the pre-regeneration city, I couldn't help but approach the transformed centre without the requisite awe. The recession has led to the indefinite shelving of major projects like the Albany and Piccadilly Towers, so the regenerated metropolis has essentially found its final form. We are dealing with an unintentionally finished product, the most complete attempt to redesign an entire city on the basis of an alliance between property development, the culture industry and ubiquitous retail. In the process, the post-punk generation, even (or especially) those who considered themselves 'Situationists', has proved to be every bit as potentially corruptible as the hippies it reviled. Much as an oppositional, independent pop music has become a new museum culture in today's Manchester, the Situationist critique of postwar urbanism has curdled into an alibi for its gentrification.

I make no apologies for the Smiths quotation that names this chapter. In the ultra-gentrified context of twenty-first-century Manchester The Smiths, along with The Fall, seem to matter much more than the Factory Records lineage of sleek Modernism. Both Morrissey's unforgiving wallowing in the grim, grotty horrors of Cottonopolis and a self-constructed world of guilt, furtive desire and miserablism, and Mark E. Smith's chaotic encryptions and denunciations are in implicit conflict with the blank

Pseudomodernism that Factory's industrial aesthetic eventually produced. The continuities are direct. The late, great Tony Wilson unfortunately spent much of the last years of his life as a propagandist for what the billboards in Ancoats call 'New Emerging Manchester', with the added Huxleyesque legend 'History–Prosperity–Technology'. However, maybe The Fall are not so disconnected from the post-IRA bomb metropolis. Among the many, many quangos who have administered the regenerated Cottonopolis is one with the acronym 'NWRA'—the North-West Regional Association, a Lancastrian regeneration quango which may just be connected with Mark E. Smith's declaration that the North Will Rise Again. There are no coincidences in New Manchester.

Property Development as the new Punk Rock

The Los Angeles-based property developer John Lydon recently opined that he'd seen what a failure socialism was, because he'd lived in a council flat. This squares with the idea that punk was a sort of counter-cultural equivalent to Thatcherism—a movement for individualism, cruelty and discipline, as against the woolly solidarity and collectivism of the postwar consensus. Council flats were always an emblem of punk, at least in its more socialist-realist variants. There was a sort of delayed cultural reaction to the cities of tower blocks and motorways built in the 1960s, to the point where their effect only really registered around ten years later, when a cultural movement defined itself as having come from those towers and walkways. It wasn't always actually true, of course, but when it was—Mick Jones's Mum's flat overlooking the Westway, for instance—it led to a curious kind of bad faith, where on the one hand the dehumanizing effect of these places was lamented, but on the other, the vertiginous new landscape was fetishized and aestheticized.

Although post-punk was always a great deal more aesthetically sophisticated, not bound by nostalgia for the old streets, this bad faith features here, too. Post-punk is usually represented in terms of concrete and piss, grim towers and blasted wastelands. This is best exemplified in the poster to Anton Corbijn's woeful Ian Curtis biopic *Control*, in which Sam Riley, fag dangling from mouth, looks wan and haunted below gigantic prefabricated tower blocks (which, as we've seen, were shot in Nottingham, not the gentrified-out-of-recognition Manchester—although there are certainly parts of Salford that could still do the trick). Decades ago, when asked by Jon Savage why Joy Division's sound had such a sense of loss and gloom, Bernard Sumner reminisced about his Salford childhood, where 'there was a huge sense of community where we lived ... I guess what happened in the sixties was that someone at the Council decided that it wasn't very healthy, and something had to go, and unfortunately it was my neighbourhood that went. We were moved over the river into a tower block. *At the time I thought it was fantastic*—now of course I realize it was a total disaster.'[41] (My italics.) This is often quoted as if it were obvious—well, *of course* it was a disaster. This is the narrative about Modernist architecture that exists in numerous reminiscences and histories: we loved it at first, in the sixties; then we realized our mistake, knocked them down, and rebuilt simulations of the old streets instead.

Decades on from the victories of punk and Thatcherism, after thirty years in which the dominant form of mass housing has been the achingly traditionalist Barratt Home or perhaps an inner-urban loft, rather than a concrete maisonette, this yearning for old certainties, cobbles and the aesthetics of *Coronation Street* has a rather different resonance. In so many cases the places punk and Thatcherism wanted to destroy were swept away, particularly over the last fifteen years, in favour of 'urban regeneration'. Yet the effect on the regenerated cities has been, in musical terms, unimpressive to say the least. In the 2000s, the very few areas to have retained a distinctive musical presence—forgotten estates in east and south-east London, depressed Yorkshire cities like Bradford or Sheffield—are those which have largely escaped regeneration. Meanwhile, Manchester—capital of regeneration with its loft apartments, its towering yuppiedromes, its titanium-clad galleries—has produced virtually no innovative music since A Guy Called Gerald's *Black Secret Technology* in 1995. Jungle, garage, grime: all largely bypassed Manchester, while 'alternative' music degenerated into the homilies of Badly Drawn Boy, into innumerable 'landfill indie' acts, with or without attendant macho Manc swagger. You could blame this on the Stone Roses, or on Oasis—or it could be blamed on the new city created by an enormous and now-pricked property bubble.

Post-Rave Urban Growth Coalition

Tony Wilson was evidently pleased that the guru of the 'Creative Class', Richard Florida, had designated the Manchester of young media professionals and loft conversions as a 'cultural capital', irrespective of the conspicuous lack of worthwhile culture created in the regenerated city—save for Mancunian auto-hagiographies like *The Alcohol Years*, *Control* or the egregious *24-Hour Party People*. At the end of the most recent and most intelligent of these, Grant Gee's *Joy Division* documentary, Wilson reflected on how Manchester had gone from being the first industrial city in the early nineteenth century to what is today: Britain's first successful post-industrial city. After the blight of the 1970s it is now a modern metropolis once again, this time based on media and property rather than something so unseemly as industrial production. The old entrepreneurs built the mills where workers toiled at twelve-hour shifts and died before they were forty; the new entrepreneurs sold the same mills to young urban professionals as industrial-aesthetic luxury housing.

Wilson squarely credited Joy Division and Factory Records with a leading role in this transformation, but he was by no means alone in doing so. Nick Johnson, one of the directors of Urban Splash, has given presentations in which he dates the beginnings of his company to the Sex Pistols' gig at the Free Trade Hall. Justin O'Connor, academic and co-founder of Urbis, the exhibition centre on 'the city' built on the IRA bombsite, claims that Wilson found Richard Florida's book and thought it said all that needed to be said about cities and that Manchester should pay circa 20k to get him to speak ... I tried (to convince him) what a complete charlatan Florida was and how a 'cutting-edge' 'creative city' should not be ninety-seventh in line to invite some tosser from Philadelphia. He completely rejected this and never really spoke to me again. The last time I saw him was in Liverpool at a RIBA do. He was saying that Liverpool was 'fucked', unlike Manchester—and the reason was that Manchester had an enlightened despot (in the figure of the unelected Howard Bernstein). Which more or less set a seal on the increasing moral and political bankruptcy of the post-rave urban growth coalition which had taken over Manchester post-1996. Simpson, Johnson, Bloxham—now all millionaires —all claimed to have the new political vision for the re-invented city. Despite the fact that Bloxham—a man of little culture and education—was given chair of the arts council and now VC of Manchester university, thus confirming the toadying of arts and education to the 'creative entrepreneur', it is Wilson who represents its saddest failures. He made little money from it all, and really believed in it. Now subject of a nauseating hagiography by the city council that kept him outside for years, until the last four or five, bringing him in when his critical faculties had been worn down by years of punditry. He used to say, of the post-rave coalition, 'the lunatics have taken over the asylum'; pigs and farm was more apposite.[42]

The narrative of Sex Pistols–Factory–IRA Bomb–Ian Simpson–Urban Splash has no room for the postwar years, decades of decline which just happened to coincide with the most fertile and exciting popular culture ever produced in the city (was it accidental, perhaps?). When Manchester is profiled or reminisced over, it is most often through a narrative which leaps from the Victorian city of 'Manchester liberalism'—a laissez-faire doctrine with distinct similarities to Thatcherism—to the city recreated and regenerated after the IRA bomb in 1996. The horrendous poverty of nineteenth-century Manchester and the gaping inequalities of today are entirely effaced. In between is a no man's land.

New Emerging Babylon

Both approaches have an essentially nineteenth-century idea of the city as a place that should rise autonomously out of the activities of entrepreneurs and businessmen. The unplanned cities of the nineteenth century have long been a touchstone of a certain school of psychogeography—a term originally derived from the Situationist International. Under the influence of English writers Iain Sinclair and Peter Ackroyd, it has come to refer to an archaeological, vaguely occult approach to the city, where that which already exists is walked through at random, the rich historical associations leading to recondite, occasionally critical chains of association and reflections on the nebulous spirit of certain areas. Although this school of psychogeography is fiercely antagonistic to the glassy, security-obsessed cities created by regeneration, they share a hostility to planning and to the planned cities of social democracy. Although they come from political antipodes, both can agree about the ghastliness of council estates and the deficient aesthetics of 1960s tower blocks. If a certain strain in punk continues in much psychogeographical writing, it is the element that laments the destruction of Victoriana—the punk and psychogeographical preservation societies, symbolized best by John Betjeman's journey from the 'Hates' list on Bernie Rhodes, Malcolm McLaren and Vivienne Westwood's 1975 'Loves/Hates' T-shirt, to 'Loves' on the remake Rhodes put together in the 2000s.

Psychogeography, as defined by the Situationist International, originally meant something rather different. While it certainly had an interest in those areas untouched by renewal, regeneration or prettification, the SI in the 1950s dared to imagine a *new* urbanism, an entirely new approach to the city which wasn't based on two up two downs or on spaced-out, rationalist tower blocks. To have an idea of what the Situationist City would have been like, you could read Ivan Chtcheglov's 'Formulary for a New Urbanism', an elliptical prose-poem imagining a self-creating world of grottoes and Gothic spaces, which, through the declaration

'You'll never see the Hacienda. It doesn't exist. The Hacienda must be built' inadvertently found its way into the annals of Manchester history.[43] Chtcheglov's city divided into pleasure-driven quarters is not as unlike contemporary Mancunia as one might assume, and a travesty of it can perhaps be found in the Green Quarter, Salford Quays or New Islington. There isn't, however, any trace of another Situationist proposal for a new urbanism, New Babylon.

This was a proposal for a genuinely new city, designed by the Dutch architect, painter and early Situationist Constant Nieuwenhuis. A ludic city dedicated to play, where 'creativity' becomes its own reward rather than a means for the accumulation of capital, New Babylon is a blueprint for a city that might exist in a future in which automation has eliminated the problem of work. Here, there are no Le Corbusier tower blocks, Constant's 'cemeteries of reinforced concrete, in which great masses of the population are condemned to die of boredom'. Nor will you find here any homilies on behalf of back to backs, red brick mills or outside privies, nor on the glories of the entrepreneurial city. If punk obsessed over the realness of the streets, New Babylon doesn't even have streets, in the old sense—it is a construction based entirely on multiple levels, walkways, skyways. It is a city in motion for a population in motion, 'a nomadic town' that functioned as a 'dynamic labyrinth' entirely through means of modern technology and construction. Models of New Babylon show tentacles of elevated bridges above the existing city, linking together megastructures that are sometimes the size of a whole town in 'a continuous spatial construction, disengaged from the ground'. The most important part of it seemed to be this element of circulation, the walkways and bridges themselves, designed to create accidents and chance encounters. Fairly obviously, for all the Situationist pretensions of Manchester's regenerators, neither the Hacienda nor New Babylon has been built there.

'Up the tenth floor, down the backstairs, into no man's land'

However, Manchester may have had a fragment of New Babylon within it without really noticing, in the form of its major example of the New Brutalism. The idea of the multi-level city, which Constant and the Situationists argued had the potential to create a new urban landscape based on chance and on play, was very much in the air in the 1950s, particularly through the international architectural group Team 10. Although as practising architects, none of Team 10 was ever likely to be accepted by the Situationists, there is evidence that they had some contacts with Dutch members of the group such as Constant. Team 10 was an oppositional grouping which set itself up in opposition to the mainstream of Modernist architecture and planning. The structures it championed, opposed to the serried ranks of tower blocks that mainstream Modernism was erecting en masse, were based on walkways and the elevation of the street above the ground, based on the urban theories of the British architects Alison and Peter Smithson. The nearest built equivalent to this in Britain, though no 'pro-Situ' or psychogeographer would dare admit it, is Sheffield's Park Hill, a building whose Mancunian offshoot has a decidedly complex history.

After leaving his post as Sheffield's City Architect, Lewis Womersley set up a private practice with another architect, Hugh Wilson. Together, the pair designed two enormous structures in Manchester at the turn of the 1970s. One of them, the Arndale Centre, which swallowed up a huge swathe of the inner city and sucked it into a private shopping centre under one roof, is the antithesis both of New Babylon—dedicated as it is to work and consumption—and of Womersley's work at Park Hill. Montage and walkways are replaced by a lumpen, grounded space topped by a lone office block, while its multiple levels benefit the car rather than the pedestrian. The other structure designed by Wilson and Womersley was the comprehensive redevelopment of the inner-city district of Hulme. The most notorious part of this, the Hulme Crescents, were a shadow, a memory of Park Hill; a series of labyrinthine blocks accessed by street decks. The relative conservatism of the Crescents can be ascertained from their names—John Nash, Charles Barry and so on, all taken from architects of the Regency period, to whose work in Bath and London this was intended to be the modern equivalent—and their prefabricated concrete construction was markedly less solidly built than Park Hill. Nonetheless, in the context of Greater Manchester, where dozens of blocks from Pendleton to Collyhurst rose out of the Victorian slums, gigantic spaced-out tombstones that amply made Constant's point about the boredom factor of postwar redevelopment, the Crescents provided a Modernist labyrinth, its street decks winding round and interconnecting four vast, semicircular blocks enclosing a no man's land of indeterminate pedestrian space. Within a couple of years of its 1971 completion, it was vermin-ridden and leaky, as a result of costs cut during the construction.

Hulme Crescents and its surrounding areas were demolished in the early 1990s. Apparently yet another example of the failures of British Modernism, its demise was seen as being nearly as pivotal for Manchester's regeneration as the Hacienda, the Commonwealth Games and the IRA bomb. *'Now of course I realize it was a total disaster.'* There's another story about what went on within the street-decks, a story which suggests that post-punk was not so conservative in its urbanism. There's no doubt that the early incarnations of Brutalist Hulme fully support the concrete and piss version of punk history. A 1978 *World in Action* documentary set out its stall early on, by describing the deck-access, streets in the sky system of the estate, then stating baldly 'it doesn't work.' The documentary depicts the new Hulme as a rabbit warren, Constant's labyrinth turned into a hotbed of crime, fear and paranoia, a place whose tortuous planning makes the seemingly simple experience of getting a pram into your flat into an ordeal, a place where rates of crime and suicide are off the national scale. Yet at the exact point that this documentary was being shot, Hulme was becoming something else entirely. Manchester City Council, which had at that point a surplus of council housing, was implementing a policy of rehousing the families that found Hulme so unnerving on housing estates with gardens in Burnage or Wythenshawe, leaving many empty flats. The Russell Club, which was home to the Factory nightclub, opened in 1978 by the embryonic record label, was surrounded by the estate's concrete walkways—and the club's clientèle would follow suit.

Liz Naylor, fanzine editor and scriptwriter of the Joy Division soundtracked film *No City Fun*, remembers how after running away from home in 1978 at the age of sixteen she asked the council for a flat. First of all, she was housed in Collyhurst, then an area with a heavy National Front presence. She asked for a flat in Hulme instead, because it had already acquired 'a population of alternatives', as 'by then the Manchester Evening News had been running stories for years about how awful it was'. Not only was the Factory based there, so were many of the bands, along with fanzines like *City Fun* and recording studios. One of the most famous images of Joy Division was taken from one of the bridges over the motorway that bisected the new Hulme. Photographer Kevin Cummins later recalled: 'the heavy bombing (of World War Two) along with an ill-conceived 1960s regeneration programme, conspired to make Manchester redolent of an eastern European city. Revisiting my photographs, I see the bleakness of a city slowly dying. A single image taken from a bridge in Hulme of Princess Parkway, the major road into Manchester, features no cars.'[44] Yet this image of a depopulated, Brutalist Manchester as a sort of English Eastern Europe resonated in a less clichéd manner with those who chose to live in Hulme—it was welcomed. Naylor remembers that the entire scene was obsessed with Berlin—'we weren't sure whether east or west Berlin'—a fixation that also dictated what they listened to: 'Iggy Pop's *The Idiot* and Bowie's "Heroes" was *the* music'. This extended to the films they saw at the Aaben, the estate's art house cinema, where Fassbinder or *Nosferatu* were eagerly consumed by the area's overcoated youth.

There was an attendant style to go with the Germanophilia. In her far from boosterist history of the area, *Various Times*, Naylor writes that 'during the early 1980s there was a "Hulme look" when the whole male population of Hulme seemed to be wearing the clothes of dead men and everyone looked as if they had stepped out of the 1930s with baggy suits and tie-less shirts.' The early eighties scene in Hulme, which included Factory bands like A Certain Ratio or 'SWP types' like Big Flame and Tools You Can Trust, was perhaps a romanticization of these surroundings, of the stark, 'eastern European' aesthetic, the sense of a Modernist utopia decaying, gone crumbled and decadent. Naylor remembers it being very comfortable in this period, 'not scary', an arty scene rather than the macho Mancunia that has dominated since the late eighties. Although post-punk Hulme could be seen as a sort of slumming, the families long since decamped to more hospitable areas, Naylor argues that rather than being just a form of urban tourism, this Hulme 'became almost an independent city, another town within a town with a shifting stream of young, single people with their own dress codes.'

Especially intriguing is that this scene constituted itself *here*, in this bastardized approximation of New Babylon, this space of walkways, streets in the sky and vertiginous pedestrian bridges, rather than amidst old terraces or in between serried tower blocks. Partly this is happenstance: the City Council were essentially giving away the empty flats left by the families who escaped. But it also has surely to do with the possibilities of the structure itself. All the things bemoaned in the *World in Action* documentary as dele-terious to family life—the labyrinthine complexity of the blocks, the noise and sense of height and dynamism, the lack of a feeling of 'ownership' in the communal areas—were perfect for the pur-poses of a self-creating urbanism. In Martin Hannett's minimal, atmospheric productions, you can hear the ambiguous spaces cre-ated by the blocks' enclosures; in tracks like A Certain Ratio's 'Flight' or Section 25's 'Friendly Fires' you can hear the light-headedness of attempting to live in crumbling edifices somewhere in the air.

This sense of space is one of the most salient things about Manchester's post-punk, a dreaminess necessitated by low land values, where the very fact that the spaces were unused or even unusable led to a sense of possibility absent from the sewn-up, high-rent city of today. Naylor stresses that rent is the great unspoken factor behind culture, and in Hulme, she points out, 'hardly anyone was even paying any rent, including the rent boys'. The very emptiness retrospectively claimed as the blight from which regeneration saved the city was instead the source from which it drew its power. 'The centre of Manchester', she says now, 'was like a ghost town. From 1979 to '81 I'd walk around it, and no-one was there. Now, if you go to the centre of Manchester at 10 a.m. there'll be a line of people from Liverpool queuing for Primark.'

Although she warns me that her views might now be coloured by nostalgia, Naylor raises the possibility that Hulme 'became functional for people in a way that hadn't been anticipated by the planners'. Or rather, in a way that was anticipated by the people the planners had drawn their ideas from, like Constant or the Smithsons, but which they had long since forgotten.

Green Brutalism

Naylor remembers the overriding feeling of Hulme's sense of itself as an enclave, embattled but cohesive: 'There's no future, but if we stay here we'll be all right'. Nonetheless, starting from the mid eighties, the drugs shifted from speed to heroin, crime became more common, Tory election landslides led to despair, 'people started being mugged for their Giro', and many of those associated with the post-punk scene moved on. Yet the New Brutalist Hulme went on to become a (fairly crusty, by many accounts) centre for the rave scene in Manchester, with the Kitchen, a club made by knocking through three council flats, being the Hacienda's hidden reverse. In the mid nineties, on the eve of the Crescents' demolition as a ritual sacrifice to New Emerging Manchester, there was another television documentary made about the place, this time for *The Late Show*. Only just over a decade later, and we're miles from the hand-wringing of the *World in Action* documentary, with no condemnations of the idiocies of planners from the inhabitants. Instead, the Crescents'

Homes for Change, Hulme

occupants fiercely defend the estates' light, air and openness, the possibilities of the streets in the sky, and the richly creative community that had established itself there, even in a context where crime and deprivation was still rife. One comments that a friend's daughter 'only found out she lived in a slum when she heard it on the news'. Meanwhile, if the streets in the sky had come full circle, back to New Babylon, then this is entirely supported by the documentary, which features images of travellers' caravans in the open space between the blocks, reminding us that the hypermodernist Situationist urbanism of New Babylon was originally inspired by gypsy camps.

When Brutalist Hulme was demolished, what was built in its stead was a mix of social and private housing, with styles ranging from Barratt rabbit hutches to 'Homes for Change', designed in 1999 by Mills Beaumont Leavey Channon—an interconnected series of small but undeniably deck-access blocks. To the planners' surprise, when the more militant of the former Crescents residents, who had formed a co-operative, were consulted, they insisted on the much derided streets in the sky. This part of Hulme at least is still very striking, and one of the very few examples of Brutalism—in terms of planning, at least—built in the last twenty-five years. If approached from the 'Joy Division bridge' photographed by Kevin Cummins (there are now proposals to rename it in memory of Ian Curtis), you can see in one direction the skyscraping Beetham Tower and Wilkinson Eyre's Hulme Arch, an 'iconic' gateway to the regenerated centre erected in 1997, and in another, a large patch of wasteland, with low concrete walls providing much potential interest for a future Brutalist episode of Time Team, some standard Blairite office architecture, and just in the distance, the jumbled yellow and grey outline of Homes for Change.

Some of the moves the architects made here, such as the mix of materials—yellow brick, dark brown wood and metallic detailing—seem to be straight from the regeneration pattern book, but there the similarity ends. First of all, the materials are used 'as found', in the brusque Brutalist manner. You can still read the labels on the bottom of some of the blocks cantilevered out over the entrances, and mortar bulges rudely out between the cheap bright yellow brickwork. The walkways, metal rather than concrete, protrude seemingly at random, though their angularity is actually designed to catch the light. Even the artificial grass hill in the middle seems like a more domestically scaled version of the Smithsons's own streets in the sky complex, Robin Hood Gardens in East London. The austere elegance of Brutalism is missing, however, with the ad-hoc look, a way of factoring into the design the adaptations tenants had made to their flats in the old Crescents,

Detailing at Homes for Change

often seeming slightly whimsical. Like New Babylon, there is still a mobile architecture attached, with several caravans parked around the complex (with 'Roma Supreme' emblazoned on one of them). This is still a politicized space, but in a milder way, albeit without having anything to do with the Blairism of the centre. The blocks include studios and a café, and there is a van offering organic coffee in the middle of the courtyard. Homes for Change is by some measure the most interesting housing scheme in contemporary Manchester, especially in the context of the drab traditionalism that makes up the overwhelming majority of the new Hulme, but it might be caught—like much green politics—between an inspiring everyday utopianism and the politics of lifestyle.

Although the redevelopment of Hulme is often cited as one of the regenerated city's successes, housing co-operatives with streets in the sky did not become the basis for the new Manchester. The place is based on an uneasy compromise, as the Homes for Change co-op were impelled to go into partnership with a Housing Association, in this case the Guinness Trust, and there have been periodic conflicts between the two over who actually owns the building. And where Wilson and Womersley's Hulme applied avant-garde ideas on a massive scale, Homes for Change is of necessity a small and perhaps somewhat embattled enclave. Contemporary Hulme is itself another enclave (less gentrified than most) of a city which has dedicated itself to the service industry and the property market, bolstered by the propagation of an ideology of culture and creativity, where it matters little what the actual cultural product is, as the glories of the past can be lived off seemingly indefinitely. Hulme Crescents was one of the places where Modernist Manchester music was truly incubated and created, and its absence coincides almost perfectly with the absence of truly Modernist Mancunian pop culture. Yet what happened here—the use of spaces intended for working-class families by musicians, artists and so forth—is a strange inverse of what has been happening in the centre of Manchester since, a gift returned and in the process transformed into its antithesis.

The Home of Credit Crunch Chic

For a picture of the New Mancunian metropolis, we start in Spinningfields, towards the river Irwell and the border with Salford. Recently zoned as the Business Quarter, it includes within it the People's History Museum, as if to quarantine the city's radical past on site. The new building for the Museum is clad in a rusty red corten steel, in some sort of ineffectual gesture against the opaque glass all around. There is in Spinningfields an alignment of Capital, in the form of buildings for barely solvent banks designed by Norman Foster's B-Team; Discipline, in the form of Denton Corker Marshall's Civil Justice Centre; and Property, in the form of Aedas's Leftbank Apartments. These last are typical of Manchester's many 'stunning developments', and a skyway adds a mildly futurist dash to the usual bet-hedging multiple materials and muddled geometries. Festooned with property adverts (a ubiquitous feature of contemporary Manchester), Leftbank is, according to the local property rag *Manchester Living*, 'the home of credit crunch chic'—which is rather remarkable, given that only a year before these would have been marketed as 'luxury apartments' or 'living solutions'. When we visit they're festooned with an ad of a leering executive couple asking 'Like what you see?'

Street sign, Spinningfields

The Civil Justice Centre and People's History Museum

In a 'marketing suite' in Salford we picked up a selection of free property magazines, which proliferate here as if they were a substitute for a real local press, something which just about survives in the form of the trenchant non-believers at the *Salford Star*, a rare voice of sanity in New Mancunia. Amongst the magazines is one called *Urban Life*, and the copy we peruse features a column by a local radio DJ, decrying the sixties redevelopment of Salford as soulless high-rises, next to hundreds of adverts for new soulless high-rises. Irony does not sit well here. There's more proof of this assertion round the corner, near the cute pop Modernism of the

Leftbank Apartments, home of credit crunch chic

Granada building, in the form of Aedas's Manchester Bauhaus, a mixed-use office and apartment complex. Walter Gropius's estate must be irked that it never copyrighted the name—the new Bauhaus even replicates Herbert Bayer's original typography. But in case we feel inclined to chart a simple, unbroken lineage of serene Modernism, it's instructive to compare slogans. The Bauhaus, Dessau, in 1926: 'Art and technology, a new unity'; The Bauhaus, Manchester, in 2009: 'Business and life in perfect harmony.'

In comparison, The Civil Justice Centre is refreshing in its sheer aesthetic fearlessness. It is a genuinely striking building, although one eventually as unnerving as everything else here: the irregular protrusions at each end and the vast sheer glass wall are sublime in scale, suggesting a decidedly New Labour combination of domination and mock-transparency. Peering in, we see the ground floor houses 'Café Neo', a shimmering, cold non-space. You can't possibly imagine something so grubby as one of the city's many acts of petty crime being processed here. Nearby, on Deansgate, are two of Ian Simpson's glazed apartment blocks. Simpson's work is undeniably superior to the run of the regeneration mill, if only by default. His first major buildings—Number 1 Deansgate, the Urbis exhibition centre—both employ a sloping

Café Neo, Civil Justice Centre

Urbis

form that has been repeated by a series of lesser works in Manchester and Salford: Assael's grandiosely named Great Northern Tower, BDP's Abito Apartments, Broadway Malyan's 'The Edge', all follow Simpson's formula of sexy name, contrived irregularity and machined sleekness with rather less success, and all appear to be half-empty.

Urbis is a curious gallery, its glass made opaque to protect the exhibits. It's a flashy, dizzy memory of Patrick Geddes's idea for an urban exhibition centre in an observation tower. Justin O'Connor, partly responsible for the idea, comments on its swift dumbing-down:

> it was my idea and picked up in the absence of any other. However, the process of choosing the name, the architect and the building were done with no input from me at all. It was about two years into the project; after Ian Simpson had unloaded his pre-prepared designs with no reference to content (glass building for an interactive museum etc) and a management team cobbled together; only then did a stray question at a council meeting ('what was going to go into this building') lead the cultural supremo of Manchester to track down the author of the original eight-page memo (me, with some input from Tony Wilson) and ask us to tell him what it was all about.[45]

In typical pseudomodernist fashion, form preceded function by several leagues. O'Connor continues: 'In effect all they had been concerned about was the building as icon. Ian Simpson exemplified the no-politics, no-intellect "intellectual"—able to strut with black polo-necked arrogance through his building refusing any signage (like, entrance and exit) in the name of aesthetic purity, even when rain was coming in from the roof.' The first time we visit, Urbis features an exhibition on video games, some photos of 'hidden Manchester', drab recent New York art, and a small exhibit on the city's (somewhat beleaguered) greasy spoon cafeterias—all with little context or information. As if as a final judgement on the ideas-above-its-station nature of a museum dedicated to a concept so abstract and arty as The City, by the end of 2009 Urbis was emptying itself of its original purpose, to become the National Football Museum. It's difficult to imagine any fate more depressing.

Ian Simpson can't be held responsible for any of this, of course, though he can be for the way his Beetham Tower dominates contemporary Manchester. In it, a mix of empty flats and footballers' penthouses looks out over Cottonopolis, the Pennines and on a clear day, out to Liverpool. The Beetham Tower is distinguished by negative virtues, its lack of the aesthetic cowardice and

Beetham Tower

The Beetham Tower Skybar (Great Northern Tower behind)

confusion of most recent high-rises. It shows a mediocre architect at the very top of his game, and the relative virtues of the pugnacious local pride can be seen here, in that a native Manc has given the city something more distinctive and thought-out than megacorps like Aedas, Broadway Malyan or BDP would be able to offer. Moreover, Simpson's towers in Birmingham and Liverpool are far, far worse, indicating that here the architect made a major effort—unsurprisingly, as he lives here. The Beetham Tower's curtain wall is confidently unencumbered by the insufferable vernacular red terracotta and slatted wood, while its top-heavy massing creates a clear, distinctive silhouette without resorting to the silly hats worn by its contemporaries. Inside, the glass greenhouse effect is offset by lightness and opulent pseudo-minimalism. The Skybar's cocktail menu offers a range of drinks named after songs by Manchester luminaries—the Buzzcocks, the Smiths, Happy Mondays (fancy a Hand in Glove?). Meanwhile, as if intent on re-enacting the plot of J.G. Ballard's *High-Rise*, Simpson himself purchased the penthouse at the top for £3 million. He proceeded to fill it with an olive grove, revealed on a short BBC film about the tower. 'It *is* aspirational', he proclaimed. Post-punk Ballardianism is, then, reborn in the Beetham Tower in a most unexpected fashion.

The Bloxham Organization

The most adroit user of Manchester's pop culture fame in the service of property development is, of course, Urban Splash, which evidently shares Wilson's opinion that the eventual point of Joy Division or Acid House was to lay the groundwork for post-industrial speculation and gentrification. After seeing how spectacularly it had fucked up Sheffield's Park Hill, it was interesting to see some of Urban Splash's successes. The redevelopment of Castlefield's mills and warehouses are stylish and well executed enough—and if nobody is going to make stuff in them I suppose there are worse things than them being occupied by what Tom Bloxham once called 'decision makers'.[46] It's marginally better than their being demolished, although the gated-off nature of much of Castlefield makes it less fun to walk around than it ought to be. Urban Splash has helped preserve what is, by any measure, one of the truly great industrial landscapes—the criss-crossing chaos of railway and canal bridges is utterly exhilarating, however marred it might be by some dull new-build flats. The true unpleasantness of the operation is, however, never far away. Along one stretch of Urban Splashed ex-industrial 'lofts' is a banner, advertising its never-begun (let alone completed) 'Tutti Frutti' self-design scheme in Ancoats. It declares: 'COME AND HAVE A GO IF YOU THINK YOU'RE HARD ENOUGH.'

This ironic thuggery has another meaning in Ancoats itself, where regeneration has led to some extremely sharp disjunctions. The area between Manchester's centre and this formerly pioneering (and famously impoverished) industrial district is already marked by the sleek modern architecture that is an arguable antecedent to the new city, an American modernism more about machined precision, minimalism and cold affluence than the earnestness and raw formalism of Brutalism. Here there's the black glass of Owen Williams's 1937 *Daily Express* printworks, and a set of excellent buildings designed for the Co-Operative movement, pioneered up the road in Rochdale, ranging from smart Dutch-issue interwar brick Modernism to the glacial monolith of Gordon

Manchester Modernism, Mk 1—The *Daily Express*

Tait's CIS Tower, which vies with London's Euston Tower and Sheffield's Arts Tower as Britain's most elegant tribute to Mies van der Rohe's Teutonic America, and has the curious honour of being Tom Bloxham's favourite building. You can't imagine him citing the Co-Op's main offices in Stockport, which take glass Modernism into bizarre kitsch, rejecting tower and podium for Giza-via-Trump pyramid. The CIS Tower's architect dabbled in politics as a Tory councillor, and while its service shaft might now

The Dutch Modernist CWS Building

be clad in solar panels, stylistically this is emphatically not the Modernism of noble social programmes. It's likely that this is what New Emerging Manchester wants to tap into, this lineage of sharp, businesslike Modernism. After crossing the road from the CIS Tower into Ancoats, a series of property billboards (white on black, in Helvetica) announce the area, trying to coax businesses into this proletarian district. 'Ancoats is a Place to Pioneer', it insists, accurately, although the many things that have been pioneered in its gargantuan factories are not wholly benign.

Just north of here is Collyhurst, and a straggling landscape which demonstrates just how shallow the regeneration of Manchester actually is. Railway viaducts with every variety of shrub growing out of them lead to collapsing warehouses and ghostly council estates which somehow manage to feel peripheral despite being in the centre of Britain's third largest city, but even they are less grim than the Green Quarter, a wall of massive new apartment blocks designed by locals Leach Rhodes Walker. A green space in the centre of this 'Quarter' provides a neat planning alibi for the relentless, domineering elevations, as profit is extracted from every other inch of the site. They're a design nightmare, a headache-inducing clash of tiny windows, 'friendly' curves and unrelieved mass. In a sorry attempt to make them look

The newly green CIS Tower

less barrack-like, green render is slathered across the façades, as if at random. Meanwhile, one cluster of derelict Collyhurst council towers was sold ('for £1 each', says local rumour) to Urban Splash, who transformed them into The Three Towers. Clad in the obligatory wood (in this case almost hyperreal in its artificiality) and given the equally obligatory irregular windows, each block is topped by a beacon with the name of one of the Pankhurst sisters—Emmeline, Sylvia and Christabel, in flowing letters painted a hot lipstick pink. Some of the Suffragettes may not have minded this towering tribute, but Sylvia Pankhurst, founder of the British Communist Party, would no doubt have been disappointed if she'd known that a century hence, her name would be used to promote a transfer of assets from the poor to the affluent. It's another example of the use of radical Mancunian history to sell Old Corruption all over again, the triad of land, property and finance given a lick of pink and lime green paint. It's surely only a matter of time before some disused factory or council block becomes Peterloo Apartments or Engels Mansions.

At its edges, visible from the main ring road, the new 'Urban Villages' of Ancoats look appropriately shiny and neat. Yet at the centre of it is an emptiness where the Cardroom Estate used to be. This was a low-rise council development of the 1970s that was demolished and re-branded by Urban Splash nearly a decade ago as 'New Islington' (what could be more 'aspirational'?), one of a government-sponsored series of 'Millennium Communities'. It is, to be frank, an awful bloody mess. Marked by huge swathes of wasteland and scattered industrial rubble, the area has as its centre a derelict pub, named—with perfect conjunctural timing—the Bank of England. There are two completed schemes, both funded by housing associations rather than the developers, both suggesting that Urban Splash's eye for architecture contrasts with their fantastical ineptitude as urban administrators. Sober Modernists dMFK and unashamed postmodernists FAT (Fashion Architecture Taste) worked closely with residents to produce contradictory results—FAT's display of cartoonish artifice, dMFK's stern Brutalism—but both show a similar sensitivity

The wastes of New Islington

towards their non-executive residents. Yet they're set amidst dereliction and blight, loomed over by vast mills (renovated or
rotting) and tower blocks in dire need of renovation, the area
dressed at the corners with mostly dismal new architecture.

The farcical attempt on the part of Urban Splash and their state
sponsors to build a 'Millennium Community' on the ruins of the
Cardroom estate is a pop-PPP farrago which has levelled an area
of social housing in one of those gentrification frontiers on the
edge of Manchester's ring-road. So far it has replaced it with one

Bank of England, Ancoats

(apparently very hard to sell) Alsop block, two small closes of houses, and a whole lot of verbiage. The promised self-build enclaves, high streets, parks, schools and health centres weren't built during the boom so sure as hell won't be now, for all the Homes & Communities Agency money flowing in its direction. Irrespective of the awfulness of the place, FAT's scheme is far more conscientious than seeming jollity might at first glance imply. In the blasted context of New Islington their houses look great, and only partly because almost everything else around them is so awful—while the use of a sort of *trompe l'oeil* wall/screen to pull together the terrace of clearly very modern houses is clever without being smug.

These houses present more actual ideas than all the other recent buildings in the city put together. Yet the low-rise nature of the scheme (something also used by the very different and similarly decent, if rather less intellectually interesting dMFK housing, also based on consultation with estate residents) makes it seem rather beleaguered, given the vastness of the mills and the yuppie-dromes, and in the context of the wasteland all around the humour could seem merely grisly to the uninitiated; laughter in the dark. There's also something deeply odd about creating a low-rise suburbia in the heart of such a huge city—but then people ask for some odd things. Sadly the furnishings left around the site—a

FAT's houses at New Islington

dMFK's houses, New Islington

cuddly little fibreglass bear, two fibreglass birds and a hedge
trimmed to resemble a dinosaur, all sat near the broken millstones
and fenced-off wastes—imply something infantilizing to the
whole affair.

This is more apparent in Urban Splash's propaganda than
FAT co-director Charles Holland's own description of the place's
rationale (entirely coincidentally, he gave a talk about it the same
day we visited). Holland explained in great detail the extent to
which the estate was an attempt to meet the Cardroom tenants'

Bear, New Islington

own desires—for houses with gardens and decoration—without patronizing them, instead treating them as thirty individual clients. Even then, his documentation of the alleged 'wrongness' of council tenants' interior furnishings as a source of architectural inspiration had (no doubt unintentionally) a queasy Martin Parr-esque side, especially given that this 'wrongness' is purely in the eyes of the architecturally educated. There was one irresistible irony. After showing a set of photos from one Cardroom resident's particularly eclectic 1970s interior furnishings, it turned out that when the FAT scheme was finished, this tenant filled his new house with Ikea-modernist new furniture. 'Because I was moving into a modern house.'

FAT's work here is an ambiguous comment on the status of the 'radical' architect today—its houses are both within and against the overarching Urban Splash plan. The residents chose them precisely because they seemed most interested in their *own* ideas, rather than in slotting them into the slick towers and their attendant loft-living lifestyle. FAT's designs were chosen precisely because they were the least Urban Splash-like of all that was on offer. At the same time, the images of these houses—with the wasteland all around invariably cropped from the shot, perhaps combined with renders of the never-built Tutti Frutti scheme—became the new fun and jolly face of real-estate speculation, of Urban Splash's infantilist Innocent Smoothie approach to urban design. Master-planning and population transfer with an irreverent touch. But, as the many hostile reactions it has caused from right-thinking aesthetes can attest, it is genuinely different to the prevailing Pseudomodernism. When I first saw these houses in a *Guardian* article, my immediate reaction was horror—post-modernism returns in the guise of urban regeneration! Yet in the context of contemporary Manchester they seem far more subversive, a return of all that is repressed from regeneration architecture—most of all, the way in which taste and aesthetics are almost invariably determined by the unspoken matter of class. They represent a serious approach to designing social housing, contrasting with the deceptively simple drolleries of the decorative embellishments. It's as if they decided to create a new aesthetic of public housing on the basis of the additions tenants made to their flats in the 1980s after they purchased them through Thatcher's Right to Buy scheme. Architectural historian Steve Parnell claimed that FAT is the 'only avant-garde architects in Britain'. If so, the avant-garde is in a strange place, where the only way to return to something resembling the original ideals of Modernism is to break every one of its formal rules. At the same time, to get their ideas built, FAT allowed them to become an emblem for one of the most spectacularly botched attempts at redevelopment in the Blairite era.

There's no doubt that the non-Splashed areas of the redevelopment are worse, without even fragments of good ideas. At the entrance is Broadway Malyan's Islington Wharf, which has a certain brash, supercity dynamism from its 'good side' (as Jonathan Meades pointed out in his regeneration diatribe *On the Brandwagon*, 'iconic' architecture always has a good side for photographs and another side blemished and pockmarked), but stodgy and lumpen from all the others. Curiously enough, its design appears to be a slicker remake of the Mathematics Tower at Manchester University, a Brutalist casualty to New Emerging Manchester, perhaps in

Islington Wharf

Skyline Apartments

some bizarre act of appeasement to the recent past. To the north, Jacobs Webber, formerly of the massive multinational corporate firm Skidmore Owings and Merrill, have produced the hilarious Skyline Apartments, a car-crash of 'luxury' new-build clichés. The proliferation of excrescences here happens all at once — the mess of materials, the inept patterning, the glass protrusion at the top, the nails-down-blackboard yellow—and is so awful that we were left incredulous. The website for the towers promises all manner of opulence, including a 'Zen Room'. 'Prepare to be

Milliners Wharf

seduced', it begins, before suggesting you have your celebratory drinks the moment you get in (it's furnished, you see!) and finally reminding you that it is aimed, of course, at 'savvy city dwellers' which presumably means buy-to-let landlords. To the south is Design Group 3's Milliners Wharf, an imposingly long, featureless, loft-living version of an Aylesbury Estate slab-block. Will Alsop's nearly completed Chips, the only other Urban Splash scheme after the housing association enclaves, appears in this context to be a more imaginative version of a generic Pseudomodernism. If dMFK or FAT had been allowed to design a whole area of social housing rather than tiny closes of ten or fifteen houses, this place could have been a genuine achievement, with or without its absurdly aspirational name, rather than what it is in the recession's unforgiving light—a failed confidence trick.

Chimney Pots and Conran Interiors—The New Salford

Salford is the constituency of the disgraced Communities Minister Hazel Blears, who resigned due to her particularly impressive venality in the expenses scandal that formed a serendipitous distraction from the bank bailouts throughout 2009. One of the most authoritarian of Labour ministers (launching the nannying Five a Day nutrition campaign as under-secretary of health, defending various repressive measures as minister of state at the Home Office, and echoing the rhetoric of the British National Party as Communities and Local Government secretary), Blears is also one of the few prominent New Labour figures from a working-class background. Accordingly, her upbringing itself is mythologized as a subject of austerity nostalgia. She grew up amongst the deserving poor of Salford, and was featured as one of the child extras in a fine instance of austere Northern mythography, Tony Richardson's film of that saddest of kitchen sink dramas, Shelagh Delaney's *A Taste of Honey*. Her somewhat Thatcheresque rhetorical combination of 1950s schoolteacher and 2000s motivational manager led to a seemingly meteoric rise in New Labour, now perhaps only temporarily halted by a resignation elicited by the thrifty if not especially austere matter of huge, and possibly criminal, mortgage fiddling. A *Times* interview in December 2008 showed that Blears's public persona was based on a curious combination of homely wartime rhetoric and utterly ruthless Blairite modernization, and as such is grimly intriguing as an exemplar of austerity nostalgia, only in her case lacking the requisite ironic distance. Much of the interview reads as a document from a country where World War Two never ended. Not only is Blears's office decorated with the 'Keep Calm and Carry On' poster, her rhetoric is pervaded by a strange combination of Victorianism and Blitz-spirit platitudes. You can see a frankly impressive performance of Blairite dialectic in her clear desire to play to every constituency at once. So she mocks bankers but laments (in a symptomatically progressivist metaphor) that the 'train' which the banks presumably commandeered didn't transport every member of society; she defends the strict working-class Salford that created her and longs for the days when foremen would teach their workers 'how to behave', but also sticks up for the ending of 'deference' and backs off from the possibility that she'd ever stand in the way of anyone's fun; and her obvious contempt for the Welfare State is combined with a belief that the working class need to be surveilled at all times. Perhaps the most interesting phrase used in the interview is that, in the recession, 'we've all got to do our bit'.[47]

In her *Times* interview Blears with austere rectitude decries the 1980s as a time when yuppies caroused and others suffered, seemingly unaware that this is by now the public perception of the boom of the last decade (while the irony that it described her behaviour too, as we now know, is another matter). She represents one of the most unequal constituencies in the country,[48] but one which has been very keen on remaking itself via a series of high-profile regeneration strategies on her watch. Most prominent among them is the transformation of the former Salford Docks into an exclusive entertainment and luxury housing enclave, soon to be occupied by a large section of the British Broadcasting Corporation. A less high-profile example is the selling of terraced houses condemned by the government's Path-finder Housing Market Renewal scheme (in which, as we saw in Sheffield, a property market was artificially stimulated in former manufacturing towns by the wholesale demolition of working-class housing) to the aforementioned Urban Splash, who turned them into 'Chimney Pot Park', a proletarian theme park for Manc media workers. Blears also talks of her love of modern buildings. What this means in the Salford context is Urban Splash's austere/luxury enclaves, or the new jerry-built condos. She certainly wasn't referring to any new housing for the Salford working class she perpetually invokes. Rather, she explicitly distanced herself from council housing in favour of the spectacularly severe solution of 'mother and baby homes'. Blears's make do and mend rhetoric was, as we now know, combined with mandarin corruption, a contradiction about which she appears oblivious.

Yet Blears is keen to exculpate herself and her government from the charge of neglecting the working class 'core vote' by referring to what they've done for Salford, so a trip over the Irwell is essential—and easy, as despite administering itself as a separate city, Salford is at the dead centre of Greater Manchester. You could cross via the swanky bridge designed by instant regenerator Santiago Calatrava, but to get the true measure of the place it's best approached through the bleak dual carriageways, retail parks,

Public art at Exchange Quays, Trafford

office complexes and industrial estates of Trafford, where you get to see the bizarre Yeltsin-Constructivism of Old Trafford Stadium, redesigned by local architects Atherden Fuller in the late 1990s. This freakish mix of domineering symmetries and bared structure is heralded by a statue of Denis Law, George Best and Bobby Charlton, the United Trinity locked in embrace. Their faithfully rendered skinny bodies and skimpy 1960s kit contrasts vividly with today's lumbering soccer supermen, leaving them looking dainty and rather camp, with a slight mince to their celebratory pose.

The area near Salford Central station is full of mediocre 2000s high-rises, the districts near Salford University loomed over by their similarly drab, if less pretentious and more spacious 1960s forebears—but at least their straightforward geometries make their failings more easily ignorable than what has been built since 1996. At least they rehoused people in something better than what they replaced—and at least nobody kidded themselves these towers were part of some elite, exclusive Lifestyle. I spent a bit of time in the company of new-build chronicler Penny Anderson, whose blog Renter Girl profiled with wit and anger 'Dovecot Towers', the block in central Salford she called home, expanding into a wider critique of the shoddy tat marketed as the height of executive chic and revealing the hidden grimness of even the new middle-class enclaves. We visited Dovecot Towers, a chillingly bleak red-brick thing shoved into a Salford side street that she insists remains anonymous, but for a real negative-equity dystopia she recommended the 'Green Quarter' over the Irwell, a super-dense mess of blocks dissolving into Cheetham Hill. We watched as a BNP van, complete with megaphone, sped past the CIS tower in that direction.

Salford has been hit especially hard by the demolitions of the Pathfinder programme, the second or third major wave of slum clearance the city has faced in the last half century, with many streets of terraces left tinned-up and derelict over the last decade. The earlier clearances led to the construction of thirty tower blocks, and a large concentration of these still survives in

Joy Division urbanism at Pendleton, Salford

Pendleton, opposite the University of Salford. They are reached by a thin concrete bridge over a wide dual carriageway. Walking over it, the sublime terror induced by 1960s planning at its worst attacks you—the bridge can seemingly only let one person past at a time, and the fences are temptingly low. On each side are huge slabs, on one side running almost as far as the eye can see. Somehow here the planners managed to combine the sensations of agoraphobia in the form of the yawning ravine of the dual carriageway, claustrophobia in the form of the bridge's mean proportions, and vertigo in the blocks' twenty-five-plus storeys. Unnerving as they may be, they're mostly now used as student accommodation. The two tallest are neighboured by a drive-thru McDonalds and a few derelict eighties vernacular brick cottages, these later accretions presumably being the reason why *Control* was not filmed here rather than in Nottingham.

These blocks are highly visible from Chimney Pot Park in nearby Langworthy, Urban Splash's old Salford theme park, and they monolithically disrupt the fantasy of enclosure. Like in Sheffield, the developers' remaking of former proletarian areas has been drastic, to say the least. The interiors have been completely stripped out, with steel frames put in their place, which provide first-floor patios at the back and black steel car parks where the

Chimney Pot Park

back alleys would once have been. Everything is scrupulously regular, with burglar alarms, street signs and of course the titular steel chimneys all in the same sober, colour-coded language—Joy Division's 'Autosuggestion' lingers over the obsessively ordered landscape: 'here, here, everything is by design ...' Despite all the car parks, there are cars everywhere in these tiny streets, and cars provide a perfect hiding place for any undesirables who might

Imperial War Museum North

The Lowry, in its natural climate

want to enter the theme park. Given how poor the surrounding area is, they appear as an invitation. The cabbie who drops us off here (after we find it, spotting the tell-tale minimalist metal chimneys: unsurprisingly, he has no idea where Chimney Pot Park is) mutters 'mind your pockets round here' when we get out. There are plenty of places to hide and to escape in these close-knit streets, unlike in the gated blocks of flats in the city centre. Such are the drawbacks of Victorian urbanism, even when occupied by a better class of resident.

Regardless of the straggling mess of much of the regenerated city, Salford Quays is where the icons are. Here is Britain's most sustained push for the Bilbao effect, built on the site of the Manchester Ship Canal, a now useless but once technically astonishing feat of Victorian engineering that turned an inland city into a port. Aside from Michael Wilford's messy but occasionally interesting Lowry, a building which, as if to prove Meades's point, is from some angles clumsy and straggling, in others sharp and striking; and Libeskind's minor but at least vaguely memorable Imperial War Museum, my main thought was 'Wow, this is bad enough to be in Southampton'. The two icons are a strange pair indeed, linked by an arched bridge, the cladding of both the Lowry and War Museum nodding with amusing blatancy at Gehry's Basque blob. The Imperial War Museum 'symbolizes' carnage through the imagery of a World Torn Asunder (it says so when you enter the building), but what Wilford's building might have to do with the miserable marionettes of L. S. Lowry's Salford is rather more mysterious. Libeskind's and Wilford's buildings might have made the magazines and brochures, but they are entirely dominated by DLA Architects' woeful stone-clad high-rises, more luxury tat by Broadway Malyan and a nondescript slab for the now-defunct City Lofts, with more enclaves to follow. The BBC's Media City is under construction, and while it's nice to see it moving at least some of its functions from the over-favoured capital, it's moving into a securitized enclave in marked contrast with the way the Granada offices insinuate themselves unassumingly into the heart of central Manchester.

Looking out through torrential rain over the Manchester Ship Canal at this, the most famous part of the most successfully regenerated ex-industrial metropolis, we can't help but wonder: is this as good as it gets? Museums, cheap speculative housing, offices for financially dysfunctional banks? What of the idea that civic pride might mean a civic architecture for the residents of Greater Manchester's crumbling tower blocks and condemned terraces? Cottonopolis might still be a vision of the future, but if so, it's only

Salford Quays

marginally less unnerving than the nineteenth century's industrial inferno. After the crash, we can see it as the ultimate failure of the very recent past, a mausoleum of Blairism. But what can be done with these ruins? The sheer stark strength of the remnants of the postwar settlement in the unforgiving light of the late 1970s inspired something equally bracing and powerful. How do you react to something which already tries incredibly hard not to offend the eye, or respond critically to an alienated landscape which bends over backwards not to alienate, with its jolly rhetoric, its 'fun' colour, its 'organic' materials? How do you find an atmosphere in something which tries everything to avoid creating a perceptible mood other than idiot optimism? It's difficult at first to imagine what the ruins of New Labour could possibly inspire—but in places like the Green Quarter or Salford Quays you can almost hear the outline of it, the sound of enclosure, of barricading oneself into a hermetically sealed, impeccably furnished prison against an outside world seldom seen but assumed to be terrifying. We await the Joy Division of the dovecots with anticipation.

Chapter Six

Tyneside: From Brasilia to Baltic

The Tyneside conurbation, or, as current branding calls it, NewcastleGateshead, is an area of wild contrasts. The first impression is of the serious urbanity of its nineteenth-century buildings. The Red-brick Gothic and Wrenaissance that denotes civic pride in so many English towns seems grasping and arriviste in comparison with the centre of Newcastle, which has far more in common with the more European urbanism of Glasgow or Edinburgh. Meanwhile, the multiple levels of the city, its bridges, walkways and steep changes of view give it a rare sense of spatial drama. Lots of this derives not just from the accidents of geology, but from planning: Richard Grainger's planned speculative town centre is enormously impressive. There are two very good things about this area which are not shared by many English cities. The first is, as mentioned, the planned centre—odd to have something this good named after a property developer, or to imagine that all this dark classicism was part of a speculative development (and Grainger was apparently not a very efficient speculator, running up massive debts and risks). Regardless, the end result is that, like Glasgow, Newcastle looks like a city that actually had an Enlightenment as well as industrial capitalism, something that certainly can't be said about Manchester or (pre-1953, post-1987) Sheffield.

Squaring this with the city I have read about in *Viz* for the last twenty years is difficult—at least until you see the remarkable women with their minuscule skirts, enormous heels and

The Tyne Bridges

imperviousness to cold, with their somewhat less glamorous, shirt-and-chinos male charges, emerge for an evening's entertainment at around 9 p.m. Nonetheless, even some awful malls and Terry Farrell's egregiously bumptious 'Centre for Life' can't spoil the centre of Newcastle, and the best postwar parts of it—the Civic Centre, MEA House and its walkways—seem to fit into it neatly. Even the accidents have a certain serendipity, as when the tower blocks and terraces seem to slot together into the same geometric pattern.

The other great thing is the Metro, and it's amazing that it is this conurbation—smaller than the urban areas centred on Birmingham, Manchester or Leeds—that has this basic urban amenity denied from all other British cities save Glasgow, the capital and, partially, Liverpool. It has more than a passing resemblance to the U-Bahn, with spacious, tile-clad subterranean stations at the centre and outright weirdness further out where it consumes earlier rail lines, such as the alternately painted and picturesquely rusting ironwork of Tynemouth. Of late there has been talk of rebuilding some of the UK's many closed rail lines, and we can only hope that if this occurs the Metro's curious combination of antique and futuristic will serve as a model—and not only because it's one of the few parts of our transport network still unprivatized (although that's not for want of trying).

'I have a terrible feeling we won't be getting our fees on this one'

If it were only for this, and the succession of increasingly power-ful, ever-more dizzyingly Constructivist bridges along the Tyne, culminating in the Tyne Bridge and the High Level Bridge, both of them more thrilling than any Thames crossing, the area would be worth visiting. There's something insufferably patronizing about the idea that a city like this needed to be made more like Bilbao/Barcelona/London (or in an earlier era, Brasilia). Yet despite its remarkable urban qualities, Newcastle and its sur-rounding area has been 'regenerated' several times. A city this good 'needs' regeneration because its industries are long dead: dented in the thirties, wounded in the sixties and finished off by Thatcher. It had to run its economy on something—tourism and the wildly unstable property racket seemed the best bet. This is, let's not forget, the home of Northern Rock.

While it's appalling to treat Newcastle as if it were some sort of backwater before the arrival of lottery money, Gateshead is argu-ably another matter. Its nominal centre is still as shabby and aesthetically stunted as Newcastle's is sweeping and sophisticated, a product of the nineteenth and twentieth centuries' more budget aesthetics. It's debatable whether its highly publicized riverside

Inside the High Level Bridge

developments have had much effect on the town itself. Gates-head's most famous buildings exemplify the area's sharp contrasts. The first of these represents what most British cities are desperately trying to suppress: the memory of the first draft of an abortive northern renaissance in the 1960s.

The late Rodney Gordon, the most mercurial and pugilistic of the New Brutalists, designed two remarkable buildings in Gates-head with Owen Luder Partnership, both now facing demolition. One of them, Trinity Square Car Park, is best known on Tyneside (and everywhere else) as 'the *Get Carter* car park'. It glowers out from its hilltop site, an abstract silhouette. Up close, it becomes one of the most visceral architectural experiences available in Britain, in terms of sheer physical power, architecture that both hits in the gut and sends shivers down the spine. Neglected for decades, it's undeniable (and irrelevant) that the detailing is decid-edly cheap, but its buckling, distorted strips of concrete remain overwhelming, storming heaven with a millennarian arrogance comparable with Newcastle's outrageous, brilliant medieval Cathedral. It's absurd that something so remarkable should be destroyed when, as we will see, several mediocre sixties buildings *are* being renovated, but part of it has already been. It is almost certain the car park will eventually go (although it still stands at

A big man, in bad shape

the time of writing, in early 2010) and similarly certain that—as with its southern cousin, Portsmouth's late, lamented Tricorn Centre—nothing of note will take its place. Nonetheless, the Tesco billboards emblazoned on the pink wall that surrounds the site try to convince us otherwise. 'I love the new Trinity Square', says one of its anonymous, regenerated ghost people, rather presumptuously.

Our New Cathedrals

To compare Trinity Square with other attempts to transform Gateshead reveals the jarring inconsistencies of the area. The 1986 Metro Centre, still the biggest mall in the EU, is far more dated than Trinity Square, to an almost cute extent—the theme-park flights of fancy like 'the Village', a Disney Tyneside, are a far cry from the slick supermodernist Westfields. The Metro Centre's unreconstructed pomo is almost charmingly dated—I went here at the age of ten, and even though I have no specific memories of it, on visiting in 2009 I felt I'd been here a thousand times. It is marked by a wonderfully contradictory tension between two models of non-place. On the one hand, the theme park approach most popular in the 1980s, with the central Village even featuring a

The Village, Metro Centre

Parish Chapel. The land on which the Metro Centre is built is owned by the church, strongly supporting The Pop Group's claim on their 1979 single 'We Are All Prostitutes' that 'department stores are our new Cathedrals'. This ridiculousness has seemingly absolutely nothing in common with the Metro Centre's new bus station by Jefferson Sheard, a Northern firm that did some fantastic Brutalist work in sixties Sheffield.

The bus station really did feel Cathedral-like in the sense of vast enclosure. However the Metro Centre itself, for all its hugeness, always feels poky and claustrophobic, always resists making the pedestrian aware of its scale. In that it's like the 'community architecture' with which the nearby district of Byker is inexplicably lumped, refusing to do any of the things with space and scale that you can do with the form and instead basically creating a series of rooms where you can shop and eat (we had a Tex-Mex buffet, incidentally). It's afraid of itself, of its own enormity. By comparison, the bus station is a Fosterian canopy seemingly designed for the personal edification of Marc Augé, where Elgar was being played loudly over the PA system, almost certainly as a means of dissuading youth from loitering there. The Metro Centre is not connected to the Metro transport system, and it's telling that these two Metros, both built in the eighties, describe the consumerist tedium we've inflicted on ourselves, and a

Metro Centre Cathedral

Descending into the Metro

possible way out. The mall's effect on the rest of Gateshead is vampiric, the direct cause of its town centre's depopulated bleakness. Not that this area isn't every bit as bleak, if not more so: looking out from the Metro Centre bus station, you see a post-industrial motorscape, bleak and straggling where central Newcastle is compact and exciting. No-one seems deterred by the post-industrial wastes they travel through to get to the Mall; it remains very successful, while the town centres in the conurbation (especially those outside the central Urban Renaissance zone) fall into dereliction. Undeterred, North Tyneside Council began in early 2010 to rectify this situation by designing fake shop fronts for the disused high streets of North Shields and Wallsend.

The Metro Centre's Thatcherite exurbanism contrasts in turn with the third New Gateshead, that quintessentially Urban Renaissance ensemble—the Baltic, the Sage, and the Millennium Bridge. This is easier to get to from Newcastle's Quayside than from Gateshead itself. Foster's Sage, though it looks beautiful from the High Level Bridge in the drizzle, opens itself out in a derisory manner to the car park, particularly unforgivable in the context of one of the few British cities with a reliable and extensive public transport system. The Baltic, undeniably aimed at tourists, is often accused of being over-scaled and irrelevant to the surrounding area, but the exhibitions and the public spaces are of a

The Sage, above the roofs

very high standard and I suspect that at least some arty young Geordies are pleased it exists. Still, whatever the merits of these buildings, they turn their back on Gateshead. The second time we visit, the poster draped over the riverside façade depicts a Miners' Strike-era banner from the Martin Parr exhibition inside, declaring 'Victory to the Miners, Victory to the Working Class'. Seen kindly, it's an irruption of the repressed, but mostly it just seems a bad joke, a sign of powerlessness, that such an object can be displayed and no longer found threatening. The Baltic's main knock-on effect is the Baltic Quays flats, arrogantly towering over the flour mills' already domineering mass. Their ineptitude is almost matched by a cliff of poor executive housing on the other side of the Tyne.

Regenerated or Dead

The remnants of an earlier attempt at regeneration sit at opposing ends of the Tyne, west of the majestic bridges. First, the tower blocks of Cruddas Park. These system-built (that is, assembled from prefabricated parts to a standard design from an engineer or builder rather than an architect) blocks exemplify the Newcastle of the corrupt, charismatic sixties city boss T. Dan Smith; not without a certain drama, better than the slums they replaced, but cheap and unimaginative compared with their contemporaries in Sheffield or their successors in Byker. Rumour has it that after his fall, Smith himself rented here. Yet Cruddas Park too must be regenerated, and the method is familiar: recladding (presumably losing the Mondrian patterns and abstract mosaics on the elevations); rebranding (as 'Riverside Dene'); and soon, social cleansing, as council flats are flogged as luxury apartments for rent and sale. Over the river in Dunston, Gateshead, is a far superior example of sixties housing, at least visually—Luder's Derwent Tower, or 'Dunston Rocket'. This is unique, bespoke public housing and like Trinity Square, Rodney Gordon's wild Constructivist-Gothic, all flying buttresses and distorted volumes, suggests Richard Rogers had he favoured shuttered concrete over neoprene. Like Trinity Square, it's scheduled for demolition, yet the bulldozers have yet to arrive. There is a Save Dunston Rocket campaign, and perhaps some hope that recession will make the council reconsider demolishing yet another structure by this outrageously talented architect.

When we were looking for the tower's entrance we were stopped by a middle-aged couple on their front patio, in the maisonettes which surround the tower. They asked if we wanted to take a picture of their front door, which we did. After all the time

The Dunston Rocket, grounded

we'd spent wandering around estates taking photos, these were the first two people to express any curiosity about what we were up to, or seemingly even to have noticed us. They lived in the last part of the estate to be cleared, and were not best pleased about being forced to move from where they'd lived for twenty-six years. They spoke well of the flats' space and how much they were liked after they were built. Nonetheless, they'd been told they would have priority for being moved to the 'town houses' that were being planned, which they expected to be like those on the riverfront. Given what we found in Sheffield, it's doubtful whether a Labour council today can be trusted on such a commitment, but the alternative, if the residents are lucky and/or atypically affluent, is just round the corner. This is Staiths South Bank, luxury and individuality enclosed by a gasworks, lots of industrial sheds and the ornamental ex-industry of the Dunston Staiths, former structures for loading coal onto ships.

Designed by Ian Derby Partnership for Wimpey, with the much vaunted input of Red or Dead boss and ubiquitous design pundit Wayne Hemingway, Staiths South Bank is mooted as a revolutionizing of spec housing. While this stuff might be rare in Tyneside, Londoners or Mancunians will find it very familiar. It has some qualities, a diversity of façade and a (fenced-off) view of

Staiths South Bank advertises itself

Dunston Staiths

the strange and beautiful Staiths; yet is deeply mediocre compared with Rogers Stirk Harbour's attempt to do the same thing in Milton Keynes. Perhaps the relative mediocrity is the point—the creation of a standard, deliberately nothing special. Yet the mannerisms imply individuality, even exclusivity. Its main claim to innovation, its attempted suppression of the private car, seems doomed in this desolate enclave served by neither Metro or train —and the public spaces are stuffed with cars. The area has a

Pedestrian Staiths South Bank

certain hint of dubiousness about it. Working Men's Clubs with extremely expensive-looking cars parked outside. Of all the cities we've been to, Gateshead was the first where we got funny looks. Not hostility so much as 'not seen you two in the Dun Cow'.

In its language of differing colours, mixed materials and contrasting scales, Staiths is (perhaps unknowingly) indebted to what might be, at least in superficial terms, the most influential housing project of the last thirty years—Ralph Erskine and Vernon Gracie's 1969–81 Byker Redevelopment, a few miles to the east. Every block of yuppiedromes with painted balconies and coloured sloping roofs is a vague memory of Byker. Accepted history alleges this was the start of vernacular, community architecture, famously based on input from and co-operation with future tenants. Yet compared with other examples of community architecture, we are dealing with something very different. There's no Poundburyesque wistful woolliness, none of the apologetic non-architecture of Militant's council semis in Liverpool or the bland suburbanism of London's Coin Street housing schemes (all the nondescript, apologetic eighties and nineties schemes which are usually used to define 'community' and 'vernacular', leading eventually in the US to New Urbanism, a school of thought which essentially rejects all urban planning and

Byker

Tower block at Byker

architecture after 1914). Byker's salient features are wholly Modernist—walkways, towers, scale, sublimity, genuinely public space, stylistic consistency, and a programme to (re)house working-class tenants, not the 'aspirational' buyers courted by Staiths. It's a product of the New Brutalist group Team 10's other Modernism (Erskine was a member of the circle), as opposed to the reactionary fantasies of the New Urbanism—the mid point between Park Hill and FAT, perhaps. Yet its Scando look, if not its ultra-modernist planning, has become as dominant as the atten- uated Corbusier that Erskine's team set itself against. It has faced social problems as much as anywhere else, and we suspect that if Anthony Kennedy, aka 'Rat Boy', the miscreant youth who trans- formed Byker's manifold ducts and decks into escape chutes, had hailed from an estate clad in concrete rather than polychrome brick and painted wood, there would have been calls for the whole place to be dynamited.

Nonetheless, this is a Modernist monument based on montage and consultation rather than master planning's imperiousness, with odd leftover details from the slums it replaced forming the area's only really postmodernist element. It retains a sweep, confi- dence, modernity and interest in sublime scale combined with small-scale intimacy that housing from the eighties onwards would completely abandon. It's especially weird that it gets bracketed with the terminally dull housing-association architecture of the seventies and eighties—this couldn't be further from the aesthetic cowardice of 'vernacular'. And much as it would have been difficult by the seventies to see the utopian aspirations of postwar Social Democratic architecture, you have to explore Byker properly to see its originality. After all, its formal language was borrowed by all manner of hacks. But what is especially interesting about the area is the way the estate abuts what looks like the remnants of a canal, now landscaped into a pedestrian path towards the Tyne, inexplicably punctuated by a collection of tiny sheds (pigeon coops? Allotments?) which either borrowed the colours and styles used by Erskine or were borrowed by him. When you get out at the other end, you're at the extraordinarily weird-mundane Ouseburn School, designed as a gesture to the Japanese businessmen who regularly visited this allegedly provincial city in the late nineteenth century.

The highly un-English Metro system takes you through an environment that can swing in minutes from density and drama to exurban desolation and back again. Tourist boards unsurprisingly favour Grainger's town more than T. Dan Smith's, yet the multi-level city created then still endures. Alongside one of these bracing plaza/walkway systems is the new library, an inoffensive glass block by Ryder Architects. This is the successor firm to Ryder and Yates, which itself grew out of Tecton, the London-based firm headed by Berthold Lubetkin through the 1930s and 1940s, responsible for Modernist 'icons' like the Highpoint flats in Highgate and the Penguin Pool at London Zoo. Yet unlike the famous post-Tecton southerners (Denys Lasdun, architect of the National Theatre, and Peter Moro, co-designer of the Royal Festival Hall) their work is relatively obscure. You can follow the walkways to their mirror-glass MEA building to see a trace of the 'Brasilia of the North' promised by Smith—or you could find it in Killingworth.

This, on the edges of the city, is a new 'township' planned in the 1960s. This really is a deeply strange place, where the remnants of

Today's Killingworth

a suburban Modernism coexist with the familiar limbo of spec homes and malls. These new spaces replaced a series of linked towers, the view of which in the distance is likened by the Pevsner guide to Fritz Lang's *Metropolis*, an office block on stilts and a Modernist shopping centre. Killingworth's current, timelessly boring incarnation had to efface something more interesting first. In the middle of the 'township' is the obligatory artificial lake. On one side of it are some small, incredibly narrowly planned houses

Killingworth Corbusier

by Ralph Erskine, with paths that could get you lost even in this small space, and on the other side the faded sleekness of Ryder and Yates's Norgas House. Round the corner is Ryder and Yates's Engineering Building. Its hieratic International Style, in a remarkable state of preservation, is utterly alien among a desert of Barratt Homes and aimless roads. It's across the road from a bus stop, so we could contemplate it for some time. The aggressive double-fencing around it was taking no chances whatsoever. It's on these outskirts that you finally find traces of the New Economy, the concomitant of the tourism of the centre—the Quorum Business Park's huge car parks and call centres, a hidden but mundane non-city, the would-be Milan or Brasilia replaced with Americanized exurbia. It's a relief to get back in the Metro and what suddenly seems a comforting urbanity.

Exhuming the Brasilia of the North

We returned to Newcastle in late autumn, to see an exhibition entitled 'City State—Towards the Brasilia of the North'. You can learn a lot about an exhibition from its comments book. In City State (helpfully subtitled 'T. Dan Smith—What Went Wrong?') the book has more arguments in it than most exhibitions have in their entirety. 'A charismatic visionary', scribbles one, 'AN ARROGANT MAN!' another; 'demolish the lot!' here, 'saddening for a lost public vision' there. Some are surprised that buildings they've always hated look so beautiful in John Davies' photographs, others express admiration for Smith's politics but note 'what a mess he made of Newcastle'. It's a reminder that no definitive judgements can be passed on Smith, save perhaps the six-year sentence passed down by the judge at his 1974 corruption trial.

Thomas Daniel Smith was of what people used to call the hard left. The son of a miner from Wallsend, after spells in the Independent Labour Party and the Revolutionary Communist Party (not to be confused with the eighties libertarian organization that continues as Spiked Online et al.), he took control of Newcastle Labour Party along with a group of fellow far-left entryists, and subsequently of the incongruously Tory Newcastle City Council in 1958, with the promise of massive rehousing programmes. Variously declaring an intention to make it a 'Brasilia of the North' or 'Milan of the North', Smith left Newcastle in 1965 to take a job heading the Northern Economic Planning Council, ran various PR companies, headed the Peterlee New Town Development Corporation, and founded a company called Open System Building, which would later be run by the architect John Poulson. In 1970, when Poulson went bankrupt, his accounts were meticulously pursued, landing Smith with a series of trials, some of which acquitted him, one of which sent him down for six years. By the 1990s he was living out his dotage on the fourteenth storey of a tower he had commissioned thirty years earlier, with enough gumption to play himself in a film, *T Dan Smith—A Funny Thing Happened On The Way To Utopia*. When thinking about Smith and Poulson, it's impossible to keep from your mind their fictional portrayals on British television. Smith became Austin Donohue, corrupt local Labour leader in *Our Friends in the North*, a snake-oil salesman of 'cities in the sky'; Poulson, meanwhile, was fictional ised as *Red Riding*'s John Dawson, portrayed by Sean Bean as a terrifying Yorkshire thug. This is the dark heart of postwar urban politics—backhanders, the threat of violence, one-time socialists forgetting they were in politics to help anyone but themselves, the tearing apart of once-great cities, the desecration of 'heritage'. What is so interesting about City State is that it ignores this narrative completely, in favour of taking Smith's urban ambitions seriously.

Newcastle's urbanism is poised tensely between classical rectitude—the planned city designed by John Dobson and others from the 1820s to 1840s, which bankrupted its developer, Richard Grainger—and the exhilaratingly aggressive industrial structures that made the city its money. Both are implicitly combined in the Literary and Philosophical Society, an extensive library and debating society housed in a serene, sharp neoclassical building by John Green. It was headed at one point by Robert Stephenson, the engineer whose proto-Constructivist High Level Bridge sliced a castle in two, something which would give any heritage watchdog today a coronary. It is, then, an appropriate place for this ambiguous half-celebration of a council leader best known for his destruction of traditional Newcastle. The images in City State show how this destruction, the domineering nature of modernity and the way its structures leap over, crush or transcend tradition, is a part of what makes the place distinctive, and not at all its opposite. The organizers hired for this the great photographer John Davies, whose book *The British Landscape* offers twenty-five years of wide-angled monochrome photographs of Britain as it actually is. Along with images of Stockport viaducts and Durham pit villages, *The British Landscape* contains astounding photographs of usually derided, master-planned postwar landscapes— the chaos of intersections in Herbert Manzoni's Birmingham, the meticulously planted hillscape of J. L. Womersley's Sheffield— taken from the planner's vantage point. That is, from above, seemingly either from the top of a tower block (where the perspective is supposedly bleak and isolating) or an office block (where it is the perspective of the lord of all he surveys). These images combine a certain classical stillness with a barely suppressed charge of excitement.

Their planner's-eye view is wholly appropriate. Under Smith,

The Lit and Phil

Newcastle's was the first English council to have a planning department (headed by one Wilfred Burns) and here you can see the brochures and PR booklets sent out to council tenants that detailed the benefits of urban motorways and point blocks. With inadvertent irony, one booklet notes that 'much of the money needed for the five year plan will be borrowed'. Davies took a book's worth of photographs of the area, and these decorate the walls of City State. Where contemporary critics like Ian Nairn saw an international style of boredom unworthy of Newcastle, he claims to have found something unique. In fact, he goes as far as to say that this is 'unlike the architecture of any city I have photographed', and sets out to prove 'the distinctiveness of Tyneside Modernism'. What makes it distinctive, according to Davies's captions, is the way the buildings support themselves on massive pillars, which allow pedestrian or vehicle traffic to pass underneath, or fire off pedestrian walkways, flyovers and overpasses from over and under. Other elements are apparent, such as a strange neo-medievalism in the design of office blocks and the Bank of England, the use of rough stone or concrete, a generalized northernness; all with a black and white palette imposed by the council. The photographs were taken in the last year or so, and they show the multilevel city in an ostensibly well-preserved state, the recent cladding and/or rotting masked by the monochrome. The finest of these buildings look breathtaking in these images. RMJM's Swan House becomes a sublime elevated grid, at the centre of a riot of walkways and highways, while Ryder and Yates's MEA House appears as the strange, angular terminus of that same system. Meanwhile, the council was every bit as ruthless about ploughing the private car through the city as their 1840s predecessors were about slicing it into pieces for the benefit of the railways. With hindsight we can see what a mistake that was, and, as we find out five minutes after leaving the exhibition, there are few places as uninviting to the pedestrian as the point where Swan House meets the Tyne Bridge. Yet this is more to do with a failure to achieve Smith and Burns's aim of completely separating pedestrian and traffic than the evils of the aim itself.

The problem with the idea of the Brasilia of the North is that Newcastle never found a northern Oscar Niemeyer. This was not for want of trying. Smith invited Le Corbusier to design what would have been his only British building, although it never worked out. He did manage to convince the Danish architect Arne Jacobsen (designer of that other icon of 1960s corruption, the curved chair which Christine Keeler famously straddled) to redesign the neoclassical set piece of Eldon Square, although he was sacked after Smith left the council, meaning at the very least that the banal mall which sits there now can't be blamed on him. As it is, Smith relied upon Scottish architects such as Robert Matthew, Johnson-Marshall (designers of the walkways and Swan House) and Basil Spence (designer of a cluster of blocks by the Tyne Bridge, and the now-demolished Central Library), along with locals Ryder and Yates. English artists were employed for the public art which accompanied the buildings, such as the Victor Pasmore murals in the Rates Hall of the new, Scando-style, no expenses spared Civic Centre ('as they fingered their chequebooks or opened their purses, I longed for [ratepayers] to snarl "this is the end!" '[50]).

It was decent enough, but where Smith's administration really succeeded (and failed) was in the rehousing of his core

The walkways to MEA House

Norgas House

constituency, the working-class voters of Newcastle. The high-rise estates take up fairly little of City State, perhaps because they don't fit the thesis of civic ambition, although one image of a Shieldfield block raising itself up on pillars fits the overarching idea of a distinctive Tyneside multilevel metropolitanism, and the cubic houses by Ryder and Yates in Kenton look extremely weird. After Smith, the Byker slums that his administration had cleared were redeveloped by Ralph Erskine in the sort of sensitive Scandinavian Modernism Smith had tried and failed to impose on Eldon Square, but couched by a Tory council as an explicit alternative to Smith's schemes like the Cruddas Park high-rises. Meanwhile, the most famous buildings of the time are in Gateshead, outside of Smith's jurisdiction, in the form of Owen Luder and Rodney Gordon's Trinity Car Park and Dunston Rocket.

All of this is photographed by Davies as part of an argument that the greater ambition of the time was to do with an intriguing fusion of regionalism—devolution, fierce local pride—and internationalism, achieved by looking out towards Europe and the Third World for ideas both architectural and political. So the architecture of the entire area makes up a wider picture of a potential enclave, a genuine city state, which Smith and his allies attempted to create through the Northern Economic Planning

Council and New Town Development Corporations. This is where Harold Wilson's Labour governments were at their most interesting, and most unlike those of Blair and Brown: where they made a serious attempt at a real reorganization of power in the United Kingdom. In the corner of the exhibition a three-hour film, *Mouth of the Tyne*,[51] shows footage of Smith in the mid 1980s, explaining the ideas on devolution he lobbied for in the 1960s: Britain divided up into eleven locally administered areas, each of which would control the 'commanding heights' of its local economy. These would elect a representative to a second chamber, replacing the House of Lords. This would then be integrated into a federal Europe, and in the process the south-eastern aristocratic biases that skew British politics would be eliminated. The failure of this is all around us, as Old Etonians dominate the government and their think tanks advocate the population of Sunderland moving to London.

Revolution via Quango

Some of Smith's ideas sound really rather similar to the 'Urban Renaissance' announced by Lord Richard Rogers. The estate he commissioned overlooking the Tyne, Cruddas Park, is currently being reclad and rebranded as luxury duplex development Riverside Dene. In these eighties interviews, meanwhile, he talks about wanting to make Tyneside into a 'science city', removing its reliance on 'yesterday's industry', i.e. coal and shipbuilding. There's no truck with nostalgia for the local past but a clear intent to build something more high-tech on top of it, partly through a massive extension of polytechnic education. Then there's his use of more civic-minded European cities as exemplars, his talk of 'science parks' rather than factories and, perhaps most importantly, his emphasis on culture. The 'philosophical background' of Labour's plans for the area was Northern Arts, an organization he founded. The discussion of the importance of arts and, by implication, of tourism, sounds like an inadvertent prophecy of the Blairite urban renaissance and its local incarnation, the ensemble of Millennium

Bridge, Sage and Baltic that is carved out of the post-industrial Gateshead Quayside. The accidental descendants of Smith's New Town science parks are no doubt the call centre colonies of Killingworth. The difference, of course, is that Smith's kind of regional boosterism had a place for democracy and for socialism, both of which are as absent from today's NewcastleGateshead as they are from everywhere else.

John Prescott may or may not have had Smith in mind when he devised plans for regional devolution in the early 2000s. Perhaps because the Greater London Authority, the Welsh Assembly and the Scottish Parliament had managed to carve out niches to the left of New Labour, the North-East Assembly was designed to be a relatively toothless creature. Nonetheless, the region's over-whelming rejection of the plan in a 2004 referendum perhaps shows that it doesn't want to become a city state, an independent metropolitan area able to step out of London's shadow. People in Teesside or Wearside would apparently rather be ruled from Thameside than Tyneside. As it is, rather than being able to reject the more unpleasant whims of New Labour, as have Scotland and Wales, the area is instead largely administered by a multitude of competing unelected Regional Development Corporations, who can pursue Pathfinder schemes more brutal than any 1960s slum clearance. Meanwhile, Newcastle became the epicentre of the financial earthquake when Northern Rock (based, incidentally, in the Regents Centre, an out-of-town office complex built under Smith) had to be nationalized to save it from collapse. The 2004 referendum and the Northern Rock collapse were a return as farce of the calling-in of accounts that did for Smith, much as the crash of Blairism was the sorry echo of the crash of social democracy in the 1970s, this time without any principles whose betrayal we could lament.

What of Socialism, presumably the reason Smith entered politics in the first place? Was he just on the make, or was the graft all a means to a definite political end? Naturally, Smith consis-tently claims the latter in *Mouth of the Tyne*. Yet the documents assembled at City State show a dizzying quantity of business ventures—in PR, engineering, design, painting and decorating—all established with the ex-Trotskyist's adroitness at setting up front organizations. They sit strangely next to his notes for speeches at ILP or RCP meetings—'workers of the world unite!' is scrawled on one of them, something you just don't get with New Labour civic dignitaries like (Sir) Bob Kerslake and (Sir) Howard Bernstein. The video footage shows Smith building up a complicated, often unconvincing but strident and intriguing defence of his, ahem, 'extracurricular' interests. He claims that the reason he established such close links with Poulson was because he was an opponent of system-building (note here the name of Poulson and Smith's former business venture, Open Systems Building, and take the following with a heavy pinch of salt). In fact, he claims, rather than being the corrupted, he was *using* Poulson all along in order to influence architecture and planning on a nationwide scale, so as to shift it in a more careful and individualistic direction. 'I wanted to influence as many British cities as I could, and Poulson was my instrument for that.' The nondescript, interchangeable curtain-walled towers that Poulson produced for British Rail, some of which still survive, are proof of just how questionable Smith's assertions here are. It sounds like a post-facto rationalization of entirely contingent alliances, yet put across with a certain gall: 'if I had been successful and Poulson had been successful, then 70 per cent of the problems of our town centres would have been avoided'; apparently none of their blocks would have been system-built. 'I have no moral qualms.'

This is as maybe, but one thing which is certain is that Smith pleaded guilty in 1974—although even this, he claims, was because of ill health brought about by a nerve-steadying diet of 'Valium and Carlsberg Export'. *Mouth of the Tyne* ends with Smith discussing the power structure of money both old (the House of Lords, the public schools, Oxbridge) and new (financial and industrial capitalism). He claims, plausibly, that he was too powerful and too influential to be allowed to continue at the top, an area strictly reserved for those who have been groomed for it, where after Eton and Cambridge 'the sign on the bus stop reads

Damien Hirst and/or Victory to the Working Class

"to the power structure".' These 'non-elected people that you never hear about' were in his day sundry Lords and civil servants. In ours we could add the multiple Regeneration Commissions and Local Development Corporations, with their names like Yorkshire Forward, Creative Sheffield, Bridging Newcastle-Gateshead, One NorthEast, Housing Market Renewal Pathfinder, and knighted, unelected council leaders like Bernstein and Kerslake. This particular variant of quango was pioneered by the Wilson government, and many of them had T. Dan Smith on their board.

In this 1980s footage, a red-faced, tired but pin-sharp and funny Smith declares that 'capitalism itself is fundamentally immoral and corrupt, and its major corruptions are all legal'. It's both utterly true and a rather poor alibi. Yet listening to him, you can't help but think how relevant his rhetoric is now. He notes that working-class movements are told by ermine-clad Lords that their politics are outdated; today, Baron Mandelson of Foy tells trade unions to move with the times. Smith claims the real corruptions are legal; while he got six years, Northern Rock chairman and enthusiastic neoliberal ideologue Matt Ridley escaped without even a fine. As the missing link between Marxism and Mandelsonism, T. Dan

Smith appears here as the ultimate political curate's egg: fascinating and charismatic, creator of an impressive but often despised landscape, both convincing and dissimulating, a corrupt mandarin who intended to create a decentralized socialist Britain. Swallow it all whole and it might poison you, but better a man who got his fingers burnt when trying to create cities in the sky than when claiming expenses for mock Tudor beams. Tyneside's first version of an urban renaissance holds out the faint promise that a city could be transformed on its own terms.

Chapter Seven

Glasgow: Looking for the Future in All the Wrong Places

This time, we travelled on the motorway. Due to a combination of cowardice and principle, but mostly our personal preference for public transport, everywhere else had been reached by the sclerotic, inept and wildly overpriced privatized rail system, but to get to Glasgow we decided to hire a car, which Joel drove for some twenty hours there and back. This was a fairly novel experience, the last time I spent anywhere near as long on a road being somewhere in childhood, so my brief observations on the experience may have the tone of a Martian visitor to the Motorway Network. The first thing you notice here, unlike on the railways, where towns, suburbs and most of all the Big Sheds provide punctuation for the countryside, is space—sheer, useless, unused space, a spectacular reproach to the notion that the island of Great Britain is overcrowded, bursting; 'Britain is Full', as the *Daily Express* and the BNP erroneously put it. Here the empty space seems to go on forever, and is seemingly featureless for long, long stretches— save for the bridges, those sometimes extraordinary concrete structures that vary from county to county. If you have the right music on and are in an appropriate frame of mind, it is thrilling, especially when you hit the M8, a grand and unnerving entrance to what is surely, regardless of the larger populations of Birmingham and Greater Manchester, the Second City.

Service Stations between the Futurist and the Organic

Going along the A1, noting the geometries of concrete bridges, skeletal pylons ('bare like nude giant girls that have no secret') and floodlights, with the green at each side as abstract as the asphalt, it's only when deep into Yorkshire that we notice a major difference from the Hertfordshire landscape where we began. There are, we know, business parks and distribution centres nearby, but they'll be off-road, reached by a complex series of junctions and slip roads. The A1 was a fine (accidental) choice of route, the relative lack of congestion enhancing the sense of space, and the services hugged the road instead of sitting at the ends of the loops round roundabouts as do true motorway service stations, something we would discover on the M1 on our return.

Rather than the Costa Coffees that besmirch the M1, the A1 is Little Chef territory, and seemingly any building can be commandeered by them and turned into succour for the traveller—1920s roadhouses, '80s vernacular, '50s futurism. We had programmed the hired car's GPS (with which the driver maintained the requisite flirtatious dialogue, which gradually degenerated into an argument between a tired married couple) to guide us to the services at Markham Moor, Nottinghamshire. Therein is a building

Sam Scorer's accidental design for Little Chef

by Sam Scorer, a local architect who was one of Britain's few representatives of Googie, the southern Californian style of irrationalist, high style mid-century Modernism. A sweeping hyperbolic paraboloid contains the Little Chef, playing all the games now expected from riverside regeneration, but for the sake of sheer spectacle and capitalist potlatch rather than edification. It is enormously striking after several hours of straight lines. Inside we note that the chain has had something of a makeover of late, in that it has become self-conscious, marketing proper English comfort food with 'classic café' imagery and a familiar Eric Gill-esque typeface on the menu. The restaurant is a later addition to the building: originally the roof enclosed nothing at all, being a mere gateway for cars on the way to a garage, a ceremonial, non-functional architecture. The roof is severely chipped and cracked, but carries its charge nonetheless.

The North is designated by the shadows of cooling towers and power stations, frequently right by the road, structures so stark and imposing that any emission-based concerns are dropped for a few minutes of awe. The landscape gradually starts to mutate and then, as we approach dusk, the motorway traverses Cumbria, a darkly cinematic landscape of burial mounds and sudden changes in scale, becoming ever more sinister until we take the M8 and get our first glimpses of Glasgow, where the motorway bisects serried rows of tower blocks like one of the relentless *Groszstadt* schemes of the rationalist twenties, only assembled in the wrong order and illuminated by seedy sodium lights. On the way back we visit what is surely the diametric opposite of the Googie Little Chef: what, with a nod to caring, sharing beverage purveyors Innocent Smoothie, can only be described as the Innocent Service Station. Tebay Services was designed in 1972 in stone and timber in order to have a proper contextual relation with the landscape, if not the abundant asphalt and concrete. The real interest is inside, where Urban Splash white walls and jolly lettering point towards a vast range of organic food, Keep Calm and Carry On chocolate bars, and numerous hoorays taking their progeny to sample what is apparently the best tea in England. That something so clearly pleased with itself should be so obviously complicit in the despoliation—by all of us in there, whether using the loos or buying local sausages—of the very countryside it fetishizes is another example of the pointlessness of irony.

On the M6 on our way back, we passed underneath the viewing bridges of T. P. Bennett's Forton Services, the most famous of the Futurist buildings that originally accompanied the motorway network, before we decided to ensure that environmental destruction was In Keeping. In order to complete the review of service stations that we had been composing accidentally, we were intent on finding an OK Diner, of which there are several along the A1, all in chrome and vitrolite, making it clear that the A1 is the S&M Café of the motoring world, a simulation of pre-1979 England for the benefit of pop culture nostalgics. Unfortunately they were all closed, so we eventually resorted, starved and nearly hallucinating, to a McDonalds next to a Travelodge somewhere near Peterborough. As we pull into the drive-in at this ungodly hour, Joel asks the middle-aged McAssistant how he is. 'I'm here' is the reply.

Theme for Great Cities

The M8's 'here' is rather different to that of the service station, in that it means *somewhere*, heralding one of the few truly unambiguously urban experiences in Britain. Unusually for the UK, Glasgow is fully metropolitan. There's a scale and grain, a (perhaps illusory) sense of the place having been thought about rather than emerging ad hoc. We only skimmed the surface on the first visit, but even our cursory three-day acquaintance revealed turn-of-the-century grandeur and a subsequent long decline—sometimes comfortable, sometimes decidedly less so. Regardless, a walk round its commercial centre attests that at the start of the twentieth century it was here, rather than in London, that architecture kept up with (and sometimes set the pace of) advances in Germany or the US. While London devolved into the pompous Champs-Elysée parodies of Kingsway, the second city excelled.[52]

Tall sandstone tenements, concrete office blocks (like the now-derelict Lion Chambers), ferro-vitreous warehouses and Crystal Palaces (restored at Glasgow Green, ruined at Springburn), and astonishing one-offs like Glasgow School of Art all showed an urban confidence which is still palpable, if faded.

Perhaps the city's bourgeois clients lost their élan when 'Red Clydeside' was occupied by tanks in 1919, perhaps something happened when Charles Rennie Mackintosh exiled himself five years earlier. For whatever reason, Glasgow fell behind, making a belated and enormously controversial stab at modernity in the 1960s, with hundreds of council towers and the M8 scything through it, giving the impression of a Ludwig Hilberseimer urban plan realized on a Lidl budget. You can see this at its best and worst in Anderston, where the Kingston Bridge emulates LA in a markedly unsympathetic climate, the impressive megastructure of Richard Seifert's Anderston Centre on one side, and East German-issue *Plattenbau* blocks on the other. Since then, the city has gone for small measures over large, an approach that brings with it some new problems.

Travelling round Glasgow, we see a city still indelibly marked by the sixties, with office blocks and (often truncated) walkways adding a sub-Fritz Lang scale to the Jules Verne of the

The Kingston Bridge

187

Truncated walkway, Anderston

St Vincent Street Church

pre-WWI city. The usual response to this is cladding, which encases practically all the city's tower blocks. At best sealing up leaks and providing insulation, in architectural terms it can be truly disastrous, as on Derek Stephenson's 1971 Heron House, now 'Pinnacles'. The way this concrete block tried to accommodate itself around the mutant classicism of Alexander 'Greek' Thomson's St Vincent Street Church may have been presumptuous, but now green glass and plastic makes it actively hostile to its

Tallest cinema in Britain!

Radisson, gm+ad

neighbour, ignoring and overpowering a (council-owned) masterpiece which is visibly becoming ruined, with shrubs poking out of the stonework. A liking for shiny tat can also be seen in the call centres that run along the Clyde, in AWW Architecture's obnoxious Cineworld, proudly the 'tallest cinema in Britain', and even in the much-lauded work of Gordon Murray and Alan Dunlop, who were, until their split in early 2010, collectively the lowercase gm+ad. Beautifully detailed, expensive and suave, buildings like their Sentinel office block and their 'iconic' Marks or Radisson hotels are also decidedly heartless. The Radisson is the best of the bunch, its verdigris angles standing out amid some terracotta-clad dreck near the glass bridge of Central Station— dreck which actually followed the hotel, after it had made the area safe for regeneration.

Redoubt on the Clyde

For a city its size, Glasgow has a striking absence of tall office blocks in the centre, meaning that the skyline is dominated by working-class housing rather than big business, something which clearly rankles with the city's notables. The nearest equivalent to a skyscraper, after the indefinite shelving of an Ian Simpson scheme, is a frankly Texan mirror-glass hotel on the Clyde next to Foster's 1997 Clyde Auditorium, designed in 1988 by local architects Cobban and Lironi. The auditorium is now looking more than a tad cheap, especially compared to the architect's later, more bulging and baroque version of the same idea on Tyneside. On the other side, there is one of those obligatory riverside culture/regeneration schemes, superior to Salford Quays but with poor public spaces compared to, say, London's South Bank. Here are

BDP's Science Centre

BBC Scotland

the titanium molluscs of BDP's Science Centre, complete with 'landmark' tower. If we really need these comprehensive redevelopment-trailing enclaves of titanium tat housing interactive experiences to patronize pre-teens (and I see no reason why we do), then this is one of the better examples, and also one of the projects where BDP proves that its corporate anonymity is fundamentally irrelevant—these examples of the Bilbao parody genre are no worse than those of Wilford and Libeskind, legitimate 'starchitects'.

In stern rectilinear contrast to the eye-snatching molluscs is David Chipperfield's BBC Scotland. Fittingly, for a structure designed by a paragon of the rectitude which is seldom found in contemporary British design, this a very BBC place in the old Reithian sense—an architectural equivalent of the Gill Sans font they still use, to the point where it has unexpectedly come back into fashion. Decent, upstanding, moderate Modernism, a surprising contrast to godawful recent BBC buildings in London and elsewhere. Its ambiguous appropriateness to a public corporation which is no longer what it was is clear, given Chipperfield's resignation halfway through construction after the BBC refused to consult him over detailing. It's as if they couldn't quite sustain the effort of completing an above-average building, and John Birt instincts took over.

Further along is the scaffolded shed of Zaha Hadid's unfinished transport museum. Scotland has two completed or half-completed Hadid buildings; England and Wales have none, after a rash of cancellations and botch jobs. There seems to be an attempt to prove Scotland's relatively enlightened nature by hiring actual 'starchitects' rather than their imitators, with the exception of BDP: think of Steven Holl's recent, and controversial, victory over Glasgow architects to win the commission for new additions to the Glasgow School of Art; or the 'Maggie's Centres', buildings for the care of cancer patients designed by everyone from Frank Gehry to less glamorous locals. These Centres have only recently travelled south of the border, in the form of Rogers Stirk Harbour's 2009 Stirling Prize winner, the Hammersmith Maggie's Centre. Buying in big international names has only really been attempted south of the border and outside the capital by Manchester with Libeskind, whose lack of interest in the UK was reflected in his fairly tossed-off design there. Hadid's approach to Glasgow seems to be similarly lackadaisical—what we see there is a rote 'parametric' design where outrageous feats of engineering support little more than a wonkier than usual roof. The architect designs a shape and the engineer makes it stand up, in an extreme version of the rigid division of labour between artist and craftsman which Modernism once tried to destroy.

Glasgow Harbour symbolizing something

Glasgow Harbour's 'Public Realm'

Then there's Glasgow Harbour, which incorporates a rather different set of clichés. This two-part housing scheme by RMJM and the ubiquitous gm+ad was, we're told, a commercial failure. The gh2o brochure, which we pick up from the marketing suite (whose staff tellingly twig straight away that we're press and not prospective buyers), shows an *American Psycho* fantasy of spotless interiors and hard bodies, promising that property can be an 'investment'. It now seems an artefact from a bygone pre-crunch age, as do the buildings, fairly typical examples of the inescapable technique of applying contrasting cladding materials in order to please everyone at once. The towers, reachable only via underpass or car, are far from shops and amenities. Persistent rumour has it that Phase Two is being bought up by Housing Associations, although officially they were refused because the development doesn't meet the 'Parker-Morris' standard for minimum room sizes established in the early 1960s which still applies in social housing, although not in private. Again, we find that the space standards of twenty-first century luxury are below the required minimum for dockworkers in 1962.

At the entrance to Glasgow Harbour we see the obligatory crass and inept public art, here worse than ever, an angel made of steel shards 'representing Glasgow's regeneration'. Across the river, some shipyards still cling on doggedly as something other than an ornament. The first high-rises constructed here for decades, Glasgow Harbour's jumbled skyline compares poorly with the visual coherence of council blocks in neighbouring Partick. Glasgow has a high-rise skyline, but not of the same sort as Leeds or London.

From Film-Set Chicago to the Glasgow Bloc

Although I'm sure I could be upbraided here for making rather too pat links between the base and the superstructure, in the recent history of architecture you can follow the passing of the baton of advanced capitalism from Britain through to Germany and/or the US, and now to the ultra-developmentalism of China. At least in the design porn you can find in British magazines like *Blueprint*, the latter shows an unforgiving confidence which is rarely to be seen in Europe. Whether that's a good thing is extremely doubtful, given the necessary corollary of extreme exploitation, but there it is. So, if you want an illustration of the decline of British capitalism and its supersession by less technologically conservative, more industrially fervent countries at the end of the nineteenth century and the start of the twentieth, architecture is a fantastic place to start. The reign of vainglory and tedium, of justly forgotten but prolific neoclassicists—E. Berry Webber, E. Vincent Harris, Herbert Baker, Reginald Blomfield; Edwardian Baroque, Wrenaissance, almost-deco—was an escape into solidity and tradition while both were being stretched to breaking point or smashed altogether on the other side of the Atlantic or in Berlin. There is an exception to this rule in England, in the form of a cluster of buildings near the Pier Head in Liverpool, the astounding Liver Building most of all—but Glasgow architecture threatens the entire theory, suggesting that unashamed British modernity died here much later than it did elsewhere.

The area around Glasgow Central station—which itself has its futurist moment with the glass bridge that barges across Argyle Street—is absolutely full of what would have been extremely advanced architecture for its date; appropriately, it's sometimes used as a double in film sets for Edwardian Chicago or New York, just before they make their leap into the stratosphere. But funnily enough this isn't a question of sheer height, but the *use* of that height. First of all, many of the most impressive buildings are fairly low iron-framed warehouses; their unambiguous techno-logical expression would never be allowed on Piccadilly. A steel-framed building of six to eight storeys in Edwardian London would generally make a big play of its own lumpen rusticated solidity, but their Glasgow equivalents stretch out their ornamen-tation, and their high windows and unashamed repetition give them that *upwards!* momentum that is as important to skyscraper design as the steel frame. There are oddities also, such as the con-crete Lion Chambers, one of the nearest things in Britain to the ultra-congested multi-functional 'delirium' Rem Koolhaas claims as the foundation of Manhattanism. This consists of an artists' studio, chambers for lawyers, a traditionalist castle and a skinny *Jugendstil* confection mashed together. So it's curious that Glasgow doesn't have a cluster of postwar office towers, as it was surely the natural place for such a thing to emerge. But what grew up instead, decades later, was the Glasgow Bloc.

Glasgow is still, at least in appearance, a city of municipal tower blocks, though it may not be for much longer. Scotland is the

The Bluevale and Whitevale Towers

perennial guinea pig for controversial policies (think of the Poll Tax, tested here years before England) and the entire council housing stock is now controlled by the Glasgow Housing Association. Leaving aside the political implications of a vast quango becoming perhaps Europe's biggest landowner, this has certain architectural consequences. Rather than merely restoring council flats, the GHA has embarked on a policy of demolition and cladding, depending on place in the pecking order. So the central Dundasvale Estate of towers and deck-access blocks is currently being made over as if it's still 1986—the contrast with the bright neo-Modernism of the recent private Matrix flats adjacent, based directly on Corbusian precedent, is telling—while many other estates lie semi-derelict, waiting for their apparently inevitable demolition.

Easy links between tower blocks in the ex-Eastern Bloc and those in Britain (because they're both so *totalitarian*, yeah?) are usually glib and ignorant, but here it makes sense. It would be silly to argue that the relative popularity of Stalinism in Scotland—Fife being one of only two places in Britain to have elected Communist MPs who were opposed by Labour candidates—had an influence on the extremely stark turn of Glasgow's municipal architecture, but there genuinely is a stylistic kinship that implies the city picked the other side in the Cold War. Only partly, of course—in fact, the uninspired *Zeilenbau* boredom of American 'projects' has more in common with the worst Glasgow 'schemes' than either has with the ambitious civic modernism of postwar Sheffield. It's interesting that the most architecturally bespoke, if by all accounts appallingly built, of the Glasgow Bloc, Basil Spence's Hutchesontown C, was demolished while hundreds of more straight-up slabs survive. Not all of them are awful, and most of them need care and decent facilities rather than clearance and demolition, but there is something bracing and cold about Glasgow's municipal Modernism. It's especially sad that the natural peaks and dips of the topography seldom seemed to be used in the way they were in Sheffield—instead it's usually slab, slab, slab.

Red Road

The slabs of all slabs are in Red Road, Sam Bunton's series of huge, steel-framed towers in Springburn that are erroneously but regularly claimed to be the highest housing blocks in Europe (they aren't, not even in Glasgow; that honour being taken by the Whitevale and Bluevale twin towers). There certainly was a sense of shame about visiting the place, camera in hand, after the example of Andrea Arnold's eponymous film—a tale of surveillance and paranoia which builds up an extraordinary tension, only to collapse into a morass of ITV humanism in its last ten minutes. Red Road is an atmospheric place, with echoing voices reverberating around the central burnt-out ex-playground. There are, or rather were, more facilities here than in Glasgow Harbour: a pub (disused), shops (derelict), playgrounds (rotting), and spectacular hilltop views. The overall effect is of a sad rather than horrifying or inhuman place. They have few more years in them as substandard, semi-ruined housing of last resort, before being demolished for something more 'mixed' in class terms, as the euphemism goes. Now, they're little more than a holding camp. In March 2010 three asylum seekers whose applications had been refused jumped to their deaths from one of the towers, after throwing down a wardrobe to break the netting pre-emptively installed to prevent suicides.

Inscription, Red Road

A taint has always lingered over certain areas of Glasgow, so to suggest that the architecture of its poorer districts might be in places very fine often needs some sort of prefix or caveat. In Ian Nairn's essay on Glasgow in the mid sixties, he prefaced his praise of the tenements with 'I can hear the cries of anguished planners already "really, this fellow Nairn has gone too far this time" '[13] He contends that they were decent buildings spoiled by overcrowding that were nonetheless easily converted into something better, but architecture provided a convenient scapegoat for political ills. In the 1960s the tenements went and their replacements are going too, for a seeming amalgam of Barratt homes and soft, sensitive, mild Modernism, both of which miss the sense of bombast and scale that makes the place seem akin to an imaginary turn-of-the-century American megacity that has somehow coexisted with an Eastern Bloc *plattenbau* expanse. Today the two parallel versions of high-rise modernity never really intersect, despite often occupying the same space. To these parallel cities can be added another unnoticed hidden city, one determined to resemble an exurban Americanism of retail parks and speculative cottages, rather than flats and skyscrapers.

The Tentative Enclaves of the New Glasgow Modernism

There has been a change in Glasgow housing over the last decade, from Postmodernism and vernacular back to Modernism, but unlike the brash identikit Pseudomodernism that is so dominant in English cities this has a certain sobriety and sensitivity to place. Its mildness, a return to the human scale after the Bloc, can sometimes be ill-fitting alongside the hardness and consistency of Glasgow's best architecture. The great exemplar for the shift in scale is Homes for the Future, near Glasgow Green, masterplanned in the late nineties by local architects Page & Park. It's a sort of Weissenhof Siedlung for twenty-first century Caledonian Modernism-lite, with the requisite mix of private and 'affordable'. There are good things here, a terrace by McKeown Alexander and some imaginative games with walkways and balconies, while it pulls into itself a fine 1960s school by Gillespie Kidd & Coia, rehabilitating the best of the postwar era rather than arrogantly setting itself up as the solution to all the problems it caused. But it's in a parlous state already, with many blocks showing their (meagre) age. Ushida Findlay's streamline effort is in particularly ghastly condition, the white render punished by the climate, the attempt to look swish and moderne mocked by the surroundings. It looks

Homes for the Future, optimistically

worse than any council block we see, unbelievable for a building only a decade old.

Following in its footsteps is the Graham Square redevelopment, the most recent part of which, planned by Richard Murphy for Moledinar Park Housing Association, was finished in 2008. This too has its virtues—the re-use of a former Meat Market's façades as propped-up ornaments is a more interesting approach than turning the original spaces into cramped but lucrative lofts, and there's also a return to openness, to shared spaces rather than the obsessive demarcation between private and public, that seems here to have stopped halfway through the process. Especially in the newer areas, there is a strange confusion as to what is public and what isn't: this is a gated community where all the gates are open, at least when we visit in the early evening. Perhaps they're slammed shut as soon as it gets dark. Otherwise, the metal and wood materials are fairly familiar, and the presence of some expensive cars suggest that the 'social' part of this 'mixed' development may be fairly minor. Still, the series of courtyards have a certain civic welcome—something notably lacking from other developments, such as the recent spec housing in Ruchill, a famously impoverished Northern district. Here you can find some schemes as bad as anything else in the country, their combination

Homes for the Future, pessimistically

Mild-Modernism at Graham Square

Pseudomodernism at Ruchill

of pretension and blandness best encapsulated in the 'Mondrian' development by Holmes Partnership. This is a truly perfect example of Pseudomodernism, a series of blocks decorated with 'Mondrian-inspired' patterns, arranged like a Basingstoke cul-de-sac, the ineffectual public space littered with cars. Adjacent are some even more uninspired developers' houses and flats. Nearby,

New Ruchill

any recent infill is mostly of a drab standard, lacking the ambition of either the city of the 1900s or the 1960s. The expanses of North and East Glasgow are relentlessly bleak—towers, with the odd exception like the striking and doomed Whitevale–Bluevale twins, are usually nondescript, always with attendant eighties cladding. The 1930s cottage estates, 1990s retail parks and 2000s wasteland awaiting 'development' are, if anything, bleaker still. Sandstone tenements poke out, in the context hugely impressive; here is a place where you could almost buy into the New Urbanist cult of Victorian city (non)planning, at least if you forget how these tenements were among the world's most hated housing. The main constant in Glasgow architecture, then, is that civic grandeur is not all it seems.

A Walk from the Past to the Future and Somewhere In Between

A second visit to the Second City consisted of a long walk with a tube journey in between, progressing from genteel Hillhead through Partick to Anderston, then through the centre of town, a quick tube trip to the Gorbals, and lastly over the river to Glasgow Cross and Glasgow Green. Our trip made it clear that

Glasgow is perhaps the only city in Britain where I could unambiguously and definitively take the view that the Victorian architecture really *is* better than that of the 1940s–70s. This is not so much because of the poverty or otherwise of the latter, but because the determinedly urban, powerful, dramatic nature of the Glasgow tenement is as hard to surpass as it is to emulate. However, given that the largest concentration of old tenements is in the West End, it's hard to guess just how bad their proletarian equivalents were, as they survive mostly in fragments. Memoirs and histories maintain that they were very bad indeed, worse presumably than the straggling wastescape of the contemporary East End, although this seems far more a matter of overcrowding than architectural quality. The West End tenements, though, are truly lovely. A Modernist get-out clause here is that their order, repetition, lack of extraneous tat and unashamed modernity exempt tenement fetishism from the peasant associations of the 'hooray for back to backs and gardens' tendency in England. New tenements seem as unconvincing as new terraces, though, as we will see.

There are a few bits of modern infill along this route which largely just seem inept. Importations from Manchester or Leeds, these little yuppiedromes use, as is customary, five or six cladding

Tenements at Hillhead

materials at once. They are far further than the sixties blocks from the regularity and focus of nineteenth-century Glaswegian architecture, standing almost entirely blind to their surroundings while scrupulously respecting the height limits set by heritage ideology. Hence they manage to be both petty and bluff. The best of them is Elder & Cannon's canted glass and stone effort, which at least attempts a serious fusion of the tenement and the current deconstructivist-lite. Others, like Cooper & Cromer's red-brick/ wood/render attempt, have escaped from the drawing boards of second-rate Lancastrian Pseudomodernism. On the way to the city centre I pass various institutional buildings. The University, for instance, has a couple of fine Brutalist compositions; none, however, match Keppie, Henderson & Partners' Western Infirmary, whose long block on stilts is bracingly warlike, its fine-grained concrete clean and gleaming in the cold sunshine. The entrance shelters a necessarily more meek and mild Maggie's Centre by Page & Park, an early example of the modesty of the current Glasgow school. The Infirmary is slated for closure, presumably because as an inner-city hospital it could be more lucrative demolished.

Metropolis at Kelvin Hall

Nearby, overshadowing all this, are the red sandstone explosions of Kelvingrove Art Gallery and Kelvin Hall, baroque nonsense of the highest order. Kelvin Hall is a prime example of a building type which seems peculiar to Glasgow and Liverpool—the near-skyscraper, the building which wants to be a skyscraper or, in this case, appears as the lost, truncated top of a skyscraper, with its preceding twenty storeys chopped off. The manner in which it dramatically forces itself upwards, its lack of tastefulness and the air of melodrama make it undeniably Americanist, the assemblage of obelisks and globes on the tower closer to Raymond Hood or Eliel Saarinen than Edwin Lutyens, in their vulgar, gimcrack metropolitan stylism.

Into the Grid

At Anderston the contradictions of Glasgow architecture break out virulently. St Vincent's Street, one of the most freakishly disparate roads in Britain, begins with a series of interlinked blocks of flats, designed in 1967 by the Sanctuary Scotland Housing Association, and the contrast with the nearby tenements of Hillhead and Partick is horribly unfair. The windows are absolutely tiny as against the generous height of the tenement ceilings, and the chromatic complexities of the red-and-blond stone precedes the cheapest of *plattenbau* concrete panels. The walkways that run between have a shadow of Futurism to them, but even they look poky. The overwhelming impression is grim, but to be frank, not uninterestingly so—the bracing Siberian air gives a patina of tragic, imposing sternness very similar to that photographers have obsessively documented in the former Eastern Bloc over the last decade. Before it all gets too stark, a 'Ladies' Hair and Beauty Salon' called 'Intrigue' reminds that this is a place where people manage to live normal lives, rather than an aesthete's dystopian dreamland. Facing these blocks across the road are a series of postmodernist tenements, designed in the mid 1980s by James Cunning, Cunningham & Associates. Despite their attempt to return to the old typology, it's clear that budgets don't

Modernist barracks

extend that far any more; the lush sandstone and high ceilings absent, the ceilings in fact as low as those of the Modernist barracks they face. Still, at least they don't declare their distrust of their inhabitants as loudly as the ubiquitous, intrusive CCTV cameras which lean out of every available outpost in the estate on the opposite side of St Vincent's Street.

Then there's a massive rupture, where the ordered, only intermittently interrupted city is torn apart in favour of the motorway

Post-tenements, Anderston

landscape where the M8 meets the Kingston Bridge. Wrong-headed as all this undoubtedly is, the first feeling on crossing it is awe, as you attempt to trace all the different directions that the traffic is going in, vertiginously aware of how puny, how easily killed you are, and how terrifyingly close you can get to these channels of motorized death. On the other side are blocks showing another America, the weirdly Mid-Western style of Glasgow's commercial Postmodernism: the Dalmore House office block, designed in 1990 by locals Miller Partnership, its mirror-glass and stone seemingly a tribute to late eighties Denver. Inside this area is a completely self-enclosed alien landscape, in amazingly close proximity to a preserved Victoriana, before you get to the Grid, and the blocks that make up commercial central Glasgow, where the one-time vigour and independence of the city's ruling class is still palpable. Here is another version of Glasgow Americanism, this time that of Miami rather than the Mid-West: The Beresford, a hulking 1938 building by Wedell & Inglis, which has variously been offices for ICI and a Halls of Residence, and is currently—*obviously*—luxury flats. Again, it appears to have weirdly little to do with Glasgow, or with the independent line of proto-skyscrapers that it developed at the turn of the century. Nonetheless, the way it has accommodated so many different functions at least partly qualifies it as an example of the 'culture of congestion' defined by Rem Koolhaas. Like many of the tallest pre-war buildings in Glasgow, it's at the bottom of a hill, as if the city didn't actually *want* a skyline.

The central grid means that Manhattanism makes more sense here than anywhere else in the UK, and the city's architects clearly knew it during the period when this became the third European city to pass one million inhabitants, after London and Paris. Today, the only attempts in the centre to skyscrape are a tallish recent hotel by gm+ad and a decent postwar curtain wall near George Square. In the grid there are, however, many examples of the halfscrapers of 1860s to 1930s Glasgow. A variety of applied styles are employed—Flemish Gothic, Beaux-Arts, etc—although you can often discern the metal frames that lie beneath, and the inspiration of the likes of Daniel Burnham or Louis Sullivan. None of them ever manage to leap out of the grid, but you can tell they want to, that they're just itching to transcend their nine or ten storeys up to twenty or thirty. Recently, some have been helped along in this ambition, with surprisingly sensitively designed extra floors added to Frank Burnet's Commercial Union and William Hunter McNab's Sutherland House sandstone mini-towers, as if to redress the mistakes of earlier building codes.

The architect James Salmon designed the two Glasgow office blocks which seem most keen to make this leap. Salmon's buildings are as *sachlich* in their technical display and as original in their ornamentation as anything by the Chicago School, who were themselves inspired by Glasgow architects like Alexander Thomson (they certainly held the latter in higher regard than Glasgow Council seem to, given that his astonishing churches in the Gorbals and St Vincent's Street remain decidedly forlorn). Salmon's 1899 Hat Rack building employs open expanses of glass and tortuous, organic curlicues of steel, its gaunt symmetry veritably pricking upwards, its bays opening the offices up to sunlight in a curious mix of utilitarian and richly decorative. Even more interesting is the now derelict 1907 Lion Chambers, one of the strangest buildings I've ever come across. Constructed using the

Halfscrapers in the Grid

The Hat Rack

then cutting-edge Hennebique Concrete system, its experimental structure is used as an excuse not to restore, although plenty of Hennebique buildings have been. Currently held up with mesh so that it won't completely fall apart, it is noticeably crumbling. A combined office block and chambers for solicitors, it includes some very dubious-looking concrete judges on the façade, canti-levered into accusatory bewigged gargoyles. The block seems to mash several different buildings together; one part seems like a glass and concrete Chicago skyscraper, another side is all Scottish baronial, with the front a bizarre composite. This fearlessly origi-nal building was surely *the* potential point of take-off for the Scottish skyscraper that never occurred.

Among the tall office blocks of Victorian Glasgow is Charles Rennie Mackintosh's office for the *Glasgow Herald*, a craggy, cranky thing which barges into a small side street. Famously, visitors to Glasgow are enthralled by the variety of available 'Mockintosh' in the gift shops and by his School of Art itself. Nonetheless, there's initially something heartening about the public esteem for the School of Art; it can't be encompassed by any one view, it doesn't photograph terribly well with the

Lion Chambers

exception of a couple of rooms, and hence is the opposite of all things 'iconic'. Sometimes startlingly direct, sometimes playing all manner of oblique, private games with light and material, this is a building out of time which was largely ignored for decades, where Modernists and revivalists all project their own ideas into its labyrinthine corridors, each finding ample justification for their positions. Yet when it won the 'Stirling of Stirlings', a recent *Sunday Times* poll to ascertain the best building of the last 150 years, it seemed that right-thinking esteem had for once matched

Glasgow School of Art

genuine quality and originality. Thing is, the cult of Mackintosh has very little to do with architecture.

This is easily gleaned from the Glasgow School of Art's own tours of the building, which are given by students—in this case, by an amiable American textile student who clearly knows next to nothing about architecture, but is keen to tell us it's all about nature, symbolism and stuff. The dizzying library, with its lighting effects borrowed from—oh yes—American skyscrapers, is worth the asking price alone, but is given about as much attention as the question of how annoying it apparently was to have been educated in the 'concrete monstrosity' of the Newbury Tower opposite, rather than 'the Mac'. They really ought to employ some of the city's architectural enthusiasts, who are now likely to be jobless, to explain this place, although that would imply that the city cares much about its architecture, that it was aware that it was among the most original in Europe.

The Lighthouse, the architecture centre that attaches itself to the *Glasgow Herald* building, recently went into administration, failing in its appeal for a grant to bail it out from financial difficulties. Its small exhibition on Mackintosh provides far more insight into his work than the tour you pay a tenner for at GSA, and for a city whose architectural inequalities are as gross as contemporary Glasgow's to be even *thinking* about closing a facility for architectural education is appalling. Nonetheless, until it is shut you can go to the Page & Park-designed viewing platform at the top and see it completely empty. It would seem that this fantastic view of the strange and complex skyline is less interesting than pondering what the ogee windows of GSA were 'about'.

One of the exhibitions at the dying Lighthouse is on labour. More specifically, it consists of a set of proposals, mainly from artists and designers, to re-industrialize this once overwhelmingly productivist city. I don't think one falls into nostalgic neo-entrepreneurialism in thinking this a marvellous idea, abandoning the pernicious tyranny of the servile service industry and the patronizing tourism represented by the Mockintosh, through creating jobs that might induce some degree of pride or purpose.

Sadly the photographic images and occasional positive proposals arranged in the exhibition, ranging from green roofs on industrial structures to some melancholy photos of abandoned mines, lack the libidinal force that could make this idea really convince. It is as if the anti-Modernist injunction against the grand scale was holding the artists and architects back. At the top of the Lighthouse extension, atop the hills that overlook the metropolis, you can see a series of wind turbines which make the same case more simply, with elegance and succinctness. As things are, this is an idea very far from anyone's agenda. On the train here, I spotted some fading graffiti alongside the vast, derelict steelworks, which closed decades ago. An SNP logo and the words 'SAVE GARTCOSH, SAVE SCOTTISH STEEL'. The steel for BDP's 2001 Glasgow Science Centre was made in Gdansk.

Palaces for the People

After this I wanted to see the People's Palace in Glasgow Green, a ferro-vitreous tribute to Glaswegian labour, but was also keen to see the Glasgow tube, so the route becomes convoluted. The tube, the notorious 'Clockwork Orange', is ... *cute*, the only architectural evidence that we are in the (musical) home of Twee, of

Norfolk Court

Public Art at a Clyde call centre

Orange Juice, Belle & Sebastian and Bis, aside perhaps from the laughably provincial pomo buildings that house Mono, the Pastels' popular vegan café and record shop. So I took a roundabout route, which entailed a visit to one of the least twee places imaginable—Laurieston, New Gorbals, dominated by the towers of Norfolk Court, which even now are the most striking thing on the way into Central Station. They're *colossal*, nearly as wide as they are high. Like the similarly gigantic Whitevale and Bluevale blocks, Sighthill or Red Road, it's hard to make a case for the

Triumphal Gate to Glasgow Green

THE NEW RUINS OF GREAT BRITAIN

towers on strictly architectural grounds: there's no clever detailing (though its shades of brown fit the climate as well as the stone
tenements), no smart angles, no richly textured surfaces and no
futuristic extrusions, just two gigantic striped slabs. What it does
do is display power, and presence. Here we are. If you don't like it
then fuck off. It's a tower about to chin ye. It's also popular with
its tenants, who are less than pleased about proposals for either
demolition and clearance[54] or recladding and transformation into
yuppiedromes.[55] This riverside site is prime real estate, and is
being left to rot until a suitable plan for cleansing is agreed.

From there, across the river, passing the arrant Mancunian
tripe on the waterfront, to Glasgow Cross and then to Glasgow
Green, I arrive at the sandstone baroque/glass and iron People's
Palace. This is next to the Doge's Palace, or rather its translit-
eration into a red-brick carpet factory. Before that, though, is a
peculiar piece of 1990s axial planning, where a triumphal arch
from a completely different eighteenth-century building serves as
a gateway to the Green. It's aligned perfectly with a stern Grecian
temple opposite the park, though certainly not with the Victorian
obelisk inside it. In the photograph we took you can see a white-
bearded gentleman wondering what on earth is going on here.
Elsewhere on the Green, unexpected sights of surviving industry
sit next to *Last Year in Marienbad* angular topiary, with Homes for
the Future on the other side pointing elsewhere.

Among its interactive exhibits the People's Palace features the
desk of John Maclean, Britain's first Bolshevik Commissar, under
some eighties neo-expressionist murals of insurgent Glasgow.
The items on the desk—pamphlets, papers, artfully scattered—
are under glass. In the Crystal Palace at the back, the huge airy
space is filled with the sound of Cliff Richard's 'Mistletoe and
Wine'. Red Clydeside seems to have been quiet since the bizarre
suicide of the Scottish Socialist Party over the pressing issue of
Tommy Sheridan's marital fidelity. This once incredibly exciting
body rose and fell with equal abruptness. At spitting distance from
Homes for the Future is a Red Bookshop where, as I stock up on
Workerist literature, the elderly owner guesses my politics (the

People's Palace

badges are a bit of a giveaway—'I used to make ones like that') and engages me in conversation about the weather in a viscous Glasgow accent. 'It's started already', he says. 'It's terrible. And from here it's only going to get worse and worse.' Afterwards, I wonder if he was talking about the bitter cold outside or actually meant, y'know, *the weather*. The landscape around is a mess of waste, surface car parks and unambitious vernacular housing, which sharpens itself up with hard, elegant tenements as you get to Glasgow Cross, and then becomes the 'Merchant City', an uneasy mix of yuppiedrome infill and more 1860s–1930s grandiosity. Here as elsewhere, you see a combined and uneven credit crunch, dereliction and shininess next to each other, trying to pretend it isn't happening: sandstone and glass office blocks alongside pound shops.

George Square is where the grid of central Glasgow opens out for some brief, much needed breathing space. It is the last place in Britain to have been occupied by the army, unless one counts the theory that the military were covertly reinforcing the police in certain battles during the Miners' Strike. In early 1919, the British government was absolutely convinced that Glasgow was where Bolshevism would erupt. A pitched battle here between police and demonstrators led to reinforcement with tanks, and a brief military occupation of the entire city. Taken by surprise, the Red

George Square's festive illuminations

Clydesiders were left wishing they'd seized Maryhill Barracks in time. It is too cramped here now to imagine an insurrection beginning on this spot. The lions and the stark, abstract cenotaph are one thing, but the festive light-architecture that fills the square in the run-up to Christmas is something else entirely. On the way up I saw countless freight trains carrying Chinese containers, a better indicator of the imminence of Christmas than any advent calendar, as we prepare to accumulate more tat from the places that still make stuff. Looking at the seasonal George Square, you have to stare very hard to imagine it as the site of revolutionary action. It's hard, but not impossible. You'd just have to utilize the carousels and decorations in some strategic manner.

Chapter Eight

Cambridge: Silicon Fences

What distinguishes Cambridge amongst the cities in this book is that it shouldn't need any kind of regenerative interventions. Not only is it the seat of the most powerful and 'best' University in Europe, it's the pulsating centre of the New Economy, and the research pivot around which the Silicon Fen of 'new settlements', business parks and science parks revolves. In Cambridge, we should find out what success looks like.

On apprehension of the area around Cambridge Station, success looks like a lower-rise version of Leeds, with all the paraphernalia of the ineptly regenerating northern industrial cities. There's a towering derelict flourmill, wasteland, cheap 'luxury flats', a gigantic leisure complex with attendant multi-storey car park, and a paucity of real public space. In the North, there might at least be a certain scale and pride in such an ensemble, but here it looks even shoddier. As an introduction to the city which has perhaps more than any other pioneered the alleged replacement for the industrial economy, it's unprepossessing to say the least. Architecturally, it gives a false picture of the city, but in its obstructive planning it harmonizes perfectly with the rest of contemporary Cambridge.

So it seems Cambridge has almost as many brownfield sites as anywhere else, but they are not always so ineptly used as they are in the area round the station. Within walking distance, on a former ad hoc government site, is Accordia or, as it calls itself, 'Accordia-Living', winner of the 2008 Stirling Prize. This is a very large

The architecture of success

housing estate developed by Countryside Properties, a volume house builder. The architecture here, by 'Humane Modernists' Fielden Clegg Bradley, Alison Brooks and Maccreanor Lavington, became a brief *cause célèbre* as the anti-icon; the clipped, no-bullshit riposte to recent fashionable nonsense, its architecture made to be lived in rather than photographed. It is extremely high-spec as these things go. Although we're under no delusion that the show homes are anything other than the largest and most well-appointed of the properties, the one we see is full of space,

The bed is made at Accordia

surprising internal arrangements and multiple balconies. It is surprising in the sense that one of the bedrooms has a little mezzanine overlooking it, for the voyeurs. The bed is picked out in purple and black. The opulent and kitsch interior decoration totally reverses the ethos of the severe but smart exterior, in that it looks expensive but also decidedly tacky—though it would be a perfect set for a future film about cynical, philandering academia, a sort of science-park update of Joseph Losey's *Accident*. However, any sexual tension is dampened by the show home's strategically placed children's wellingtons.

The Pretence to the Proletarian

Accordia's style, meanwhile, is the most recent example of the contextual Modernism introduced by Leslie Martin in the 1950s when he transferred from the London County Council to Cambridge as architectural overseer—yellow brick, a very obvious Alvar Aalto influence, quadrangles and courts rather than houses and gardens. It's totally devoid of amenities of any sort, but then nobody worries whether social atomization will ensue if a few hundred wealthy people are shoved together in an area without a grocery shop or a nursery school. There is a rhythm and strength to the buildings here which is extremely rare in speculative

Accordia

Bling at Accordia

developments, but the language taken up from Leslie Martin rankles somewhat: this 'post-war pretence of a proletarian humilitude', as John Outram mockingly called it, hence his maniacally aristocratic riposte, the Judge Institute, of which more presently. Accordia, like its postwar forbears, is a modest councilhouse Brutalism for an area which is, if anything, upper class. There is (relatively) 'affordable' housing here, so diminutive it can be spotted a mile off, and unfinished flats whose cladding shines golden—finally owning up to how expensive the whole project actually is, a brief flash of unashamed bling before it weathers into the dun of the rest of Accordia. The essentially kitsch nature of the place is made clear in the property brochures, where each of the building types is given its own name—'Accordia Dawn', 'Accordia Vista', or for the more petite parts of the estate, 'Accordia Light'. At one corner is the real utilitarianism of a 1960s fallout bunker, apparently converted to storage, though given Cambridge's air of paranoia we suspect it was retained just in case. The affordable housing abuts it, and the roofs harmonize with the angles of the bunker in the most peculiar example of contextualism.

Accordia is for sale, so it encourages visitors. This in itself marks it off from the rest of Cambridge, which outside of the tiny centre is one of the most unwelcoming cities I've ever visited. Nonetheless, that centre is not without interest. Here you can find remnants of a quaint university town, the expected and frequently breathtaking tourist attractions (King's College Chapel and so forth), and some pugnacious irruptions of modernity which are the result of either Baedeker Raids or the University's 'progressive' reputation. This leads to some very surreal juxtapositions—Silicon Fen business parks slotted between Gothic churches and Span estates. In one passageway, you have in sequence J.T. Design Build's Vegas-Palladian Crowne Plaza; the functionalist backside of Chapman Taylor's desperately nondescript John Lewis store; and clambering over them all, Arup Associates' 1971 Computer Laboratory, a lanky, fearful creature reminding the heritage city of the technocratic reason for its national prominence.

The tastefulness is broken up by Arup's lab, but not as much as it is by the 1995 Judge Institute. Outram, easily the most original of British postmodernists, a one-time associate of Archigram who brought some of its garish extremism into this generally lumpen restoration style, was clearly unimpressed by the city. In a hilarious and slightly crazed attack on its humble modernism-lite, he wrote, accurately:

Bunker at Accordia

the Dons and Fellows disliked being exposed as being possessed of recherché cultural qualities; more especially as they had no secure means of judging whether this 'difference' was properly mediated by an Architectural Medium whose dominant, and spuriously 'local', qualities, since 1945, had been to deny itself capable of any rhetoric except that of the 'honest, proletarian, woodworker and bricklayer'. This was the so-called 'Cambridge Style', as it was known from the 1960s onwards ... more suited to the pedagogy of milking-cows than the most brilliant young minds of Britain.[56]

Indeed. We are unable to go into the Judge Institute, which I rather regret, and pause only at its puzzling, oblique gates, but it looks spectacularly bonkers in Outram's own drawings and photographs: a garish, Piranesian, wilfully tasteless mock-aristocratic extremism in 'blitzcrete' that can clearly *épater les bourgeois* as much as a Tricorn Centre would. Visually, that is. Functionally, it's one of the world's most prestigious business schools, and the Judge of the title is Sir Paul Judge, a Tory grandee with links to everything from The City to Nuclear Power, who once lost a libel

Door into the Judge Institute

case against the *Guardian* over 'financial irregularities'. Judge funded his own list for the 2010 general election, under the umbrella of the Alliance for Democracy, along with dubious rightists like the English Democrats and Christian Voice. Judge is the Alliance's chairman. The Judge Institute can be seen as an expression of the old kind of buccaneering, wilfully malevolent Toryism as against the soft-left soft-modernism of 1960s (and 2000s) Cambridge, hence Outram's quasi-Thatcherite blasts against the aesthetics of 'welfare', building a fitting home for the managerial 'Olympians'—but at least here all Cambridge's contradictions are displayed rather than effaced.

Hiding in Plain Sight

Across the Cam you find modern Cambridge proper, as opposed to these little irruptions. This is a land of complex gated quadrangles with only one exit, 20ft hedges, security gates, dead ends and, as we're out of season, it's peopled mainly by the workers who are stopping the whole thing from falling down. This other Cambridge has as its landmark Giles Gilbert Scott's sombre skyscraping library tower, a fine example of a supposed traditionalism that actually marks off divisions rather than continuities.

There is one semi-public area, the 'Sidgwick Site', and it's a fascinating battleground, a series of architectural grudge matches. At its centre is James Stirling's notorious History Faculty, slamming together two poles of the industrial aesthetic, Manchester circa 1827 and Moscow circa 1927, showing no compromise whatsoever with its genteel setting. This is a very powerful building, if one which looks even more impressive in photos, which give no clue as to how compact and cranky it actually is, far from the dynastic monolith familiar from the architecture history books. Around it some buildings try to compete; others are more introverted. Allies and Morrison's Criminology and English Faculties are cowardly business-park buildings cowering from Stirling, perhaps taking their cue instead from the buttoned-up courtyards of Casson and Conder's Arts Faculty, though lacking the latter's subtle, flowing

Librarian's Gotham

Stirling and Cullinan at the Sidgwick Site

Undergrowth at the Criminology Faculty

circulation. More prepared to put up a fight is Norman Foster's Law Faculty, which is elegant from one angle, its faceted roof running along the impeccably manicured grass, evoking Foster's one-time mentor Buckminster Fuller, but for the most part a mere premonition of the standard Silicon Fen PFI Modernism. Far more impressive is Edward Cullinan's Divinity Faculty, which snakes around Stirling at one point, opens out to embrace him at another, and rises into a watchtower to give it a vertical counterpoint.

The pleasing thing about the Sidgwick Site is that you can actually walk round it if you're a mere plebeian without feeling like you're about to get arrested. The History Faculty is famously functionally dysfunctional. An anonymous anecdote has it that the Law Faculty was amused by the way the historians had allowed themselves to be sold a fashionable glass pup in the sixties, and mocked them for decades. Then the lawyers moved into the Foster building, which soon proved to have all of the same problems, but with few of the architectural virtues. Maybe because of this, the later buildings here take no chances. A moment of minor interest can be found in the Criminology Faculty. As a building it is drab Modernism-lite, but in its courtyard are a series of glass saucers, sticking up out of scrubland, suggesting secret things occurring underground.

Scientists and Their Bloody Childish Living Habits

Nearby, Leslie Martin and Colin St John Wilson's Harvey Court is the only place we actually get thrown out of, a few seconds after wandering in to catch a glimpse of its apparently 'dynastic' staircases—so a decision is made to sneak past the Porters' Lodges from then on. North and west of here are the new colleges that emerged after the war, and hence more wonderful architecture and awful urbanism. The finest is surely Gillespie Kidd and Coia's Robinson College, a wildly imaginative and spatially thrilling place that somehow manages to also be rather self-effacing. Totally nondescript when seen from the street, once inside you find something that effortlessly fuses ideas from Brutalism, the Amsterdam School, the amorphous seventies and eighties vernacular style and collegiate planning into something coherent. For all the austerity the omnipresent deep red is rich and intoxicating, as are the vistas of walkways, overhead bridges and angular extrusions. Walking round it, we can't decide whether the red brick is, like Stirling's, a mocking industrial challenge to Cambridge, or another example of the faux-proletarian—but here at least the effect is so powerful that objections fall by the wayside, even when we have to dodge back past the Porters' Lodge, realizing there

Walkways at Robinson

Selwyn College, built in the twenty-first century

is no other exit. As if to inoculate against Robinson, Demetri Porphyrios's new buildings for Selwyn College nearby are entirely Prince Charles-friendly.

Meanwhile, the antipode to the tight cohesion of Robinson is Sheppard Robson's airily expansive Churchill College, an engineering-based school, again in light-Brutalist idiom and similarly impeccably finished. It's clearly very regularly renovated; would that the many council estates that resemble it were so well treated.

Learning English at Churchill College

At its centre is the Baroness Thatcher Archive. Fittingly, given her role in the destruction of industrial Britain, the workmanship here is poorer than in the surrounding sixties blocks, with fussy glass detailing. Like Accordia, it is wholly an estate in disguise, whose elegance, manicured lawns and regularly cleaned materials are evidence not of its superiority, but of changed priorities. When we were there, a group of Chinese teenagers, one of whom was wearing a cape, were being taught English on the green.

Then there's the New Hall, a women's college designed as an odd mixture of boxes (some of which are new and vaguely 'in keeping') and domes, linked by walkways, paths and the usual utterly private courtyards. New Hall (now the Murray Edwards College, after a former student donated £30 million to it), with its curiously Islamic-looking centre, is an unexpected example of Louis Kahn-style Third Worldist modernism in a suburban corner, but it was becoming hard to enjoy the strangeness of the architecture. By this point we were sick of locked doors and getting lost in quadrangles, so Chamberlin Powell & Bon's work here was mostly ignored by us as we tried to get out, though we noted the breeze block walls, akin to their Vanbrugh Estate for Greenwich Council, rather than to the obsessively sculpted, bristling concrete of their Barbican in the City of London.

Porte cochère at Churchill College

The watchtowers of the Mathematical Centre

The edges of Cambridge are devoted to science parks, executive housing and gated exurbia, but tasters for it exist in the city. Facing Churchill is The Crescent, neoclassical housing that, while at least more honest in its aristocratic affiliations, is hopelessly provincial, a preview for the New Town of Cambourne, which provides electronic cottages for IT professionals who can't quite afford to live in the city itself. The blandness of these places is a reminder that the 'two cultures' divide works both ways, with scientists perfectly content to be utterly ignorant about architecture.

But at least one of these suburban enclaves is positively breathtaking—Edward Cullinan's Centre for Mathematical Sciences. It's mysterious how Cullinan and his firm managed to get a reputation as meek and mild organicists, given their propensity for obliqueness, terror and scale. The first glimpse of this Centre is of one of its sinister watchtowers peeping through the ubiquitous high hedges. Inside, we find a tangle of unnerving lookouts, walkways and roof terraces held together by obsessive symmetries, featuring a bench with the numbers '2000' carved out on it, which seems futuristic for a split second until we remember the decade. We found it wholly by accident, by following the watchtowers. The eerie calm again suggests a film set rather than a place, a vision of paranoid, eccentric English technocracy which awaits its

The gates of English Heritage

Alan J. Pakula. Here Cullinan has managed to produce some sort of summation of modern Cambridge. The gestures at vernacular, the concrete and yellow brick, are barely noticed in among its technocratic devices and an aesthetic of surveillance. It is admirable in its refusal to kowtow to the past, and dubious in the way that its many, varied and impressive spaces are only pseudo-public. More than anything else, it is an enclave—a place for the privileged to hide from the rest of the country. What exactly is Cambridge so afraid of?

Chapter Nine

The West Riding: Instead of a Supercity

Will Alsop's proposal for a northern 'Supercity' was perhaps the boom's only good idea, and was practically lost amidst its many vacuities. Unveiled in 2005 at an exhibition in Urbis, Manchester, and subsequently published as a book, Supercity entailed string-ing public infrastructure along the M62 corridor to create a twenty-first-century metropolis out of Victorian industrial towns. Alsop placed the North at the centre of the UK, apparently with the brief support of John Prescott in his vague role as overseer for architecture and urbanism.[57] Yet Supercity was easily reduced to cliché: what commentators remembered were the actual buildings proposed by Alsop, rather than the far more interesting abstrac-tions behind them; Tuscan hill-towns and signature museums rather than travel networks, piers and viaducts. The 'West York-shire Urban Area', a conurbation of up to 2.5 million people, exemplifies a good part of what exists instead. Despite having two great and greatly contrasting cities, Leeds and Bradford, at its heart, and a multitude of smaller but often equally architec-turally rich towns packed close together, the West Riding is far from unified. Disparities are both its weakness and its greatest strength.

I mainly use the term 'West Riding', ignoring its southern part centred on Sheffield, to describe the government-defined 'West Yorkshire Urban Area'. This is made up of Bradford, Leeds and their many satellites, along with Wakefield and Huddersfield, sometimes with Halifax added to the list; a conurbation that, unlike those other unofficial supercities, the West Midlands, Greater Glasgow, Tyneside or Greater Manchester—all these potential rivals to the bloated, absurdly over-favoured capital which never quite manage to get their act together—is hardly continuous. One part can appear to be on a different planet to another part, which is presumably one reason why, other than the ingrained opposition to planning, the places are all treated as discrete areas, despite the fact it's easier and quicker (if seldom cheaper) to get from one of these towns to another than it is to get from South-West to South-East London. If this is a Supercity in waiting, it's an extraordinarily strange one, a multi-centred mess, marked by sharp, shocking geographical and urban/rural contrasts. Although Alsop's M62 Supercity is a genuinely smart idea, something which, as he rightly points out, is already happening in an exurban, car-driven, environmentally destructive manner but could, if planned, be far more powerful, it should be noted that his actual town plans are less interesting. The plan for Bradford, for instance, is a peculiar bit of whimsy, advocating the recreation of long-covered stretches of river; let's add a few water features, then it'll be more like Manchester. There is, however, *plenty* of water in the Westfield Crater, the huge hole left by Bradford's most recent and most ill-advised exercise in town planning.

Near the centre of the potential Supercity is the Emley Moor TV tower, the tallest free-standing structure in Britain, which sits alone in the midst of open country, a *Stadtkrone* monument without a *Stadt*. So the most obvious thing would be for the hypothetical West Riding Metropolis to be centred around Emley Moor, much as Berlin, Seattle or Toronto cluster round their space-age beacons. Here we will travel around this stretch of the urban West Riding as if it were already a city rather than a cluster of cities and towns, arranging the observations by theme rather than by town.

The Marketplace

Surely one of the many reasons the West Riding seems to have produced great urban writers—among them David Peace, Laura Oldfield Ford, Jarvis Cocker and even the now all-but-forgotten J.B. Priestley—is the presence of actual Parisian ferro-vitreous arcades in its cities, something which is otherwise largely limited to outposts in Piccadilly, Deansgate and central Cardiff. Few are as good as these. Leeds has the most obvious examples, and given Leeds' status as the local mecca for The New Economy—i.e. the post-industrial triad of finance, property and shopping—its examples are best looked after, as a northern Knightsbridge. In 2006 Simon Jenkins hailed Leeds as a traditionalist exemplar for the rest of the country, curious given its inner urban motorway and many towers, but looking round the shopping spaces of the immediate centre, you can see why.[58] Civic grandeur and commercial opulence make decidedly comfortable partners, giving streets a similar feel to Regent Street or Deansgate—but fittingly, given the weather, the enclosed spaces are special. The Arcades, mostly restored to an almost suffocating level of opulence, are fantastical, as is the Edwardian megastructure of J. Bagshaw & Sons' City Markets, while the 1938 concourse of the City Station is a calmer version of the same principle.

Eggs, Butter and Cheese in Halifax Markets

Within the ring road, Leeds is as elegant as it is proud, largely because of these semi-hidden spaces. Normally they are entered through buildings that are not especially interesting, standard if high-spec Victorian piles, which when penetrated reveal their prophecy of the total retail environments of the twentieth century and after. Leeds Arcades, like everything else in the city, appear to be hierarchical. There are two tucked away in places where you wouldn't know to look unless you're with a local, and which are relatively down at heel. Yet the rebranded 'Victoria Quarter', centred on Frank Matcham's 1898 County Arcade, is the ferro-vitreous fulcrum, where Vivienne Westwood, Harvey Nichols and, with tragic aptness, a boutique called 'The French Revolution' make their home. It's wonderfully effeminate for (in the southern imaginary) macho and stolid Yorkshire, prettily dressed as it is with Parisian ornament and lurid art nouveau mosaics.

Much more exciting, however, are the City Markets, a lanky and gaunt, complex and brightly painted piece of spindly orna-mental proto-high-tech, which contains within it a mingled smell of old sweets, paint and wrapping paper, and a welcome bustle and mess absent from the slick opulence of the Victoria Quarter. Again, it's impossible not to be struck by the formal daring of the interiors and the retardataire pomp of the exterior, Modernist

The Victoria Quarter

Leeds City Markets

cliché though this may be. The bombastic, imperial stripped classical 1930s Queen's Hotel contains within it the elegant, deeply
American-moderne station concourse, where a restoration job by
local architects Carey Jones (of whom more later) has given
Wetherspoons et al. an inappropriately Reithian typeface, and
advertisements for the Calder Hall business park stress the white-
collar nature of the new Leeds. At this point the city that Simon
Jenkins thinks is so wonderful effectively ends—although no

Moderne Wetherspoons

doubt he is pleased that many back-to-backs, a form of housing considered unfit for human habitation for 150 years, still exist in the city. The other arcades are the Arndales and their contemporaries: Gillinson, Barnett & Allen's 1964 Merrion Centre, say, with its lost, abandoned basement of greasy spoon cafés and a tiled tower which is a comparative masterpiece by the standards of the post-1997 Leeds Skyline. Inside, the use of mirrored glass creates an imaginary geometric space that reflects the uninteresting collection of chain stores therein in odd ways. The Merrion Centre argues that Modernists couldn't quite invest commerce with the same drama as the Victorians could. That theory is belied in Huddersfield, where the Seymour Harris Partnership's Queensgate Market, with its Mesoamerican ornaments and concrete vaults, creates an ambitious space that makes everyday market trading suddenly surreal.

Wakefield must have wanted a piece of all this when it commissioned David Adjaye, the young and recently bankrupted architect best known for his London 'Idea Stores', a pair of barcode-façaded libraries in East London, to design its new market. To Adjaye Associates' credit, they provided a striking but far from ostentatious or meretricious structure, clearly designed as a mere backdrop to the more important action of the stalls themselves,

Merrion Centre

Adjaye's new Wakefield Market

admittedly the opposite approach to the Arcades of Leeds and Halifax, which impress through opulence rather than rectitude. If the complaints in the local press are any indication, the market is loathed in Wakefield—a place where, for the first time, I felt like I was somewhere familiar, which is why I haven't given that town as much attention as others. It felt like a southern city. I appreciate this is probably the worst thing anyone could say to Wakefield, so it has my apologies.

Wakefield's Ridings

The city's main new shopping centre, aside from the Market Halls, is The Ridings, a standard-issue mall which occupies part of a 1960s megastructure, several towers, arranged in zig-zags on top of a shopping street. I have no idea whether the complex was once impressive or whether it was shoddily done, but today—like all the tower blocks in Wakefield—it is painted in desperately jolly colours, and wears an absurd hat. No doubt if the blocks were falling apart before this is a preferable condition, but it should be noted that as in cladding-crazy Glasgow, the entire housing stock has been sold to a housing association, which seems keen on these kinds of 'solutions'. The end result is that Wakefield becomes bleakly surreal in its total lack of all-over planning. Take the exit from the all but ruined Wakefield Kirkgate—reckoned to be the worst major rail station in Britain, and where part of the station wall collapsed last year, smashing a parked car. You emerge to find a large, burnt-out and boarded-up pub and tower blocks seemingly redesigned by a five-year-old as an entrance. Regardless, Wakefield feels *normal*, just a bleaker version of normality— and perhaps the council knows this, hence the hiring of Adjaye (and at the unfinished Hepworth Gallery, David Chipperfield) to sprinkle starchitect fairy dust. This approach has been embraced even more extensively in Castleford, where Channel 4 and Kevin McCloud descended to foist wonky bridges and public art on a depressed mining village.

Bradford, meanwhile, is a relief after contemporary Leeds, with a sense of real strangeness, drama and uniqueness. Its railway stations may be pathetic and its Portland stone postwar towers might seem to think they're in Plymouth, but there's no denying the murky beauty of the city, which supports its one-time claim that while Leeds was famous locally, Bradford is famed internationally. The local stone is as sombre and powerful as the architecture (usually by local firms such as Lockwood & Mawson), which is mostly neoclassical with experiments in Gothic and Moderne. Yet presumably because of its reputation for poverty and civil unrest, Bradford was largely deprived of the boom's dubious benefits. From the raised park adjoining the

The first view of Wakefield from Kirkgate

excellent Telegraph & Argus building (and its recent imitation, the Gatehaus) you can survey the vast hole torn in the centre of Bradford which is Blairism's main Bradfordian legacy. Australian retail developers Westfield had planned to have built and finished a mall here by early 2008, as some local signs still proclaim. In early 2010 they still haven't started work, nor do they expect to. This failure gives the city the exceptional chance to reject the shopping obsession that has torn the heart out of so many others. The space potentially awaits a park and public housing, if Bradford has the guts.

The Westfield Hole

Aside from the hole, the city has gingerly attempted the Mancunian approach to regeneration (Bradford's industrial buildings are often better; less prettified, more striking in their fusion of utility and sombre classicism), adapting and reusing some warehouses and mills. This works reasonably well in Little Germany, a warehouse district where the likes of the Behrens family traded for decades. This hilltop area is marked by a mural celebrating the foundation of the Independent Labour Party nearby, and presents a series of canyon-like views and rich juxtapositions, particularly at night when it is utterly deserted. As it is, all roads lead to the Westfield Hole, a purple-fenced mass that is impossible to miss, which reorients the city's geography, its propaganda posters practically insulting Bradford. 'Urban Energy', 'Café Culture', 'City Living'; all those Blairite Urban Renaissance clichés. One of them was defaced when we visited by the graffito 'BEST AMONG RUINS'.

'"It's like Hell, isn't it?" he said enthusiastically'

For a southerner, Halifax is another world, a place where 'Belladonna', John Cooper Clarke's paean to an opiated urban Pennine landscape, comes immediately to mind: 'where the panorama looks like Mars ... to the dying gardens, down below ...' The high hills around served as the setting for Wyndham Lewis's introduction to the North in the 1910s, courtesy of the Vorticist painter and Huddersfield native Edward Wadsworth: '[He took] me in his car on a tour of some of Yorkshire's cities. In due course we arrived on a hill above Halifax. He stopped the car and we gazed down into its industrial labyrinth. I could see he was proud of it. "It's like Hell, isn't it?" he said enthusiastically.'[59]

A century later, waiting at a road junction, looking around at the tower blocks, derelict mills and two-up-two-downs, the sombre local stone, all surrounded by freakishly high impassable hills, themselves enclosed by hedges as if hundreds of miles from a city, the smell of the Nestlé factory wafting over, all under a looming, threatening sky, I said to Joel: 'This is *indubitably* the North.'

Where the panorama looks like Mars

A voice from a car waiting at the junction agrees, yelling 'THE NORTH!' as it drives off. Next to this junction is a pub with the name The Running Man, which fits the general sense of fear and tension perfectly. The Running Man has a rather Googie roof, and a view over the seemingly untouched 1960s estates which have mercifully escaped the hatting given to Wakefield. As we board the Halifax to Wakefield train, some youths ask us 'Are you FBI?' Aside from being quite a funny question to ask two men in long coats with neat hair taking pictures, this says more about the Special Relationship between the UK and US than any BBC2 teleplay ever could.

The Running Man

Quite honestly, anyone who knows and/or comes from the industrial towns of the south—say, Southampton, Portsmouth, Reading, Slough or Luton—can't help being *jealous* of the sheer strangeness of their Northern equivalents; their hills, their scale, the closeness of open country, the amount of extraordinarily serious, world-class architecture, the lack of 1980s and '90s tat. Of course, relatively little of this applies in Leeds, which conjured the postmodernist 'Leeds Look' in the eighties to simulate Victorian grandeur, with the presumably unexpected end result that much of its outer centre looks like Reading. This is perhaps why it's the token 'successful' northern city along with Manchester, because it's boring enough for southerners to understand. Civic pride has bizarre, impressive results—inexplicably, Halifax, a town about half the size of Luton, has a Town Hall by the architect of the Houses of Parliament; the rural England/Renaissance Italy Piece Hall; Arcades as good as those in London, Leeds or Manchester; a 'People's Park' which is a model of municipal munificence; and yet you can see where it stops, when the Moors rear up in front of you. And yet all this (admittedly *jolie-laide*) beauty seems to have no effect. There's no sense here that city air is free air, but rather an almost all-pervasive air of latent violence that could explode at any moment. We watch indie kids with black eyes cluster together

People's Park, Halifax

in the Arcades, we get called 'shirtlifters' by shell-suited youth. Halifax is the most racially segregated place I've ever seen, something that, as Joel points out, even extends to the way the windows in the old terraces are treated—UPVC frames in white areas, new wooden frames in the second/third-generation Kashmiri districts. There's a certain historical justice that the spaces of imperial philanthropy are well used by the formerly colonized, while the descendants of the colonizers prefer to live in the middle of nowhere, seemingly refusing to take advantage of the extremely impressive town their great-grandparents toiled to create.

Building Society Design

The epicentres of late British neoliberalism and its subsequent crash have been those areas once considered resistant to Thatcherism. Scotland with RBS and half of HBOS, Tyneside with Northern Rock, the City of London running riot with the support of a Ken Livingstone administration, and Manchester morphing into a Blairite ceremonial capital. The former Mutuals in the West Riding, Halifax Building Society/HBOS and Bradford & Bingley, are perfect examples of this process; one utterly dysfunctional and propped up by the state, the other now reluctantly entirely nationalized, due in both cases to their over-identification with, their arriviste over-investment in, the new financial architecture of derivatives, credit default swaps and suchlike. Both of these entities have a deeply corporeal, brutally physical presence in their respective towns, expressions of bourgeois civic pride, reminders of the close interlinking of finance and industrial capital in the (post)industrial north. Halifax's headquarters is genuinely one of the most unbelievable postwar buildings in the country, all the more so for being an early work by BDP, when it was still an idealistic socialist experiment rather than the corporate colossus it is now. To call it dominant would be an understatement, the way it juts out across a Victorian street, but it also harmonizes chromatically with Halifax's Yorkshire stone, brown and coal-stained black. Finished in 1974, largely designed by BDP collective member Bill Pearson, it combines every possible device in the 1970s architectural arsenal, everything that was in the magazines at that point: flying walkways; black glass Seagram curtain walls; postmodernist incorporation of heritage (the original Victorian façade of their first headquarters can be viewed as an object stripped from its context, behind a glass screen); neo-Constructivist public sculpture; and a series of jarring jigsaw angles which are clearly indebted either to Russian Constructivism itself or the variants upon it which were soon to be known as Deconstructivism. It is all reached by a series of platforms and walkways which replicate the sharp changes in scale of the local landscape. It's an astonishing building, proof that finance capital was, even over a decade before Lloyds, quite capable of using the devices of 'left' architecture.

Bradford & Bingley's offices, the 'Hanging Gardens of Bingley', are relatively normal by comparison but a powerful statement nevertheless, designed by the local firm of John Brunton and Partners, of whom more presently. Sharing Halifax's grounding in the work of Denys Lasdun (his fusion of the English baroque and Brutalism in buildings like London's National

BDP's Halifax HQ

Constructivist sculpture, Halifax

Theatre or the University of East Anglia in Norwich is so perfect for the West Riding that it's a minor tragedy he didn't design anything here himself), Bradford & Bingley's ziggurat was once planted with creepers, to make this most ancient of architectural forms look appropriately ruined and eternal. Interestingly, now that the building is up for sale and under threat of demolition, the creepers have died, a reminder that ruination is not always picturesque. Otherwise Bingley is an almost-suburban encampment

The avant-contextualism of the Halifax HQ

Hanging Gardens of Bingley

looking out over an (award-winning!) new motorway and the Moors. It's also now up for sale.

One body which has positively thrived after the financial crash is the Co-Operative, a sometimes surprising survivor, its mix of Fabianism and neither-a-borrower-nor-lender-be moralism now combined with Fair Trade ethical consumerism (I write this as a proud member). Its roots are not far away in Rochdale, and West Yorkshire has plenty of monuments to its one-time local power and influence, although for the most part, like any other financial

Bradford's former Co-Operative

institution, its business is administrated in less high-street places. Apart from its Mancunian HQ, the Co-Op seems wholly uninterested in the fate of its old buildings, which here are striking adaptations of Erich Mendelsohn's Weimar Republic department stores to the drizzly climate and the local stone, designed by W. A. Johnson and J. W. Cropper. The latter studied radical architecture in the USSR, bringing Communist aesthetics to Fabian functions. The glazed stair tower of the Bradford Co-Op is covered up internally, so we can't see the no doubt terribly secret operations of its current owners, T. J. Hughes. At least it has escaped the fate of Johnson and Cropper's other Co-Ops: in Huddersfield, a more original building now threatened with demolition, or the very similar branch in Southport, now occupied by McDonalds. The only one of Johnson and Cropper's buildings which has been treated with any respect is the one actually still occupied by the Co-Op itself, the CWS headquarters in Manchester.

Local Architecture for Local People

In southern towns, except for Bristol (almost an honorary Northern city in its independence from the capital) and Camden-on-Sea (or 'Brighton and Hove', as it prefers to be known), arty and ambitious youth tend to escape for London if they possibly can. This is one of many reasons why these places are so aesthetically stunted: all manner of rubbish can be foisted upon them as nobody really cares enough to propose anything better. Local architects in the south are a source of grotesque comedy. This isn't quite true up north, where the general standard appears once to have been rather extraordinary. Compare the aggressive work of Lockwood and Mawson or John Brunton, who designed much of High Victorian and sixties Brutalist Bradford, with the pallid mediocrity of Southampton's nineteenth- and twentieth-century hacks Gutteridge & Gutteridge, or W. H. Saunders—these are cities of comparable size and (one-time) importance, after all.

Being commercially driven non-side-takers in the style wars, Lockwood and Mawson were able to indulge in a wide variety of seemingly conflicting manners without fear of contradiction: Ruskinian Gothic (with the explicit disapproval of Ruskin himself) for the Wool Exchange and the Bradford Club; 'debased' (according to Pevsner) classicism for St George's Hall; and an amplified, time-stretched utilitarian man–machine Italianate for the mammoth industrial structures at Saltaire. Planned and designed entirely by the firm on behalf of the Wool Magnate and philanthropist Titus Salt, Saltaire serves as one of the more complete examples of a settlement completely formed by the rationale of early industrial capitalism in its more 'improving' variant: a *gesamtarbeitstadt*, with churches, social centres, libraries but, of course, no pubs, at least originally—the local is called 'Titus Wouldn't Like It'. More recently, his other inadvertent legacy is the Titus Salt School. One of two functionally deficient PFI complexes by Anshen + Allen, it was initially boycotted by teachers who were concerned that the buildings compromised the health of their students, a reminder that although the authoritarianism continues, today's architecture for the deserving poor is of an inferior standard.[60] Although the conditions in Saltaire's housing were far better than those of the surrounding areas—with space, inside loos, orientation to the sun, etc—there's little attempt to prettify the process, which may explain why it is that its later equivalents, such as Bournville or the Garden Suburbs, massively increased the level of verdancy.

Salt's Mill, Saltaire

Urban and rural Bradford

For those of us who mourn the passing of the visible world of engineering and design, Halifax, Bradford and Saltaire are exemplary. The city does not pretend to be the country, but the surrounding country, wild and dramatic, is always visible and reachable on foot. Accordingly, Saltaire does not pretend to be a rural village, does not have winding streets, big gardens, gables and beams as do its successors. It is completely unambiguous about its industrial nature. Strangely, then, Salt's Mill is heaving with cottage industries, as after closing in 1986 and being regenerated over the last decade this became its new function—inside the mills are businesses, galleries, luxury flats and (comfortingly) an NHS centre. A similar transformation has been wreaked upon Dean Clough Mills in Halifax, but Saltaire seems to have as its demographic something that could only exist near to a large city like Bradford: *Guardian* readers, many of whom are in attendance for a beer festival in Salt's teetotal temperance outpost (Hebden Bridge has a similar concentration of liberals). The only other ex-factory of a comparable scale is Andrews and Pepper's Manningham Mills, built two decades later in 1873 by the less philanthropic wool baron Samuel Lister. Almost accidentally, we found ourselves on the trail of the Independent Labour Party that was born here. We ate pizza in the room where the ILP was formed, admired the mural and Terry Hamill's Constructivistic statue of a

Terry Hamill, 'Untitled'

worker rising like a lion after slumber, both of which rot outside
the buildings where the Party was 'officially' founded, and later
visited the mills where a long, bitter strike presaged the party's
formation.

'Socialism is the Hope of the World', says the mural, if you
look very closely. The ILP was an enormously admirable organization, always to the left of the compromised Labour Party to
which it gave its name and helped to create; leaving it in the 1930s
out of anger and frustration with its dogged conformism, it subsequently disappeared within fifteen years. The legacy of New
Labour, meanwhile, is best expressed in Manningham by Urban
Splash, one of its finest architectural embodiments. Joel is from
Manningham, so he was able to show me exactly where the line of
burning tyres were placed in front of the fortress-like RUC-esque
police station during the 1995 riots, as well as the block of vernacular shops and flats that sits on the site of the car showroom burnt
to the ground in the more extensive riots of 2001, when the army
was on standby. Manningham is overwhelmingly low-rise and
Victorian, something strangely unmentioned in the hand-wringing over the riots; we all know only 1960s buildings cause civil
disorder. By far the largest and tallest building is the now Urban
Splashed Lister's Mill. Dressed with a Fosterian series of steel

rooftop penthouses designed by David Morley Architects, it looks out on an eerily spacious row of small council houses, with a scrubby park in between. Inside, through the gating that protects it from the surrounding hordes, is a series of red ventilators that are treated as pieces of public art, the most striking example of which is the graffiti round the corner, outside the gates, where it appears the Wu-Tang Clan haunt the area. Deep down in the back streets, in the heart of Medina, about to set off something more deep than a misdemeanour. I always hear about how 'brave' Urban Splash are in restoring and privatizing factories and council estates, as if gutting and selling well-constructed city centre buildings is a thankless, risky task (in a recession it suddenly becomes one, hence their current 'troubles' and Bloxham's demotion to a lower rung on the Rich List). There is certainly a daring of some sort in taking one of the most notoriously divided places in the country and building *more* gates, *more* walls, reinforcing its divisions—although locals tell us that the division between the new Manningham Mills and the surrounding area is more a question of class than race, with wealthier Bradfordian Asians moving in. So while the best buildings go private, the Victorian situation is replicated, the well-off literally look down upon the poor, who remain

Manningham Mills

Inside the Lister's Mill gated community

in their hovels, left to their sectarian fights while their birthright is stolen in front of their eyes.

This process is particularly shocking in Saxton Gardens, Leeds. Joel, admittedly a Bradfordian, dismisses Leeds as 'a bosses' city', and there's an alignment in one particular site which is truly alarming. Once, on Quarry Hill sat an extremely carefully designed council estate full of facilities and public space. It was Britain's first major casualty of post-sixties municipal anti-Modernism, demolished in the late 1970s. Now a BDP office block nicknamed 'the Kremlin' (but resembling more closely Farrell's

Manningham Wu

Two ways to redesign a council block, Saxton

MI6 Building) occupies most of the site. In the 1950s the same architect, R. H. Livett, designed the less dramatic, more CIAM standard-issue blocks of Saxton. The juxtaposition there now shows that while the not so poor get ethereal barcode façades and gated-off car parks, the poor get plastic balconies seemingly designed by the same five-year-old who worked on Wakefield. The Urban Splash propaganda apparatus—website, brochure, hoardings—has as its motif garden gnomes, which are apparently going to be everywhere when they finish cladding their second private block, as they will, out of the kindness of their hearts, be

A soon-to-be-bailed-out empty frame at Saxton

253

laying on allotments. Whether these allotments will remain as imaginary as their oft-praised, never-started Tutti Frutti in Ancoats is worth speculating over. The other local architects worth mentioning here are from the eras of Wilson and Blair; each is equally symptomatic of its time. First, John Brunton and Partners, designers of the aforementioned Bradford and Bingley along with High Point and the Arndale in Bradford. A huge swathe of Victorian Bradford was levelled to make way for the Arndale (now the Kirkgate Centre), and for the Arndale House tower. Local monitors of design like the Bradford Civic Society loathe the Arndale, but in its harsh physicality and its confusion of forms it fits the city far better than, say, the appalling decorated sheds which sit next to Forster Square railway station. It is a mess, full of tat, although the markets in the basement have a certain bazaar-like quality that only seems to exist in the north, and are another place where the oft-alleged racial segregation of Bradford is conspicuous by its absence. It's all full of almost Barbican-like gridded ceilings and walkways, but in organization is identical to any 1980s mall. There's another, newer market building in Bradford, where shiny cladding shuns rather than embraces Bradford's still remarkable architectural cohesion. This is aided in a rather staid, traditionalist manner by buildings like the recent Jamiyat Tabligh-ul-Islam Mosque, whose domes and prickly ornament harmonize with that of the Alhambra theatre and the art deco Odeon. Despite a long-running preservation campaign, the latter is scheduled for demolition and replacement with an obligatory mixed use scheme designed by Leeds' currently dominant firm, Carey Jones. But all this is overlooked and overshadowed by Brunton's most unnervingly brilliant building.

High Point, too, is ritually loathed by right-thinking Bradfordians, and was also built for a local financial institution, the somewhat less notorious Yorkshire Building Society. It's utterly freakish, the severed head of some Japanese giant robot clad in a West Yorkshire stone aggregate, glaring out at the city through blood-red windows, the strangest urban artefact in a city which does not lack for architectural interest. The work of

High Point, rising above Bradford Markets

Brunton seems almost too appropriate for the combination of wild technological daring, Cold War paranoia, shabby corruption and crushed dreams that defined the Wilson era. In a similarly neat manner, Carey Jones's new skyscraper, Sky Plaza, a hall of residence for the extremely prolific developers Unite, was completed in summer 2009 and was receiving its first undergraduate inmates when we visited.

The earliest building of Carey Jones's that we see, the 1999 Princes Exchange just by the Queens Hotel, is a decent bit of

Sky Plaza

corporate slick-tech, well-scaled, cool and confident, from the time when Blair's rhetoric about a 'young country' might almost have seemed convincing. It's actually better than some of the 1990s Richard Rogers buildings that it pinches its ideas from. After this, it all goes rapidly downhill. The 2000s redevelopment of Clarence Dock was done mostly by said firm, although it includes Derek Walker's earlier fierce, bleak Royal Armouries, which we first assume (by now inured to these sorts of shocks) to be flats. Thankfully, even in Leeds the idea of a block with virtu-ally no windows at all couldn't get through planning. Yet. Leeds is full of Carey Jones's towers, most of them more or less like Clarence Dock or the ever so slightly more jagged and *outré* Gateway—not *awful*, they'd get to that later, just woefully un-imaginative. The towers tend to sit by congested, looping main roads, in a city marked by a huge amount of empty inner-urban flats, with none of the oh-so-inhumane underpasses or walkways that could relieve the enormously unpleasant road crossings. Sky Plaza marks the point where they go from dull to positively abysmal.

The plan is ambitious, pulling together several blocks of stu-dent flats to form a skyline, and it fails on every possible level, with its mean, tiny windows, its chillingly blank façade, its desper-ate boredom. To design a tower as minimal as this means that at

The eerie calm of Clarence Dock

least some effort must be made with proportions and materials, some attempt at elegance; but here grey cladding and a green lift tower seem almost calculatedly crap. Students are a captive market, and by providing extremely tight security (the Unite 'village', of which Sky Plaza is the centre, is gated), developers like Unite appeal to middle-class parents worried about the many appalling things that could happen to their children in the inner city. Given that this formula is enormously successful, what with the expansion both of university education and of paranoia, the architecture doesn't have to be particularly interesting. This is, however, the first time an ex-industrial city has had a building for students as its tallest structure, and what it says about the 'knowledge economy' is incomparably depressing.

Blake's Seven, Leeds Nil

It was not always thus. Leeds University in particular can boast one of the most impressive attempts to design an inner-city campus as a total, coherent environment, albeit without the need for CCTV and gating—the complex of university buildings designed by Chamberlin Powell and Bon between 1958 and 1968. Today it is alternately mutilated and commemorated. "The New Monumentality', running through much of 2009 at the Henry Moore Institute, was an exhibition both about the Leeds campus and about architecture and everyday life, or rather about the disjunction between the two. The three artists represented, Dominique Gonzalez-Foerster, Gerard Byrne and Dorit Margreiter, all engaged with the fact that the strangest of buildings actually have to be lived in, and the latter two do so in the context of a building just round the corner from the gallery.

Local rumour has it that this complex served as a set for the seventies science fiction series *Blake's 7*. This should come as no surprise. There is a divide in the perception of these buildings between the future they seem to suggest—a space-age society with egalitarian buildings that make no reference to anything so prosaic as local materials, human scale or history, which some of

The Leeds Campus

us may find liberating, others unnerving—and the past they are most often seen to represent. That is, the *other* 1960s, not the now very familiar decade reminisced over by ageing *soixante-huitards* but the decade of a new landscape of towers and slabs, walkways and motorways, which is only very slowly starting to come back into favour after decades in which it was abhorred by many as an example of top-down quasi-totalitarianism, often better known for its transformation into film-set dystopias at the hands of Kubrick, Truffaut or Antonioni.

At the Henry Moore Institute, the most appropriately cinematic of the three works is Gerard Byrne's film *subject*. On three screens, in glorious, lustrous monochrome, earnest Yorkshire youth talk to the camera. They're dressed in seventies clothing, though you can't quite guess whether this is because they're in period costume or are merely fans of vintage fashion. They're reading contemporary texts on familiar, kitsch sixties matters— ESP, promiscuity, the legalization of cannabis, taken from the student press of the time—in a bracingly unusual space. Byrne tries to normalize the campus, make it part of history once again, rather than the heavily contested remnant of the future's past that it so clearly is. Yet as his camera lingers round the flying walkways, the jutting lecture theatres and the scintillating artificial surfaces, the eye is drawn to exactly this impossible strangeness, resisting the attempt to impose the signifiers of the sixties onto it, refusing to be made retro.

That the University doesn't know what to do with the campus is obvious enough. In early photos, you can see the central space occupied by the sculpted nature of a planned garden, akin to the designs of the Brazilian landscape artist Roberto Burle Marx. In recent years the University filled the whole space with such a quantity of street furniture, foliage and inelegant public art that you can *almost* ignore the building. Meanwhile the concrete—sculptural, shuttered stuff similar to that used in Chamberlin Powell and Bon's hugely successful Barbican complex in London —was painted in estate-agent magnolia, and the halls of residence are being demolished, it being easier to house students in the barracks provided by the likes of Unite. The old campus is a place that simply cannot make sense in the present, yet this might be what is most valuable about it. In Dorit Margreiter's *Aporia* the unreadable abstraction of the campus is juxtaposed with an itinerary of theme parks and reconstructions, these hypercapitalist spaces a sharp contrast to a barely remembered social democracy and its abhorred architecture. The surrounding area provides its own argument, with the underpasses leading to enclaves like Sky

Metropolitan University Tower

Plaza. The University itself is still capable of commissioning good buildings—the twisted tower of Leeds Metropolitan University's Arts and Humanities Department, designed by Fielden Clegg Bradley, is easily the best new tower in Leeds, although the competition is not exactly stiff. It's clad, like all the others, but here the corten steel panels are designed to age gracefully, while the other towers seem not to be aware of the concept of 'weathering'.

Best Among Ruins

Both Leeds and Bradford have extremely aggressive ring roads, but somehow Leeds' underpasses do less damage, while the wide dual carriageways and inexplicably Portland stone-clad sixties towers in Bradford create ghettos as easily as any housing allocation policy. The Leeds system feels more permeable, less like a barrier, because you pass *over* the traffic, you are not directly inconvenienced by it—though the pedestrian bridges can be decidedly bracing. What makes it unpleasant is not the planning so much as the architecture. It's an enduring irony that John Thorp, Leeds' city architect, the last of his kind in any major city and mainly employed as a designer of 'public realm' rather than buildings, has personally authorized the development of these towers. Not because it's a bad idea in principle, but because of the relentlessly shabby quality of the results.

Sky Plaza I've mentioned, but there are others almost as bad, and from their vicinity we literally see the destruction of the Leeds International Pool, by far the finest work of Leeds' most famous architectural firm—John Poulson, the corrupter of Maudling, British Rail and T. Dan Smith, headed by a man who may apparently have barely held a pencil, let alone designed a whole building. *Ambitious young journalist like yourself*... We had a good view of the diving board from the walkway over the underpass. Preserved nearby above the central station is the hopelessly lumpen tower Poulson bribed his way to designing, as if to prove the irrelevance of quality or originality in the architectural pecking order. The International Pool was originally supposed to be

The demise of Leeds International Pool

succeeded by an Iconic tower called 'The Spiracle'. That was cancelled, but the demolition proceeded as planned, as an incentive to any future developer.

At the ring road, outside the Simon Jenkins-friendly Victoriana, you are faced with what is indisputably the worst new architecture of any major British city. What makes it even more worrying is its massive, unavoidable scale. There are several reclads of sixties towers, with the hat worn by 'K2 The Cube' easily the silliest, but the new towers are worse. The Opal Tower, a design and build project nominally by Morrison Design, is nearly as tall and as mean as Sky Plaza, again providing en-suite bedrooms for the city's ruthlessly exploited student population, but this time more clunky than horrifying. Then there are innumerable fifteen-storey blocks by Carey Jones, devoid of real public spaces but clad in contextual terracotta. By comparison to this lot, Aedas's reviled Carbuncle Cup-nominated Bridgewater Place is not so bad—at least its clash of shapes has a vestigial futurism, the ghost of an idea. The combination of local references, incredibly clumsy massing and the walled-off wasteland in front of Carey Jones's West Point constitutes one of the clearest images we could find of the results of the financial crisis and the thinking that led to it. Leeds has been in the grip of a bitter strike over rubbish collection, with the city council taking a hard-line

Opal Tower and a rehabilitated sixties block

Bridgewater Place

class war approach to the binmen, but we don't notice it until we check the local press that evening. 2009 is a 'reverse 1979', so the images are different: 'luxury' turning empty and desolate rather than the collapses of council housing and consensus that marked punk mythology; no mountains of rubbish in the street, at least not yet. Surely the worst of all is Halliday Clark's Mill Street Student

West Point

Leeds' nadir

Accommodation, like a PFI hospital stretched vertically into a block of flats, a wavy blue roof atop an incredibly badly built chequerboard façade. The designers call the building 'vibrant and purposefully controversial', which is one way of putting it. The windows are again horribly mean—for some reason students are not allowed normal-sized windows in their flats, and must instead look out of these tiny slits, presumably designed to discourage auto-defenestration.

While central Leeds' ring roads and inhospitable corners are impeccably regenerated via this sort of hostile, pedestrian-unfriendly architecture, there is one end of central Bradford that regeneration has barely even scraped, despite having unimpeachable traditional urban credentials that would warm Simon Jenkins' heart. A Bradford Civic Society brochure entitled *Common Sense Regeneration* that we pick up from the Bradford Club, the Lockwood and Mawson-designed Old Liberal Club which we manage to blag our way into for lunch (apparently it hasn't been distributed far outside of such rarefied circles), calls it 'Goitside' (no Bradfordian we mention this to admits to using the term). In between blasts at most of what has happened since 1939, the writers recognize the remarkable quality of Goitside in architectural terms, and the depths to which it has sunk.[61] From here you get an awesome view, with the Yorkshire stone sides of BDP's late sixties Bradford University tower fitting perfectly with the landscape (on the other side, sky-blue cladding has been added in an act of sheer architectural illiteracy). There are several derelict wool warehouses, but what really hits you is the city's earliest council housing—1900s tenements, low-rise, arts and crafts. They are littered both with bright, well-meaning public art from when people did live here, and the needles and foil left by those who are using in the flats' derelict shells. The smell is foul.

Bradford's first council housing

'Best Among Ruins'

We gradually twig that there's something we've been seeing practically everywhere in West Yorkshire, and which we then realize we've seen nearly everywhere else as well—the ubiquitous fences, usually marking off sites 'for development', customarily painted a pinkish purple, with graffiti usually scrubbed off as quickly as possible and heavy security patrolling the weeds. The ultimate example of this is the snaking wall that encloses the Westfield Hole in Bradford, but we find so many others: by West Point in Leeds; in front of Halifax Town Hall next to a sign pointing towards its regenerated 'quarters'; and enclosing random spots in Wakefield. The realization comes after we visit an exhibition in Bradford's National Media Museum on Don McCullin, who is quoted there saying 'visually, you just can't lose in Bradford'. He photographed the area in the late 1970s, showing huge amounts of dead and derelict space. At first we wonder where this has all gone, given the rash of cancelled projects, but the bright fences are the explanation, the happy result no doubt of health and safety regulations. They screen the wasteland—the most obvious sign of failure—from the public. After the Blitz and at massive human cost, the scarred cities created a feeling of 'light and openness' in the formerly overcrowded areas. These holes run through postwar art, music and architecture, creating a new conception of space, a sense of airiness and possibility which is still palpable in parts of Sheffield or Manchester where the fence-makers haven't arrived yet. Mostly, however, these bright barriers dressed with property propaganda practically scream at pedestrians to move on, telling them not to pause to look at what's behind the door, assuring them with grinning desperation that EVERYTHING IS GOING TO BE OK. The anonymous sloganeers of Bradford know exactly what's going on, however, and they subjected the fence to a relentless campaign of ridicule via graffito for as long as it stood. At the time of writing, in early 2010, there are plans to remove the fences and sculpt the wasteland into a new park. Officially, it will be temporary, the site still owned by Westfield in case they ever decide they do want to build a mall in Bradford, but nonetheless this is a small victory that Bradford ought to savour. This place is still being dumped upon from a great height, and they know it. Maybe they ought to found an Independent Labour Party.

Chapter Ten

Cardiff: Manufacturing a Capital

Cardiff is a capital of some sort. Architecturally and topographically it feels internationalist yet utterly local, dynamic but afraid of the unfamiliar. If it resembles another European city, it is Brussels, albeit on a far smaller scale: a reluctant, bureaucratic capital, largely aloof from the linguistic and nationalistic conflicts that surround it, its industrial base mostly dead, but with a thriving sideline in administration. Yet in British terms it feels somewhere between Southampton (not quite so mean, a bit more ambitious, freer) and Liverpool (whose port metropolis grandeur it sometimes attempts, but tentatively). It's a puzzle of a city, and mostly a very worthwhile one, if not always for architectural reasons. Sadly a lamentable provincialism and parsimony means that in places, we have a ceremonial capital designed by such giants as Benoy, Crapita and, if we're feeling a bit naughty, BDP. It's pathetic, and when criticized is invariably justified via a strange circular argument—how dare some jumped-up ponce from London come here and slag off our brilliant buildings? Anyway, the reason they're so shit is because of our clients and it's not our fault, so there.

Two parts of central Cardiff appear to be competing for the role of the Welsh capital's administrative centre, both of them built from scratch—one of the early twentieth century, another of the early twenty-first. The earlier of the two is at Cathays Park, near Cardiff Castle's Gothic fantasia. Laid out in wide, tree-lined

Cathays Park

boulevards, with plenty of green space, reached by the appropriately francophone Boulevard de Nantes, it's what I imagine imperialist capitals in Africa or Australia to look like, something which says odd things about Wales' status in the United Kingdom but complimentary things about the ambition of its politicians. The ensemble feels a bit dated for its period, the buildings mostly examples of an imperial neoclassicism already outmoded by the time of completion in the thirties, but at this distance it's thoroughly impressive, the free baroque of Lanchester, Stewart & Rickards's City Hall especially. This really feels like a capital,

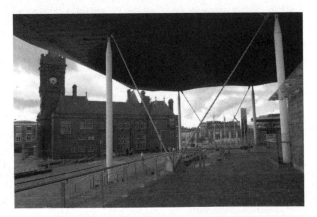

Senedd meets Pierhead

albeit a colonial one, but the Welsh Assembly's Senedd is at the other end of the city, overlooking the port at Cardiff Bay. Here is a staggeringly different urban experience, in a fashion which is not kind to the twenty-first century.

A Capital Done on Design and Build

'Cardiff Bay' was once the beautifully named Tiger Bay, for decades the UK's most multiracial area outside London. The name has been obliterated, along with much else; in a city scrabbling around for any shred of heritage, this effacement is bitterly ironic. Defining it are two major buildings by the architectural wing of *Private Eye* favourites Capita—a thuggishly dull, spirit-crushing, dead-eyed Police Station by Capita Symonds, and the less appalling Millennium Centre, of which more anon. While it may be dressed with volkish public art and rubble stone, the Police Station is a veritable behemoth of punishment—it increased the amount of cells in the previous central station from four to sixty. It also has a range of exciting security features. Apparently, 'full integration allows for the operation of multiple systems from one holistic front end with high levels of control'. Comforting, no?

The New Police Station

We were given a clue as to the reasons for this when we watched 'Cardiff Carnage' sweeping through the centre. This militarized pub crawl was a thing to behold—hundreds of freshers, all clad in promotional T-shirts with writing all over both T-shirts and themselves—marker pens were given out so they could cross off each pub on the list. They were doing all the expected things —drink fall over be sick snog knee-trembler if you're lucky, etc—but on such an enormous scale that there were fluorescent-jacketed stewards on hand, as if this was a political demonstration. The stewards seemed to be there to channel and watch the students, ringing ambulances if necessary, but in the context it seemed more as if, along with the traditional role of providing liaison with the police, they were there to protect the youth from the possible wrath of Cardiff. I've never before seen fun of such a weirdly desperate, over-organized yet nonetheless spectacularly dissolute sort. Without getting too *Daily Mail* about it, it was hard not to feel terribly sorry for them all: even the defenders of this curious event know it's done to blot out the imminence of impending debt and temp hell. You can be as hedonistic as you like, as long as you're prepared to be indentured for it for the rest of your life.

The place we saw all this occur was St Mary's Street. Architecturally this really is a fabulous place, its impressiveness barely affected—possibly improved, for some—by hordes of screeching petit-bourgeois virgins covered in marker pen groping each other before being sick in the gutter. This street is a great, complex urban object, a continuous block with each of its buildings differently styled (hence the comparison to Belgium, where by-laws ensure diversity), ranging from loud low countries Gothic to two massive Americanized neoclassical department stores, one of which was once the hulking headquarters of the local Co-Operative; on the other side of the road, the buildings lead into markets and arcades. Not all of central Cardiff is this interesting, but there's a tendency not to take architecture too seriously, a sentiment which, while perhaps at the root of the cut-price botch job of Cardiff Bay and the invariably dreadful towers, can be quite entertaining. The Cardiff Cineworld and the cluster of buildings

Cardiff Cineworld

Stadium struts

near the Millennium Stadium, while never quite being *good*, have at least a bit of fun with our prevailing Modernism on the cheap, dressing themselves up in neon when night falls—similar low pleasures can be found in HOK's Millennium Stadium itself, although it's a shame the struts are painted white, when black or red would have taken the admirable tastelessness to a more charismatic level. In the middle of this is one fine bit of late Brutalism, Seymour Harris Partnership's 1982 St David's Hall, looking improbably chic and European Grey by comparison. The St Mary's Street area is one of two really very good things in Cardiff, the other being the aforementioned imperialistic Beaux-Arts pleasures of Cathays Park—which, interestingly, was planned decades before Cardiff was designated 'capital' of Wales, and yet it is laid out with confident gusto as if it already were. It's this which makes the comparison between Cathays Park and Cardiff Bay so irresistible, in that both were explicitly laid out as bureaucratic and cultural centres (with some retail added in the new version). The former Tiger Bay became, as with Greenwich Peninsula and the Cardroom Estate in Ancoats, a Blairite tabula rasa, and like them it remains fundamentally unfinished a decade later. Even Lloyd George Avenue, the ceremonial boulevard towards the new district, was botched and is likely to remain unfinished, with anything slightly adventurous in the original proposals—interesting planning, light transit—replaced with a mere road from A to B. Still, it's all there at Cardiff Bay—wonky sub-decon, New Urbanist-indebted 'proper streets', yuppie-dromes; and upriver, lots of call centres—and none of it seems to notice its fellow buildings, let alone exhibit a spark of personality. But among the more innovative things done here was the creation of a new Barrage at enormous expense, the sole reason for which seems to have been the assumption that muddy water would have deterred people from moving into the adjacent condos.[62]

Capita Percy Thomas's Millennium Centre suggests that Crapita has managed to absorb some moderately talented architects. Best known for replacing Zaha Hadid's competition-winning opera house, it's oft reviled but far from all bad—its futuristic vernacularisms are populist and original, if ever so slightly patronizing. There are another two 'landmark' buildings here, William Frame's fine, rather Liverpudlian Pierhead, and Richard Rogers's Senedd. Rogers Stirk Harbour too often temper their Gothic impulses in favour of 'nice' architecture, and from the outside the

St David's Hall, trying to look cool

National Museum and Gallery of Wales, Cathays Park

Future vernacular at the Millennium Centre

Alsop's Visitor Centre

Senedd is decidedly low-voltage for its site, giving little to those who treat architecture as objects to look at and enjoy, although the interior is reputedly impressive. What is around it, however, is motley, to put it politely. The washed-up tube of Will Alsop's rusty visitor centre and a reconstructed Norwegian Church at one end are the good side of this chaos, but are dwarfed by Benoy's Mermaid Quay on the other side. Here are manifold fashionable gestures of the 2000s at their most banal—vaguely nautical, vaguely decon roofs aligned on 'real streets', often looking curiously like budget versions of the Senedd's wonky roof over glass box approach. What is especially noticeable here is how badly

Harry Ramsden's, Mermaid Quay

planned all this is, how disconnected each cluster is from the other, how each completely ignores its neighbour. None of the buildings have the architectural courage to make a virtue of this disconnection. The abundant and lumpenly literal public art is really not enough to stitch it all together, and so this gift of a site is wasted.

Along the River Taff, there are two routes back to the centre. The western route goes along the well-preserved Victoriana of Grangetown—the houses are set back from the river, and behind there are squares, a Hindu temple and a welcoming liveliness coexisting with seaside town sleepiness, marred only by the clogging up of the streets by parked cars; something which those who hanker after the Real Streets of the nineteenth century always fail to notice. This pleasant averageness is rudely interrupted by Wildig Lammie's Fitzhamon Embankment, a block of student housing that improbably combines neo-Victorian postmodernism in cheap stained stone and brick, 'nautical' porthole windows, and regeneration-signifying Iconic jagged roofs. It's quite possibly the worst new building we've seen all year, but it's so cheerfully awful that it's hard to hate it entirely.

Although overlooked by Cardiff's few postwar municipal towers, surviving industry and call centres, the eastern route would no doubt consider itself rather classier. Its main interest is WYG's Century Wharf, riverside yuppiedromes with no public access to the river. The flats are now going pretty cheap, revealing

Architectural comedy at Fitzhamon Embankment

'Strata'

that these are no longer the exclusive enclaves they present themselves as, though they still retain their aggressive gating against
the city around. No surprises here, you know the drill—render,
concrete balconies, irregular windows, sub-Parker Morris standards, lots of materials. Yet as it taketh away, Blairism also giveth.
Strata, the newest part of the development, features an 'Animal
Wall' to accommodate the creatures that may otherwise have been
displaced, and it's curious to see that in terms of both interesting
design and social policy the birds have been having a better time
of it than the humans. The Wall achieved the rare accolade of
an article at the website of architectural pornographers *Dezeen*.
Amusingly, one commenter compares the bird wall to a 'socialistic concrete apartment block'. Perhaps the birds and bats need
something in their vernacular?

Libraries Gave Us Power (and Concessions)

The commercial centre, meanwhile, is better in details than from a
distance; while at first you notice the tacky new or clad towers,
closer inspection is chaotically rewarding, with layer upon layer
of conflicting styles. It's currently centred round St Davids 2, the
latest outgrowth of the covered shopping centres that were built
here as early as the 1850s. There's a juxtaposition which clearly

Inside the new library

wants to be a new civic 'hub', where BDP's new library meets Benoy's (mainly unlet) Hayes Apartments and John Lewis. The prow-like corner apparently represents the port—an easier device to justify here than in the many inland British buildings that employ it. The library, part of the same development (they're giving something back, so kind), is mannered on the outside; a barcode façade that is clearly indebted to David Adjaye's similarly striped east London 'Idea Stores', meeting copper cladding, with a vaguely organic bulging floor-plan. The entrance to Wagamama is clearer than that of the library itself. The interior is better, balancing activity, quietness and abundant natural light, with a hint of Brutalism about the bare concrete circulation spaces, slightly making up for the desperation outside. From here you can survey the most striking object on the Cardiff skyline, the Millennium Stadium, which is audaciously crammed right into the area's bustle, huge girders and cantilevers single-handedly providing the dramatic skyline which would otherwise be absent from the city. On the ground it clips itself onto the earlier Cardiff Arms Park, its 1969 concrete structure still impressively harsh.

The shopping spaces are by a considerable measure most interesting in the Arcades and markets hidden along St Mary's Street, which boast some wonderfully imaginative moments—the point where the ferro-vitreous roof of Edwin Seward's 1879 Morgan

Learning and retail

Arcade curves round the street line is fantastical, as is the second-hand bookshop adjacent, despite an incongruously twee Wedgwood paintjob. The City Market, designed by William Harpur in 1891, and the other Arcades are similarly diverse, especially compared with the identikit fare in the St David's Malls. Near here, a couple of edifices suggest a world beyond shopping: the complex late Brutalism of St David's Hall, and a forlorn statue of Aneurin Bevan, now stuck between McDonalds and Bradford & Bingley. Pigeons may have relieved themselves on him, but at least the great man didn't have to see Cardiff Carnage.

Morgan Arcade

Cardiff is marvellously rootless and cosmopolitan. It *has* no vernacular. At its edge, St Fagans pointedly brings authentic Welsh architecture to the capital. It's a park full of reconstructed rural buildings set up from the 1940s onwards, commissioned by the Earl of Plymouth, who was worried about the possible expropriation of his land by Bevan's Labour government. Maybe he was influenced by the similarly anti-socialist Henry Ford's proto-theme park Greenfield Village, an open-air museum of the American vernacular, but this—assembled by Welsh nationalist Iorwerth Cyfeiliog Peate—would be more about scholarship than entertainment. Heralded by a neat, clean-lined visitor centre in the style of the day (the day being 1968), St Fagans is like a spacious, studious version of Clough Williams Ellis's North Wales fantasy village Portmeirion, only with all the joy extracted. It started off with North Walian farmhouses, mills, speculative prehistoric Brythonic villages and timber circles, but has since reconstructed fragments of industrial South Wales: a row of shockingly mean miners' cottages from Merthyr, a wonderfully imaginative Miners' Institute torn out of Oakdale, Caerphilly, all decontextualized and rebuilt for our comfortable exploration. It's Baudrillard at the Eisteddfod. Some of it implies there might have been a real vernacular a very long time ago, with steeply overhanging roofs and lots of whitewashed stone in evidence; in the case of a pit for

Cardiff Central Market

The transplanted Miners' Institute

cockfighting, there's some impressively complex wood framing. Nonetheless, the reason why this poverty ought to be emulated as a model for today—as it is with similar studiousness in Poundbury, not too far away in the West Country—remains entirely mysterious.

Its paths loop around a couple of reconstructions of the future, too—a 1948 prefab and, cordoned off near the entrance, the House for the Future. Obviously a rather ambitious gesture for a place devoted to reconstructing the past, the construction of the future has been enduringly controversial. A large house designed

The House for the Future

by Jestico & Whiles and paid for by developers Redrow, like the Merthyr cottages it's flat at one end and dramatically sloping at another. It went through a series of metamorphoses, rebranded in more vernacular fashion as Tŷ Gwyrdd, the House for Sustainable Living. The combination of green technology with luxury didn't provide a realistic model of the future, so it closed recently because of 'technical problems and a negative reaction from the public' (according to an extremely helpful staff member who lets us sneak in when the Park is closing). It is not altogether surprising that a constructed past has no room for the future, but the centre of Cardiff ought to be able to offer a more convincing idea of where we should go from here. Although its civic ambitions coexist with commercial blandness, I have more hope in it than I could ever have in St Fagans and all it represents.

Past the visitor centre (as we stood taking a picture of it, the CCTV camera swung round to look at us), St Fagans provides the Vernacular Experience, a park where you can look at everything from piggeries to prefabs. Although the prevailing implicit argument is for the 'authentic' (and, as you can find out for yourself, the unfit-for-human-habitation) architecture of rural Wales, plonked in a capital which voted an overwhelming No in the referendum for the Welsh Assembly, the excursions into industrial south Wales are the most tragic. There's the House for the Future,

St Fagans Visitor Centre

the miners' terrace, and most of all the Oakdale Miners' Institute: now that the coalfields in the Valleys have gone from being Cardiff's reason for existence to being its outer suburbs, they can be safely commemorated, their institutions of self-education torn out and re-rooted in the fallow soil of compulsory heritage. I have a mole in St Fagans, and he told me the following about the failure of the House for the Future:

> the negative reaction to the House of the Future was, I think, a recent thing (it closed this year). For one thing, its contents had ceased to look futuristic after seven, eight years. The museum rejigged it, but half-heartedly, as Tŷ Gwyrdd—this meant new displays on the walls etc but no major changes otherwise. The public picked up on this and were always pointing things out to us—such as the two combi ovens 'for flexibility', necessary due to a sponsorship deal with AEG—and, quite fairly, saying 'but that's not sustainable'. Also, they now expected us to be know-ledgeable about environmental issues about which we'd have to bullshit; we weren't trained to talk about such things. We actually hated the place. It would have worked if the change of emphasis had been addressed properly (there were no recycling or compost bins) and if the technology had been kept up to date, but neither is in the museum's culture … can we safely assume that none of Redrow's actual houses of the future will look like it?

Finally, the mole informs us of the following telling exchange about the Miners' Institute: 'Small girl, in the Institute library, asks her mother what sort of books the miners would have read. Answer: "Oh … books about making things, I suppose, do it yourself and that sort of thing".' No subversive literature in the former 'Little Moscows' of South Wales, then. Oakdale adjoins Blackwood, where the Manic Street Preachers come from. They opened the new Cardiff Central Library a few months ago, a pro-ject whose adherence to the ethos that 'Libraries Gave Us Power' is rather negated by becoming part of the 'planning gain' in a new shopping scheme. In front of it are new blocks of flats sitting empty, leading the way into a similarly derelict new shopping mall. A design for life.

Chapter Eleven

Greenwich: Estuarine Enclaves

It's hard now to capture the excitement of the Millennium. Whether the fear of the mythical Bug or the light-headed optimism of New Labour's honeymoon years, symbolized nicely in the 'River of Fire' that failed to ignite the Thames, it's all something we'd rather forget. Yet it survives as an anachronistic Blairite nomenclature in the 'Millennium Communities' designed to herald the new age.[63] The only one anywhere near completion over a decade later is in Greenwich, a borough in south-east London, where I have lived for several years. Greenwich was christened and re-signposted as the 'Millennium Borough', and a trace of the pride and anticipation of this clings to Millennium Pizza and Millennium Kebab on Woolwich Road, or the renaming of the Vanbrugh Health Centre as Vanbrugh 2000, not to mention London's biggest publicly funded entertainment enormodome, the O2, the remnant of 1999's Millennium Exhibition. Hence there are few better places to assess what has happened in London in the first decade of said millennium. Greenwich is also the westernmost part of the Thames Gateway, the vague expansion zone where the redevelopment of former military and industrial wastes into a new suburbia was actively encouraged and subsidized by the government, so is also an apt spot to think about what legacy, if any, the New Labour non-plan has left.

The London Borough of Greenwich (soon to become, thanks to a proposal from Lord Mandelson, The *Royal* Borough of

Greenwich, in reference to the fact that the blue-bloods lived here four centuries ago) merges two once independent towns, Greenwich and Woolwich, each with their own histories, their own distinctive architecture and mood. Yet both were happy to subsume themselves in London from the inception of the London County Council in the 1890s. The refusal of once autonomous towns—of West Bridgford, Salford or Gateshead—to admit to being part of something larger than themselves was never a factor in the capital, where it was a source of pride instead. It all became something even more centralized when the two were merged in the sixties into the London Borough of Greenwich, in the process creating one of the capital's most disparate administrative areas, a place where everything about the environment can change in a matter of seconds and yards, where the cleared GLC ghost town of the Ferrier Estate, Kidbrooke is in spitting distance from Blackheath's preserved Georgiana. At its heart is a tourist outpost where bewildered Americans wonder where the Cutty Sark disappeared to, amidst multiple Tex-Mex restaurants.

Greenwich's Shifting Borders

Curiously, the tourists seldom seem to make it to the Royal Naval College, despite it being one of the most astonishing architectural ensembles in Britain, except to view it from the hill. John Webb, Christopher Wren, Nicholas Hawksmoor and John Vanbrugh's staggering achievement here—aligned with Inigo Jones's Queen's House and Wren's wilfully off-axis Observatory, now filled in when looking north by a view of the glass trading floors of Canary Wharf—stands as one of those rare moments (another being the 1960s) where England was in the European mainstream, adapting continental ideas to its own ends. It's a remnant of an earlier change in function—presumably too good for its original purpose as Naval Hospital, it became a school for Naval Officers, and is currently occupied by the former Greenwich Polytechnic, which gives it a life which would otherwise be absent from its de Chirico colonnades and wide open spaces. Architecturally, it's

Royal Naval College, Greenwich

such a towering achievement that almost everything around prefers to doff its cap rather than attempt to compete. The buildings
around this set piece include some recent neo-Georgian houses,
defaced for a time with the legend 'NODDYLAND', and
Corvette Square, an introverted, badly altered block by James
Stirling and James Gowan, showing that even architectural egos
this huge affected deference here. The only object which doesn't
is the vast Edwardian Power Station that lords it over seventeenth-
century almshouses, its skyline of towers actually adding to rather
than detracting from the ensemble.

Stirling & Gowan's Corvette Square, with added pitched roofs

There is another monument on the Greenwich skyline. Set back at a respectable distance, the Greenwich Town Hall, designed by Clifford Culpin in 1938, is a soft-Modernist complex in expertly, scrupulously detailed brick. This material stands in for all things stereotypically English in recent building, a material to use when you aren't really interested in 'materials', in much the same way as concrete stands for the alleged mistakes of the 1960s. Yet much as it is glib to dismiss a material so plastic, so tactile, so varied as concrete simply because it gets a bit soggy in the rain, brick is often considerably more complex. Although it's even worse when the builder decides to do something a bit fancy with it, hence those Cotswoldy worn and scuffed yellow bricks used often, for some reason, for Halls of Residence, there are major exceptions. In the 1930s, architects who were not fully paid-up members of the Modern Movement often used brick in order not to offend, but they could do some wonderful things with it too, using it as a complex modern material in itself rather than a default stack. This is a legacy of the Amsterdam school, the Socialist-Expressionist architects who remodelled the city in the 1910s and '20s, and the adaptation of it by Wilhelm Marinus Dudok into a moderate Modern, rectilinear but not aggressive.

The disused public viewing area of Greenwich Town Hall

This style has had a raw deal from the historians, though—I've heard tales of respected architects looking at buildings like the Greenwich Town Hall and proclaiming: 'That's not modern architecture, it's *Dudokery*'. Today, it seems as much a prefiguring of the unpretentious robustness of much 1950s and '60s building, and hence it doesn't feature in the *Grand Designs/Wallpaper* white-rendered world of Brit Corbusians. There were more attempts to Anglicize Dutch Modernism than for the purer equivalents, making it relatively prosaic and hard to notice. For years I've lived in the vicinity of the Greenwich Town Hall, one of the best examples of this lost style. I signed on there for a couple of months, and it was a rare pleasure to pass through its murals on my way to the endless queue. It's an asymmetrical, reddish brick series of wings culminating in a tall clock tower in a corner of the borough's nice bit, ignoring the Georgiana without making a fuss about it, rising to a tower that would once have been the tallest thing in the area by some measure. At the top is a razor-cut window, presumably with a public observation post inside, although since the town hall was let out to a motley variety of private enterprises, it's closed to the public. Like any good civic monument, the Town Hall now houses all manner of wrongness, from a dance school to MBA courses to Alpha god-botherers. Still, the clock tower is one of the least sung but most important kinds of building: something you see day in day out without really thinking too much about it, and only gradually realize is an extraordinary work of art.

It looks over an immediate hinterland which has mostly avoided major redevelopment. Aside from the pallid urban renaissance new build of Lovells Wharf, the sold-off, Scandoed-up former flats for NHS workers at Seren Park and the wasteland which was once the District Hospital, awaiting Make's infinitely deferred 'Heart of East Greenwich', Millennial Greenwich is a good mile downriver. 'The Heart', as the local press call this gigantic cleared waste ground, is worth attention. For years now the site has been screened off by another of the current ubiquitous bright fences (this time picked out in blue), to the point where nobody seems to notice the erasure. That, of course, is the point: the fences are supposed to efface what was there before, until the shiny new buildings arrive. So, walking past it a little while ago, I was taken aback to see 'Greenwich District Hospital Was Here' scrawled on the bright blue fence. Oh, so *that's* what used to be here. I had almost forgotten.

Odd that I would forget, given the morbid entertainment it provided several years before, watching the District Hospital's concrete megastructure being demolished, panel by panel. Greenwich District Hospital was one of the huge general hospitals built in the sixties to service the burgeoning NHS, before being sold off and demolished by its New Labour council in favour of another 'mixed-use scheme'. Sometimes a hole opens in the fence and you can peek in at a vast, overgrown wasteland. For a time, a couple of lonely boxes and portaloos suggested minor activity, but even they've gone at time of writing. This is south-east London's equivalent to the Westfield Hole in Bradford, a gigantic scar which everyone has given up expecting to heal. At the end of it is Vanbrugh 2000, a still-extant NHS doctor's surgery. It's an angular A-framed Brutalist beast ('architect—DHSS', notes Pevsner) which is by far the most striking piece of architecture in

'Watch it come down.' The end of Greenwich District Hospital

The heart of East Greenwich

the immediate area, unconcerned about polite opinion, fittingly named after the seventeenth century's leading proto-Brutalist. It's slated for demolition upon the commencement of the 'Heart'.

A wholly blank fence would have been far too *oppressive*, so at one corner, there's that most egregious of public-art impositions, subsidized graffiti. Unlike 'Greenwich District Hospital was here', this one won't get cleaned off. It cutely depicts 'The Changing Face of East Greenwich', from muddy-faced flat-

Vanbrugh 2000

capped Morlocks erecting gas holders to the cleanly utopian teflon Dome. The benefits of the post-industrial knowledge economy in one vaguely 'street' image—if this were in North Korea we'd call it propaganda. Just round the corner from the mural, meanwhile, you can see some panels declaring 'My City Too!' Each of them details just what London's kids want from regeneration. Children demand fountains, apparently. Otherwise, the only perceptible movement was in the shifting of the signs when the quangos changed their names—originally First Base and English Partnerships, then the Homes and Communities Agency, now with the added legend 'Building Britain's Future'—accompanied one morning in February 2010 by the equally pithy 'THIS IS SHIT'.

Looking at the wasteland inside the fence, you might forget the 'vision' for the hospital site. The owners—nominally, the caring, sharing, it's-good-for-you property developers First Base—are perhaps a bit chary, given the ethics of flattening a general hospital for flats. Nonetheless, Make were hired, residents 'consulted' (memorably, one asked the unanswerable question: 'Why are all buildings at the moment covered in this brightly coloured slatted wood?'), and some of it will be 'affordable', although none of it will be council housing, irrespective of the size of the waiting list and the fact that the project is basically state-funded. It will include some replacements for functions provided perfectly adequately nearby: a new library (the East Greenwich Library, a listed baroque confection down the road, will no longer be required); a new health centre (the Vanbrugh Centre will be demolished); and perhaps a new Jobcentre as the recession bites (the Jobcentre in the old Town Hall closed a couple of years ago). Make's publicity images show CGI folk wandering around the shiny plastic and pine surfaces, clearly delighted with the availability of coffee. As the crash seems to have finished it off, it's even possible they'll leave it like this, an indistinct green space twinned with Blackheath just up the road.

The 'Heart' is something of an exception, being relatively far from the river. As if to tempt fate when the gleaming Thames Barrier in Charlton becomes insufficient, it is along the Thames itself that development has been concentrated. This begins in Deptford, on the other side of the creek, a sliver of which is in Greenwich Borough. There's Millennium Quay, bland late-nineties new build with a hilarious statue of one-time resident Peter the Great, Czar of the Russias in a three-cornered hat with a deformed flunky, the work of a Russian sculptor and anatomically so bizarre that his elbow is larger than his head. More interesting is the area around the Creek itself. On one side, a redeveloped and yuppiedromed council estate, and on the other the Laban Centre, that most prestigious of things, a Stirling Prizewinner. These often have very direct effects on their surrounding areas, which seldom feature in the brochures and television programmes.

The Laban Centre, Herzog & De Meuron's dance school on the Deptford side of the Creek, is not, contrary to what stereotype would suggest, blind to its light-industrial surroundings. The corrugated metal walls act as a new version of that ubiquitous industrial material, and its drizzly metallic skin curves around the murky trickle of the Creek. Thing is, that context would itself disappear quickly enough, and because of its precedent. Adjacent, under construction, are a series of blocks of flats of significantly inferior architectural quality, which with their opaque coloured glass are nevertheless vaguely 'in keeping' with the Laban. They claim on their hoarding to be 'inspired by dance', proclaiming their sponsorship by RBS and, inaccurately, their presence in Greenwich despite being firmly on the Deptford side. As with so many other iconic buildings, the prizewinning architectural masterpiece has become the advance guard of gentrification, and the 'icon' brings in its train a familiar menagerie of property developers' 'stunning developments', aiming to change the area's demographics. Over the road from that is the Macmillan Student Village, a high-security complex that sticks to the rule that all Halls of Residence must be architecturally negligible. For the really dramatic changes, however, you have to go along the Thames to the drastic curve where the Isle of Dogs meets the Greenwich Peninsula.

The Pursuit of the Millennium—Greenwich Peninsula as a Blairite Tabula Rasa

As recently as fifteen years ago, this place was called Bugsby's Marshes. Downriver from Greenwich, with its baroque master-pieces and gift shops, a moonscape of blasted, smoking industry: the largest gasworks in the world, an internal railway ferrying goods and effluent from the river out to the suburbs, and a cata-logue of toxic waste, known from the early nineteenth century as an area of 'corrosive vapours', something only added to by the autogeddon of the Blackwall Tunnel, which sweeps a roaring fleet of cars under the Thames at rush hour.

In the post-industrial city, what we do with these places, with their memories of the grotesque mutations that ushered in its industrial precursor (after moving production out to China), is to clean them up and make them safe for property-owning democ-racy. Accordingly, by the 1990s this by now unproductive wasteland was ready for redevelopment, after a mammoth decon-tamination effort. Just over the river is an example of what this could have been like, the Canary Wharf development on the Isle of Dogs, where dead industry was rebranded in the 1980s as the 'Docklands Enterprise Zone'. Architecturally, it was given the treatment pioneered in New York's post-industrial Battery Park,

The Blackwall Tunnel approach road

a postmodernist simulation of a metropolis that never truly existed, populated by banks and newspapers. It even used the same architect, Cesar Pelli. Yet after the early 1990s recession, perhaps this was considered rather foolhardy for the Peninsula: at this point Docklands' *Stadtkrone* at Canary Wharf ('Thatcher's Cock', as it was nicknamed) was an empty, melancholic monument to neoliberal hubris, as opposed to today's rapaciously successful second City of London. Something else had to be done: the 'entertainment' variant of the same schema swung into operation.

The Greenwich Meridian just upriver made it an obvious centre for the Millennium Celebrations in 1999, so Major's terminal Tory government drew up plans that were swiftly adopted by New Labour when they came to power in 1997. This time, though, the then vaunted Vision Thing would be key. Mike Davies at the Richard Rogers Partnership, as it was then known, devised a PVC Tent that looked akin to a squashed version of the neighbouring gasholders, with yellow supports stretching themselves out like an industrial crown. The form was borrowed from an earlier, abortive master plan for the Royal Docks on the other side of the Thames, where several smaller tents were planned before the last recession. Initially devised as temporary, the tent's PVC was demoted to Teflon when Green campaigners complained of 'waste', landing them with a semi-permanent structure they would subsequently loudly abhor. Inside would be an exhibition divided into zones on culture, science, the body. When Blair's government won the first Labour landslide since Clement Attlee's in 1945, some compared this Millennium Dome to the 1951 Festival of Britain, a parade of Modernist design and popular futurism mounted on the South Bank of the Thames. 'Three-dimensional socialist propaganda', as it was called by Churchill, who hated and demolished it, leaving nothing after Tory re-election but the Royal Festival Hall, which would be encased in Portland stone in the 1960s to harmonize with the conservative restoration architecture of the Shell Centre.

As if in answer to criticism that the Dome, as the tent was erroneously named, was mere decadence in the face of a housing shortage, a residential area was planned just south of it. The commission for this Millennium Village was given to Ralph Erskine, still held in high esteem for Byker Wall in Newcastle. Millennium Village carries a faint trace of the vain hope that New Labour could have continued that project, and in the process brought Britain back into Europe. The symbolic gesture of hiring Erskine, architect of the last great public housing scheme that was interrupted by Thatcher in 1981, was scuppered when Erskine's partners Hunt Thompson quit over compromises made both in the design and in the social 'mix'; and Erskine's plans were very loosely interpreted, especially after his death in 2005. This was not going to be true public housing, but a redoubt for Canary Wharf employees, 'key workers' and absentee landlords.

A spacious, well-finished and dynamic tube station was designed by Will Alsop, fresh from the success of his Peckham Library, as part of the Jubilee Line extension, and optimists thought this might not be the Tory farrago originally planned after all. Instead, it could be a twenty-first-century equivalent to both the Great Expositions of 1851 and 1951, and the dreams of utopian communities envisaged by previous Labour governments, only without making their paternalist mistakes, all rising out of a formerly poisoned industrial wasteland.

Millennium Village Phase One, Ralph Erskine & Hunt Thompson

The David Beckham Academy

Predictably, but no less sadly for that, things did not pan out that way. The Dome's exhibition turned out to house a vast McDonalds and array of corporate advertainment, holding it up to a public ridicule that has only recently subsided. Within a few years, the area had taken on a definite identity, albeit not the one that was in the original brochure, and for most of the 2000s this was the place London forgot; a desolate landscape, one that was fascinatingly *wrong*, given the ecological and social-democratic ideas that had initially been thrown around in relation to it. A holding pen for Canary Wharf, yet somehow so much weirder than the usual Thames-side developments that they inhabit. Alongside Erskine's buildings—a staggered skyline of rendered concrete towers that would clearly be more at home in Malmö—was a nature reserve and a beach full of discarded shopping trolleys. The views were of industry either abandoned or clinging on, and pervaded by the sickly-sweet smell of the Tate & Lyle works. People were seldom seen, and the highways for cars en route to the Dome were utterly empty. Something resembling a dual hangar housed the 'David Beckham Football Academy', while concrete grain silos that would make Corbusier weep in admiration surveyed the area like sentries. The only part of the old Bugsby's Marshes was a reservation of listed Georgian houses, and a blue steel bridge with blind corners (but doubling as an iconic arch) that provided the only link with East Greenwich proper. Adjoining Erskine's blocks was Millennium Village South by Proctor Matthews, a bricolage of girders, pine and tile, sometimes giving way to De Stijl-like row houses—yet the render on the concrete was flaking with impressive swiftness. Further down, two rote retail-park buildings: a monstrous drum of a multiplex with a crassly exciting *Laserquest*-style dystopian interior; a nondescript hotel with a giant, heterotopian Chinese restaurant on the ground floor; and two strip malls, one containing that oxymoronic thing, an ecologically friendly supermarket, designed by Chetwood Associates and nominated for the 2000 Stirling Prize. While this place was clearly a resounding failure on any social measure, it was a compellingly alien interzone in London's cityscape. Neighbouring areas might be wracked by seething poverty and violence, but this enclave gave off a post-apocalyptic calm.

This would all change when the Dome was bought by Christian Fundamentalist magnate Philip Anschutz, who planned 'Britain's First Supercasino' and entertainment complex, while the phone company paid for it to be rebranded 'the O2'. I attended Open House here in 2006, hoping to be able to see inside this famously enormous, hubristic space, able to fit several football pitches inside it, Canary Wharf laid flat, amongst other dubious statistical feats. The reality was rather more disappointing, as Anschutz employees showed nonplussed architecture buffs nothing but the small space where the Casino was being constructed—to no avail, as the Supercasino permission was given to New Emerging Manchester instead, until the plans for these gambling cathedrals were cancelled by Gordon Brown upon taking power. Nonetheless, the Dome was reopened in June 2006, its ceremonial opening a concert by bafflingly enduring hair metal act Bon Jovi.

Around the time the Dome was reopened as the O2, the renovated Royal Festival Hall had also just reopened upriver to much fanfare. This fragment of the 1951 exhibition appears as the upscale, upriver entertainment centre, with the Dome as the prolefeed

Industrial relics at Greenwich Peninsula

The bridge back to civilization

The Odeon's interior

The O2

easterly equivalent. Inside, the newly reopened Dome resembles
an Arizona shopping mall, only sheathed in greying Teflon. The
whole area is 'themed' in a *Grand Theft Auto* art deco, and I
wonder what Richard Rogers and Mike Davies think about what
happened to their building. A 'chill-out zone' consists of a tent
filled with iPods. Decorated guitars and fibreglass palm trees
punctuate the 'streets', while outside a billboard proclaims a little
history of entertainment—1951 Frank Sinatra, 1983 'Metallica
invents Speed Metal', 1995 Blur vs Oasis—emblazoned on a series
of gurning crowds.

Chill-Out Zone, O2

This place was a Blairite tabula rasa. Faced with an area the size of a small town, freshly decontaminated and waiting to have all manner of ideas laid down upon it, what did they create—or rather, what did the companies and corporations that they subsidized create? A couple of areas of luxury housing (typically, with fairly minuscule apartments), a couple of shopping centres, several car parks, and now a gigantic Entertainment Complex to finally get those car parks filled. Amusingly, given that the area was once so keen to trumpet its eco credentials (a supermarket partly run on wind power), it has since become another of London's locked traffic grids, as well it might having the Blackwall Tunnel nearby. Blairites, and neoliberals in general, have always posited some sort of 'force of Conservatism', some entrenched opposition either from the remnants of organized Labour or woolly traditionalists, that prevents their vision from being realized. Here there was nothing but blasted wasteland when they got hold of it. Yet a more astounding failure of vision is difficult to imagine. If there is a vision here, it's of a transplant of America at its worst—gated communities, entertainment hangars and malls criss-crossed by carbon-spewing roads; a vision of a future alienated, blankly consumerist, class-ridden and anomic. The 'corrosive humours' turned out to be more difficult to erase than might have been imagined.

A Good Idea, Fallen Among Fabians

By 2010 a few new buildings could be added to the list above—new phases of the Millennium Village, and some new development around the Dome. Foreign Office Architects' Ravensbourne College building—a whimsically portholed, painstakingly ornamental construction unreachable by anything other than motorized transport for all but the 'villagers'—is going up next to TfL offices by Terry Farrell, where clever barcoding attempts to hide a hulking mass. The O2 now bills itself improbably as the most successful entertainment venue in the world, and the Village made a brief return in the news as part of a Fabian Society report.

Due to the contortions of New Labour, the Fabians are now probably somewhere on the far left of the Labour Party, and their 2009 report on council housing, *In The Mix*, had a walk-on part for this estuarine enclave.[64] One of its central ideas was that council housing once catered for a wide cross-section of people, and is now an emergency redoubt, creating what are rather hysterically described as 'social concentration camps', and more convincingly an 'apartheid' system in housing. This, as far as it goes, is true enough. If you delve into the history of council housing, you notice that it was originally aimed at the 'deserving' poor: the first and arguably finest of London estates, the 1890–1900 Boundary Estate, merely displaced most of the residents of the famously horrendous Old Nichol slum that it replaced, while George Orwell once spoke of the 'upper level' of the working class being 'skilled workers and council tenants'. Meanwhile, if you shove a lot of the very poor together in an enclosed area then the results, as a general rule (*very* general—there are many well-managed and well-looked-after council estates) are not going to be pleasant. The Fabian report also appears to be entirely sensible in pointing the finger at, first, the system-built estates of the sixties, with their lack of attention to much other than stacking 'em up cheap, and second, the right to buy, as the culprits for the current state of council housing.

After that, sadly, if predictably, it returns to New Labour ideology. When they talk about making council estates more 'mixed' (and the report is titled *In the Mix* in order to flag this up), politicians aren't planning to build more council housing. This is despite the vastness of waiting lists, now including many prospective tenants who were entirely 'respectable' before the 2008 property crash made their house/investment completely worthless. Yet when there was more council housing than there is now, it rather unsurprisingly had far less of a stigma—so, one would think, more council housing would be the best solution, and the easiest way to ensure 'mixed communities'. However 'mixed' almost always means 'mixed tenure'; what this usually means in practice is the selling off of council housing to be replaced with a mixture of private homes, a quota of 'affordable' homes (a meaningless phrase, usually meaning affordable to buy—and even that is resisted by property developers) and perhaps a small percentage of Housing Association homes. This merely increases council waiting lists, making estates even more overcrowded and yet more full of people who are utterly desperate, with even 'priority' tenants sitting on waiting lists for years. The introduction to the Fabian report was written by Nick Raynsford, MP for Greenwich and Woolwich. His offices are on the street where I live; a street where a few years ago, there was a post office, a general hospital and a primary school. Now all of these have gone, but it does have three blocks of tiny, speculative 'luxury' flats, one of which is a gated community.

In a Radio 4 interview to promote the Fabian report, Raynsford contrasted the GLC new town of Thamesmead with the Greenwich Millennium Village, built under his watch. Thamesmead is undoubtedly a melancholic place, but in a remarkably shallow comparison it stood in once again for 'the failures of the past'. First came a few clichés about the place, mentioning among other things 'dark alleyways', which either refers to a scene in *A Clockwork Orange* actually filmed in Battersea, or the system whereby the housing blocks are raised on stilts with underground car parks beneath—actually a very sensible way of building on a floodplain, something wholly ignored across the rest of the Thames Gateway. Still, it conforms to stereotype, so never mind the actual reasoning behind it. Yet Thamesmead was itself *intended* to include a mixture of public and private housing, without an obvious difference between the two, and the reasons why it didn't are both political and architectural. The concrete walkways and lakes of the Tavy Bridge area were originally supposed to be the model for the whole semi-new town, but the backlash against Modernism led to later phases being constructed first in council house vernacular (often snapped up with right-to-buy), second in Barratt Homes neo-whatever, which never had any pretensions to being public housing, and third in the tacky new build brownfield aesthetic of the Blair boom. So at the centre is the much-mythologized 'concrete jungle', which stands alone for fairly obvious reasons. Meanwhile the alternative, Greenwich Millennium Village, held up as a great example of a 'mixed community', is similarly skewed, this time to the middle-class side of the 'mix'.

It's almost as isolated as Thamesmead—an impressive achievement for a place that is on the edges of Zone 2 rather than the outer reaches of Zone 5. The only way to get from GMV to Greenwich itself is by the notoriously infrequent 129 bus. It's cut off from the surrounding Edwardian and Victorian areas by the Blackwall flyover, but it *is* very well connected to Canary Wharf. It may have a token bit of affordable and key worker housing (in the teeth of much opposition), but there are no council tenancies. At its centre is the amusingly named Oval Square, the obligatory piazza, ostentatiously lacking any facilities other than an estate agent, not that it matters, as there are two huge strip malls with huge car parks just around the corner (and did I mention that this is a 'sustainable community'?). It's not at all homogeneous in racial terms—far from it—and you do sometimes see a handful of families in the area, but generally it's a young professional enclave set in wasteland, with absurd rents and flat prices to match. That this mix is considered a model for anything other than a prospective posthumous Ballard novel tells us a lot about what 'mixed communities' really entail.

Architecturally, the Village is the perfect example of Blairite urbanism as it would like to see itself. It prefigures most of what would come next: the use of a formerly toxic brownfield site; lots of wood detailing; a rhetoric of sustainability that is rather undermined by the huge car parks and malls built adjacent; water features; brightly coloured rendered concrete; irregular windows; and the estate agent cliché of the 'urban village'. The estate agent misnomer is also appropriate—like Ballard's Chelsea Marina in *Millennium People*, for which it was almost certainly the original inspiration, the Village is not quite where it says it is. Yet most luxury flats that have reused the Village's elements are mere parodies of this first effort. What we have here is really the best and worst of Blairism in architecture, as in places, the Millennium

Cullinan, Proctor Matthews and Tovatt at The Village

Village works very well indeed. The original Erskine blocks over-look a relatively untamed, swampy nature reserve (sorry, 'Ecology Park') and a curious boathouse which seems to merge into the steel chutes and jetties of the industry that clings on nearby. The Village's flats are dense and complex, but with an order that would be absent from their successors, and even the touches that scream hypocrisy (the car parks are hidden in little pine alcoves) are at least ingenious.

The Proctor-Matthews parts across the road are less cloying than Erskine's, and are also more interesting than the run-of-the-Docklands des res. There's a variety of tall blocks and low-rise terraces that, if stretched out on a larger scale, would be quite something: curious tech-eco De Stijl hybrids of metal and wood. Unfortunately, they are never quite given the space to set up a rhythm, stopping abruptly after five or six units. A shame, as if any part of it could do with extension, it is this, rather than the simpler perimeter blocks. Perhaps because these are complicated structures, with a tendency to become flimsy if not well built. The most recent sections, by the Erskine successor firm Tovatt and John Robertson Architects, stuck on the ends of the first phases, are clumsier, brighter, flatter, even more top-heavy versions of the riverside blocks, with cubic executive 'Überhauses' sticking out ostentatiously.

But the real horror show is Edward Cullinan Architects' 'Millennium Primary School' (which famously had to import children from far-off areas of the borough, something aided by the closure of the Annandale School on Woolwich Road). It never ceases to amaze me that Cullinan is presented as a humanist architect, when the effects of his buildings are so often, as we've already seen in Cambridge, practically dynastic in their sense of intimidation. The expected undulating, pine-clad walls are punctuated by concrete watchtowers which are redolent of nothing more than the West Bank Separation Wall. Nearby, a square is filled with 'interactive' sculptures, but the sense of being constantly overseen overrides the intended jollity.

The place might be becoming 'normalized', now that Oval Square has acquired a pharmacy and a corner shop, the industrial zones on both sides of the Village have been closed down and sold off, and the sublime concrete silos that act as ceremonial gateposts have started to come down. Nonetheless, there's still a persistent hint of the not-right in the Village, of civility on the surface and other tensions not far below. Once, when the lifts were being renovated and the walls covered in padding, there was a sudden flurry of violent, illiterate graffiti. In 2009 there were stories of groups of Indian Canary Wharf workers, at the banks' lowest rung, living four to a bed in the chic executive microflats, and tales of the all-but-unused roads being used for drag racing. Little by little, the Village is being dragged back into London.

Alternatives (1)—The Architecture of Climate Camp

Another enclave, very different to that of the Millennium Village but even more temporary, sprang up in summer 2009 in the south of the borough. In a corner of Blackheath, at the point where the greenery fades into the messy urbanism of Lewisham, materialized the Climate Camp, an Instant City looked over by police with a cheekily opportunistic ice cream van at one end and a funfair at the other. The Camp for Climate Action is an activist group known for its pickets of particular sites where carbon is most

The temporary architecture of the Climate Camp

likely to be belched into the atmosphere—the site of the Heathrow expansion, the Kingsnorth Power Station. But the pickets aren't solely about protesting and then going home. Rather, they attempt to carve out some sort of oppositional, independent space. Whether consciously or not, the Climate Camp echoes the idea of the 'temporary autonomous zone' popularized by nineties cyber-theorist Hakim Bey. The 'TAZ' is usually used in terms of raves, or more politicized actions such as Reclaim the Streets in the late nineties—immediate, participatory events. Yet the Climate Camp is deeply media-conscious, aware of the need to broadcast outside of that 'zone', as was obvious on its camp against the G20 meeting on 1 April 2009. The Camp made sure that, unlike the crusties smashing up banks half a mile away, the images of *its* event in the news were of peaceful campers with their hands in the air chanting 'This is not a riot', while riot police walloped them with truncheons.

In Blackheath, picketing nothing in particular, the camp became a demonstration of itself, a discussion space aimed at the metropolitan public, deliberately drawing attention to itself precisely as a Temporary Autonomous Zone—although one walled off both from the police, and inadvertently from this (well-heeled) corner of south London. What's intriguing about the Climate Camp is its interest both in protest and an actual proposition of another way of living. In a time when utopianism of any sort is thin on the ground other than as an object for nostalgia, this alone makes it worth taking seriously. Many in the camp are clear that the autonomous zone itself provides at least a potential model of a post-carbon, post-growth world.

So what is it like, this new world? Well, it's very well organized indeed, clean and civilized. The Mayor of Lewisham haplessly moaned that 'taxpayers' would have to clean up after the camp, while in reality the campers were even picking up KFC boxes and used condoms on the areas of the heath they weren't occupying. There's a lot of talking, yet nobody is being lectured—there's much argument, especially over whether 'technofixes' or 'life-style' are the best way to adapt to a world without fossil fuels. The rejection of these 'technofixes' often means a rejection of modern architecture. In the leaflet that explains why they chose Blackheath, the campers have as number one on the list the 'Tall Buildings' of Canary Wharf that the camp has a panoramic view of, with their ad hoc, low-rise settlement the explicit alternative.

The main part of the camp is a series of marquees: one showing films, others with speakers and seminars, a tent for 'tranquility', another that broadcasts to the outside world, a medical tent, and a

Clean living under difficult circumstances

sound system, all of which use electricity generated on-site. So the camp clearly uses advanced technology of a sort; solar panels and laptops are in evidence. Yet it was the low-tech elements which seemed most striking. There are the notorious compost toilets, a wood frame partly painted blue with random bits of table and door affixed for privacy and steps up to the loos themselves (mercifully they're for sitting, not squatting), with all waste to be reused as fertilizer; a wall on which various slogans are scrawled, providing a spectacularly incoherent picture of an inchoate movement that makes a somewhat disingenuous virtue of disorganization; and several hay bales, used both at the entrances in case of rain and mud and more whimsically for seating. That's before we get to the acoustic guitars and earnest conversations. Though it's by no means a camp of crusties, an adherent to the Modernist ideal of clean living under difficult circumstances might find it all a bit too hairy.

It's easy to miss just how technologically savvy the camp actually is, because its aesthetic makes a virtue of necessity. The Climate Camp's serious politics make it far more worthwhile than, say, the windmill erected in Dalston that summer to much ceremony, and it has aims other than giving green consumers a warm glow of virtuousness. Instead it recognizes the need for enormous structural changes, both in wider politics and in everyday life, and by association, in the way we design our lives. Yet it is precisely here that the camp is at its most flawed—it inadvertently becomes an aestheticization of emergency. As a way to support an entire society, rather than a thousand or so campers, the camp describes dystopia, not utopia. There's an instructive contrast between the goodwill, intelligence and participation in these marquees and the viciousness, atomization and stupidity that occurs in the glass and steel office blocks they look out on. Yet a world run on pedal-powered generators, with no system of drainage, would be nearer to Mike Davis's *Planet of Slums* than the healed planet imagined by some of the campers. What is enjoyable, in fact pretty laudable, in a corner of south-east London would be terrifying on a larger scale.

Alternatives (2)—Greenwich Mural Workshop and London's Hidden Socialist Realism

London is a mercantile city, a colonial city, and a place whose radical history is easily suppressed. Hence, you can walk past a particular object a thousand times without really noticing just how strange and jarring it actually is; how ill it sits with the desperately accumulating city all around. In Greenwich there is a painting on the wall of an interwar council estate. It's somewhat faded, and placed behind a school playground just by the traffic and Tex-Mex emporia-clogged UNESCO World Heritage Site that is 'Maritime Greenwich'. The mural has little to do with the area, and its glorious imperial past. Rather, we see an insurgent crowd, the word 'Co-Operativa', some Aztec characters, and about to be crushed under a gigantic roll of canvas are oil refineries and sundry reactionaries. In the corner is the name 'EL SALVADOR'. This is 'Changing the Picture', a mural by Jane Gifford, Sergio Navarro, Nick Cattermole and Rosie Skaife d'Ingerthorpe. Painted in 1985, it was in celebration of the Salvadorean insurgents who were at that point being fought by a CIA-funded military government. The picture, its colours weathered to dun blues and browns, with the tenants' satellite dishes protruding at the

The El Salvador mural

corners, places itself squarely in the tradition of the Mexican muralists, of Rivera, Orozco, Siqueiros. Heroic workers and peasants, their bodies distorted but never abstracted, on an unreal but easily understandable space, heavily symbolic but not esoteric. But what on earth is it doing here? Public art is supposed to be either sententiously mysterious (there's an Antony Gormley half-a-mile away) or a grinningly optimistic symbol of 'regeneration'—but not didactic, not concerned with complex political struggles in faraway countries of which we know little.

'Changing the Picture' was one of several large-scale murals carried out in the late seventies and especially in the early to mid eighties in the British capital, partly under the auspices and with the funding of the local authorities that were characterized by the tabloids at the time as 'loony left', most of all the Greater London Council, which for a few years in the eighties became such a threat to the Conservative government in Westminster that London became the only major world capital without its own governing body. Said tabloids were often keen to point out the alleged profligacy of these councils, doling out Taxpayers' Money to various political and cultural projects. Yet this GLC, unlike its precursor the London County Council, did not (for financial and political reasons) leave a legacy of great public buildings, or of social housing estates. Its presence can be seen in these murals more than anywhere else; their naïvety, earnestness, daring and enthusiasm speak for the politics of the time. Although some of these, the 'GLC Peace Murals', were directly commissioned, more of them came from groups like the Greenwich Mural Workshop, an influential (and still extant) group who left this borough with one of the best, if most badly treated legacies of this all but forgotten public art.

There are a few antecedents for this peculiar outbreak of fantastical socialist realism on London's streets. Inside the Marx Memorial Library in Clerkenwell is a 1935 mural by Jack (or rather Viscount) Hastings depicting a burly British worker presiding over a transfigured world, flanked by the figures of Marx, Lenin (who used to work in the same building) and William Morris, produced contemporaneously with its Mexican or WPA source—but this is safely indoors. Yet, despite their presence on the streets, the only one of the 1980s murals to have achieved any major fame is 'The Battle of Cable Street', painted by Dave Binnington, Paul Butler, Des Rochfort and Ray Walker. Here, the 'battle' where eastenders and socialist activists prevented a Fascist march from entering Jewish areas is commemorated by an explosive mass of fighting figures and banners in a cracked, panoramic perspective, packed with surrealistic details like an underwear-clad Hitler thrown aside by a marcher. Some fame clings to the Hackney Peace Carnival Mural in Dalston, painted by Ray Walker, Anna Walker and Mick Jones—perhaps because, if looked at casually, it depicts a jollily carnivalesque multiracial crowd of the sort which no longer seems threatening to local power, although if examined more closely the paraphernalia of eighties leftism is all present and correct: Communist Party and trade union banners; GLC 'jobs not bombs' balloons; the slogan 'Nuclear-Free Zone'. Yet Greenwich has the most numerous and most intriguing examples, which speak clunkily but enthusiastically of a time when Londoners were actively political—a radicalism in recent memory, rather than the heritage leftism of the 1930s.

The Greenwich Mural Workshop was founded in 1975 by Carol Kenna, Stephen Lobb, Rick Walker and others. Kenna still runs the Workshop, which continues to produce public art in the area, though of a less immediately political sort. She recalls being inspired by the work of the Chicago muralist Bill Walker on a visit to the United States, and aimed to produce something similar in London—a kind of public art that had little to do with fine art, in response to other more participatory movements. It was 'very deliberately tied in with political movements over workers' control, community architecture and planning, health, tenants' rights', an attempt to inspire people to take control over their environment. So the art was necessarily simplified, in order to make it easy for locals to work on the murals. As many as twelve people would work on them at any one time, meaning that the communities it mythologized on walls were directly involved:

the Workshop would, early on, advertise itself to tenants and residents' associations, seemingly as a self-mythologization service for council estates. The result bore little resemblance to the public art of the 1960s, the Henry Moores, Barbara Hepworths and imitations that were enigmatically attached to public buildings— instead, this offered something more immediately interventionist, less conventionally 'artistic'. At the same time that they returned to figuration, their rhetoric echoed Russian Constructivism. Kenna says that they always referred to themselves as 'art workers' rather than artists, and the painting of murals would happen between 9 a.m. and 5 p.m., so that the council tenants they were working for could see that this was 'a proper working day', rather than the play of aesthetes at leisure.

Naturally this 'attempt to take art out of the galleries' was in explicit opposition to a fine art that had begun to find Constructivism acceptable, although not the didactic, simple and garish murals. Asked today if they regarded what they were doing as Socialist Realism, Kenna says 'Yes, quite deliberately so, though not in the sense of happy workers with muscles five times the size of normal people.' Their inspirations were still impeccably aesthetic in derivation—she mentions Stanley Spencer's expressionist frescoes for a church in Burghclere, Hampshire as an inspiration, showing that a spectacular public art that was direct and figurative was possible without lapsing into cliché. The Mural Workshop itself followed the arts and crafts movement in trying to return art to some pre-Renaissance collectivity—'where a master would have with him a group of students where one would do the clouds, another the portraits, and so on'.

One of their first efforts, and one of the few still extant, was the Floyd Road mural, painted by Kenna and Stephen Lobb in 1976. Here, the Workshop's ideas of empowerment through artistic representation were used to celebrate the victory of local residents over a council proposal to demolish their homes. Kenna recalls that they initially offered the residents two different suggestions, one subtle and one strident. They chose the latter, and so this ordinary Victorian wall near the Charlton Athletic football ground features a class war around the bay windows, where the builders and bulldozers face an insurrectionary south London crowd. In their 1983 pamphlet on their own work, the Workshop's didactic intent was made clear. Not only was this mural intended to represent, it was supposed to inspire, through—the modesty here is touching—'showing the people of the street working together and enjoying each other's company'. In similarly Hispanic vein to this south London *muralismo*, the 'Rathmore Benches' nearby borrowed the concrete and mosaic forms of Antoni Gaudí's Park Güell. Stephen Lobb's work here represented the 'past, present and future of Charlton'. There is dock work, not to imply the past but to argue for the retention of the Thames as a working river; there are local people harrying politicians and portraits of said locals inset into the concrete; but the prettiness of the benches means the didactic intent never becomes shrill.

There was once a cluster of murals in the Meridian Estate, just by the Heritage Zone. Nearly adjacent to the faded fury of the El Salvador mural was 'Towards A Good Planet', painted in 1978. Again, looked at casually it seemed to be something acceptable to contemporary eyes, a vaguely hippieish circle of life spinning round a mandala. Just below it is something weirder: a group of space travellers repairing their craft. The Mural Workshop's

The Rathmore benches

Ex-mural, Woolwich High Street

pamphlet describes it in strikingly odd, categorical terms: 'The circles of the mandala are—a through-the-day sequence; international co-operation, trade, cultural exchange sequence; a plant cycle, a central sun. The space ship and crew are metaphors for the estate and its tenants. The planet is utopian.' So while Stanley Spencer restaged the resurrection in Surrey, here interstellar yearning found a home amongst the stock-brick and access galleries of a 1930s council estate. Nearby was the 1983 'Wind of Peace', where, with the Heritage landmarks by Christopher Wren and Inigo Jones at the centre, the people of Greenwich and the tenants of the Meridian Estate destroyed a stockpile of nuclear weapons. This disappeared when the building was demolished to make way for the miserable, and now horribly dilapidated heritage urbanism of the Cutty Sark Station redevelopment. Its site is now a Wetherspoons.

Until recently, another of these insurgent crowds could be found on the side of a wall in Woolwich High Street, near to a free ferry and the local council offices. The owner of the site was clearly not keen on the artwork, and at one point painted over all the faces and hands of the figures in a weirdly precise act of defacement. Finally, almost the entire work was whitewashed over around a year ago, leaving a strip of mural where the ladder could

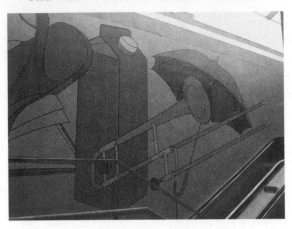

Michael Craig-Martin's Woolwich mural

not reach, which turned the super-realist mural into an accidental abstract. Around the same time, the new Woolwich Arsenal DLR Station was opened. Inside was a mural by Michael Craig-Martin, who was in the eighties just the kind of conceptualist who would have abhorred the literalism and social intent of the Mural Workshop. It depicts in a bright, child-like manner a series of consumer objects that can be obtained in the centre of Woolwich—a cafetière, buckets, guitars and more. The work is intended to be 'democratic' and 'everyday', but it speaks of a democracy and an everyday life which revolve entirely around the next purchase, the precise opposite of the hopeful, active and conscious crowds whitewashed away nearby.

Are You Arsenal in Disguise?

Woolwich, even more than Greenwich, is a place where London's contradictions are built-in. As somewhere that has always existed for the purposes of war, you'd think it would be flourishing around now, what with the endless War on Terror. But despite the barracks at one end and the (long since disused) Arsenal at the other, and some piecemeal attempts at regeneration/gentrification, it's a very depressed place, with all the noise and mess that the middle-class tourist always takes for 'vibrancy' but which could just as easily be desperation. Yet Woolwich is not like other places, and still retains a certain independence. For Ian Nairn, in his peerless city guide *Nairn's London*, it is one of London's highlights: an independent industrial city plonked into South East London, 'thumping self-centred vitality, a complete freedom from the morning train into work', and the main shopping street, Powis St, a cornucopia of odd shops and bustle. Forty years later much of Powis St is a slough of despond, yet at the edges there's still a strangeness that marks it out from the stockbrokers' dockland on the other side of the river.

Coming down the hill from Charlton, for instance, you reach the barracks: 'no need to go to Leningrad', writes Nairn, when this rationalist quarter-mile of classical accommodation for war is in a corner of London. Up a bit from that is John Nash's creepy iron rotunda and, inexplicably, a black geodesic dome, screened by a high wall from those who might wonder what it's doing there. Further on into Powis St itself are a pair of brilliantly demonstrative architectural curios, both built by the Royal Arsenal Co-Operative Society, the most militant of the co-ops. The earlier 1903 building is a red-brick and terracotta eccentricity, featuring amid the curlicues some inset screaming heads (the cry of the

Woolwich

toiling workers? Of the capitalists about to be expropriated? Some oblique tribute to Munch?) and at its centre a statue of some tremendously side-burned co-op worthy staring grandly at its counterpart across the street, with 'EACH FOR ALL AND ALL FOR EACH' inscribed above him as if he were a Fabian Musketeer. The other Co-Op building is a heartbreakingly dilapidated 1938 Art Deco confection, its tiles flaking off and in some places missing entirely; an adaptation of the picture palace to some sort of palace of social democracy—so its desuetude is politically appropriate. The aforementioned slogan can be seen in there somewhere, just below a rectilinear tower that is still visible in most parts of Woolwich.

It's almost inevitable, then, that this melancholy beauty is on the way out: if all goes to plan, it will be the first thing to fall to the march of gentrification, as Greenwich Council plans its demolition prior to the replacement with luxury flats/retail/whatever. Meanwhile, the axe of regeneration preserves nearby Riverside House, the Council's truly horrible 1960s offices, a hopelessly dull tower with a blue pattern drawn on it in crayon. There is more of the same round the corner. Two Picture Palaces, still in decent enough condition, albeit dedicated to rather depressing practices: the former Odeon, now the 'New Wine Church' (presumably as

The well-kept Powis Street

Royal Arsenal Co-Operative, Powis Street

in 'into old bottles'), a fantastical faïence confection; and opposite
the ex-Granada, now Gala Bingo. When opened in the late thirties
it declared itself to be 'THE MOST ROMANTIC THEATRE
EVER BUILT', its elegant Dutch Modernist Dudokery masking
a Gothic interior by the Russian theatre designer Theodore
Komisarjevsky. Walk on a little further and you're opposite the
Ferry: a gloriously pointless free boat that gets you to the 'London
Teleport', a field of satellite dishes opening themselves out at
the Thames. Unlike the North side, the South is still all turrets,
chimneys and towers, smoke-blackened and crumbling. Nairn
describes North Woolwich as 'a good private place to hatch a
revolution', but the south side fits the bill rather better today.

Nil Scrap Value

The Woolwich Ferry is one of the few signs of life on a dead river.
Save for the aquatic police, a stray tourist boat, and the Tate ferry
that goes from one branch of Nicholas Serota's World of

Adventures to the other, London's huge, majestic river is almost entirely unused; even in 'Docklands' it's difficult to find any sign that it ever was. Not only is the ferry a strange fragment of a past in which the river had some sort of function rather than being the backdrop to the ubiquitous 'stunning developments', it's also gloriously free. Just queue up at either side of the river, Woolwich SE18 or North Woolwich E16—there's a concrete shelter in case of rain—and at no point will anyone ask who you are or what you're doing there, let alone ask for money. The Woolwich Free Ferry was introduced in the 1880s by Joseph Bazalgette as one of his 'improvements', and the current terminus and ferries date from the mid sixties. The terminus is in shuttered concrete, with an angular staircase poking out, while the boats themselves are named after local politicians: all of a Labourist bent, given Woolwich's history as a socialist stronghold. One of the three is called the 'Ernest Bevin', after the union boss and Cold Warring foreign secretary in the Attlee government.

Go in the daytime or the weekend and the ferries are bracingly empty, with lines of benches sitting forlorn, while red-walled rooms labelled 'SMOKING' have their doors definitively locked. Until recently, the ferry filled up at rush hour, people getting off at the DLR station on the North Side to go to the (until 2009) tubeless South. You can also stand on the traffic deck and gaze at this desolate stretch of river: the Tate sugar refinery and the Thames Barrier dominate the riverscape here, the leftovers of industry now overwhelmed by those riverside flats that cling to even the poorest stretches of Thames, Canary Wharf looming in the distance. At the front of each of the ferries is a little cylindrical lookout pod, creating a peculiar arch that frames Woolwich Reach.

This crossing was earmarked for the Thames Gateway Bridge, a project of Ken Livingstone's Mayoralty subsequently cancelled by Boris Johnson, along with a bus that was planned to traverse this stretch of riverside. But if for some reason one finds the ferry's laconic, unhurried river crossing a little perverse, there is a foot tunnel, or a tube connection of a sort in the form of the Docklands

Light Railway. London's transport system is beautiful and strange, and it's oddly pleasing that because of it, most of the best modern buildings in the city are in the outer reaches of the Piccadilly Line, in unprepossessing suburbs like Sudbury or Oakwood rather than in the fashionable East End. Just as good is the 1999 Jubilee Line extension, easily the single most impressive work of architecture in London for the last twenty years. It might seem, with its muted colours and late high-tech stylings, to be a quintessential bit of Pseudomodernism, but the surface is deceptive. These are huge, unnecessarily generous spaces, where the luxury flats and sundry Blairite *grands projets* of the last decade have been poky and mean. Richard McCormac's Southwark is a silvery series of passageways which suddenly open out into functionless, high-ceilinged vaults, North Greenwich an uncharacteristically sober bit of Alsop which inside reveals itself to be a weird, oversized space of slanting columns and optical illusions. Norman Foster's grandiose Canary Wharf station creates such anticipation that when you get out of it, the windy collection of half-hearted skyscrapers always disappoints. Finest of all is Michael Hopkins's truly incredible Westminster station, a feverish Constructivist/Piranesian dream or nightmare of gigantic concrete pillars and criss-crossing escalators. The latter even reproduces the Modernist canard of the Victorian distinction between retrograde architecture and futurist engineering; on top is Portcullis House, a woefully pompous stone fortress, while the inside could even convince that the Millennium was not such a crushing disappointment after all.

Because of this as much as its Frank Pick-era pedigree, a new station is one of the few exciting events in London architecture, although part-privatization has caused a perceptible dip in quality. The Docklands Light Railway is at a slight remove from the Underground proper, but its stations are usually imaginative, if never hitting the heights of the Jubilee or thirties Piccadilly. West Silvertown, Pontoon Dock, Deptford Bridge are all clever and diverse structures, albeit coloured somewhat by the large 'Nil Scrap Value' signs on their steel railings, a response to a rash of stolen steel sold off by illicit traders to China. So when a station at Woolwich Arsenal, which is more or less local for me, opened, I felt an obligation to go there. It's clearly a good thing that it's there, although the possibility it might mark an early step in the supersession of the free ferry is a minor worry, as is the fact that it aids the heritage horror of the nearby Arsenal riverside developments (more of that later); but nonetheless, a good thing. You go in under a DLR standard-issue canopy, down the escalators and onto a concrete platform; in between are the aforementioned mural and a branch of Costa Coffee, facing off across Powis Street. The building joins Woolwich Arsenal DLR in a pathetic act of genuflection, swapping concrete and steel for unconvincing stock brick. From there, one can trace a route to the new riverside enclaves for which this new station is a long-awaited lifeline.

What's All This I Hear about a 'New Way'?

Due to the presence of the eighteenth-century Arsenal buildings, the Royal Arsenal, Woolwich's large new development on former Ministry of Defence land, had to market itself via appeals to heritage rather than newness. The infill is sometimes in keeping, sometimes not, but the entire area, with its affluence, the obligatory Gormleyesque sculptures (by Peter Burke rather than Ecce Homo himself) and vast unused spaces, feels a million miles, not a few yards from the bustle of Woolwich proper. It's a place which feels as if it might be popular with Tories who prefer not to leave the capital, but who would rather not live in the multiracial montage city that most of London has become. I once saw Jeffrey Archer walking briskly in this direction, and the leaked BNP membership list showed a concentration of members in this enclave, a wide dual carriageway and a world away from a densely mixed area of West African takeaways and cavernous greasy spoon cafés. Here, new space contains its own specific inequalities, both architecturally and socially. A&Q's Royal Arsenal is the high-end version—clean, tidy, stolid and sometimes well-designed—but the real horror show starts with the eight towers of

Gormleyism, Royal Arsenal

RMA Architects' Royal Artillery Quays, where Woolwich fades into Thamesmead, the Greater London Council's botched 'Town for Tomorrow'.

This development's vagaries have had an enormous effect on the surrounding area, in a way that is more subtle than Fabian Society reports would suggest. When the GLC (who built and owned the place) was destroyed in 1986 on the grounds that it was a threat to central government, the housing was subsequently administered by Thamesmead Town, a resident-run organization whose appropriately Modernist signs still decorate many of the blocks. This in turn was wound up in 2000, and its functions were spread between two organizations, the Gallions Housing Association and Tilfen Land. The former is one of the fundamentally unaccountable philanthropic organizations who are now the sole builders of 'social' housing in Britain; the latter a private company which owns much of the land in SE28. On Tilfen Land's land everything from riverside stunning developments to vast out-of-town distribution sheds, from Barratt Homes-style mock-traditionalism to an experimental 'Ecopark' can be found.

Walking east from Woolwich, Royal Artillery Quays is the first of their enclaves. It's one of the most unambiguously old-school Modernist developments of the 2000s—white serried towers on a *zeilenbau* layout, hard concrete and, astonishingly, no wood cladding whatsoever; the usual ingratiating features are limited to the glazed stair towers. They're somehow imposing and flimsy: in a 2009 BBC story about the impact of the credit crunch on the area, they were tellingly described as 'tower blocks' rather than the 'stunning developments' they would have been a year earlier —the system-built towers of the sixties returned, this time with even fewer facilities and smaller flats.

Even so, in terms of notoriety Royal Artillery Quays has nothing on the neighbouring 'Pinnacles'. These inexplicably named stubby blocks were the epicentre of the London property crash. In one block, eighty-two out of eighty-four flats were repossessed, and the development is apparently riddled with vermin. As a piece of design it's the Millennium Village language of bright render and brick at its most inept, with as much relation to Ralph Erskine as Riverside House has to Le Corbusier—the death of a good idea at the hands of the capital's love for the cheap and banal. Of course, much of the horror the place has caused was due to the development suddenly being affordable for the original buyers'

Royal Artillery Quays

The Pinnacles

cleaners. As a piece of planning, the blocks curving round a central space work reasonably well, and we see children playing there on one visit—but this makes it feel only marginally less sinister. There is something horribly wrong here, and it's not just a matter of architecture or mortgage fraud. One of the 'Pinnacles' is blocked off by no less than three metal fences.

A pathway leads from there to a 'Tor', a heathen mound where the surrounding area can be surveyed: World War Two pillboxes in the fenced-off MOD marshes, possibly not yet cleared of mines; Belmarsh Prison, where fans of the vernacular will be pleased to

The view from the Tor

see that 'Britain's Guantanamo' is in stock brick; the Beaux Arts
planned Barratt Noddyland of Broadwater Green, where a sym-
metrical arrangement and pointy roofs presumably based on
Kentish oast houses lead to endlessly looping cul-de-sacs and one
huge pub; the vast, empty distribution complex of White Hart
Triangle, one gigantic white shed surrounded by swamp-like
wasteland. This is another Blairite tabula rasa, and only one small
part of it, Splinter Architecten's Ecopark, accords with 'official'
policy, a sustainable fragment in an area mostly developed as
cheaply and quickly as possible.

The Ecopark is one of Gallions Housing Association's pet projects, an 'urban village' designed by Dutch architects, an enclave
of sustainable Eurozone aesthetics amidst some typical English
crapness. The Eco credentials are compromised somewhat by the
way the development organizes itself around a car park, with no
public transport in the vicinity bar Belmarsh's bus stop. This little
close is presumably one of those attempts to get 'planning gain'. In
a development of yuppiedromes, leave 20 per cent aside for 'key
workers'; in a huge swathe of land untouched by public transport,
make sure 10 per cent of the homes are carbon neutral. It's a kind
of urban offsetting, spectacularly infantile.

The original new town, which actually went over budget rather
than being done as cheaply as possible, is something that you can

The Ecopark's car park

CCTV at the Southern Outfall

arrive at gradually. It never quite dominates the landscape until you suddenly find that you've been walking along walkways through concrete buildings more than on the ground past red brick houses; it can also be reached by walking along the ridgeway of Bazalgette's Southern Outfall Sewer, which has its own strange microclimate, a rough, scrubby, knobbly landscape which seems to turn an area of fifties stock-brick council houses into somewhere on the outskirts of Bradford. In the middle of it, a single CCTV camera stands guard over what otherwise looks impeccably *rus in urbe*. It's a terrifying sight.

Here, you can contrast the ruins of the postwar attempt to build a futuristic, socialistic new London with the ruins of the attempt to create a slightly nicer version of neoliberal capitalism in the 1990s and 2000s—a failure without even the dramatic qualities of tragedy, as the defeat of something so woefully unambitious is merely pathetic. Thamesmead proper consists of a series of developers' cottages which could be absolutely anywhere, the walkway-maisonette-tower complex of Tavy Bridge, and the unbelievably long interconnected block of central Thamesmead, the latter of which indulges in some bleakly comic nomenclatural games. One part is named after socialists, another after liberals, so that there is a council block called Malthus House. It's on the cusp of

Greenwich and neighbouring outer-suburban Bexley, and on the border is some recent infill by Gallions. Known collectively as 'Poplar Place', these are two very different blocks of flats, both designed by Stefan Zins Architects. One is a rotunda, converted from what used to be the boiler house for the new town, a squat version of Canary Wharf's stockbroker-stackers, with all the terracotta and inexplicable fiddly overhangs we've found everywhere from Southampton to Leeds; the other, much stranger, is a stepped block with aluminium and wood detailing, a green roof and metal pedestrian walkways, in what can only be a reference to the circulation systems of the surrounding estates.

It's impossible to praise the original Thamesmead without caveats. There were never enough facilities, the transport links to the centre were always appalling, and the development was always shockingly urban for its outer-suburban context. Regardless, it is something special, a truly unique place. It always was, and remains so in its current amputated form. The walkways run all the way from a sharply elegant pedestrian road bridge to the legit ruins of twelfth-century Lesnes Abbey, passing on the way a lake, a nature reserve with wild horses, and the hack director's urban decay set of choice. It's more like Millennium Village than anyone would like to admit, with Gallions even rebranding Tavy Bridge as 'Southmere Village'. What with all the maisonettes

Near miss, Central Thamesmead

New walkways of Thamesmead

given mock-Tudor detailing by their tenants, it sometimes even looks like Byker, by accident rather than design. Unlike its successors, it's flood-proof and still architecturally cohesive after decades of abuse. Around Southmere Lake you can see, just about, how with some decent upkeep and had tenants been given the choice rather than being dumped here, this could have been a fantastic place; something that could never be said about Pinnacles. This is basically a working-class Barbican, and if it were in EC1 rather than SE28 the price of a flat would be astronomical. Today it feels beaten and downcast, and it only ever gets into the

The bridge from here to there

Tavy Bridge

news through vaguely racist stories about the Nigerian fraudsters apparently based here; but its architectural imagination, civic coherence and thoughtful detail, its nature reserves and wild birds, have everything that the 'luxury flats' lack.

The destruction of these qualities continues today, in a botched regeneration job. Gallions would no doubt prefer to level the whole bloody thing, as it's clearly too vast, too complicated, too isolated and harsh in design terms to be sold to the much-wanted better class of resident. It's too big for that, and too many people live here, so they've settled for small surgical interventions instead. At random points, walkways and stairwells are painted pink and blue, and UPVC drastically shortens the once floor-to-ceiling windows (funny how something which symbolizes wealth in one place signifies poverty in another). Two of the towers have been painted white, immediately marking them out as superior to the others where the concrete is still bare. Finally, the Pyramid Centre, an NHS building that would almost certainly have been listed were it somewhere more prominent, a futuristic gem akin to but more powerful than the now entirely accepted Brunswick Centre in Bloomsbury, was demolished entirely and a modern centre in white render and wood built in its place, only this time without the anti-flood stilts. The car park around it is surrounded by the crumbly, abrupt stumps of the walkways that were ripped off to create it. Thamesmead does not want to be what it is, which makes it hard to argue that the rest of London should want to be like it.

The only new building here that has been noticed by the architectural press is Norman Foster's Bexley Business Academy. In its finance-capital flashiness and Canary Wharfian atria, it neatly embodies the Academies' managerial ideology of 'aiming high', their apparent attempt to solve the problems of the nation's youth by setting up mini-business schools on the ashes of the social-democratic comprehensives—the Academy replaces an earlier school, and sits at the furthest corner of the Tavy Bridge estate. Foster's first London building, a tiny light-industrial unit designed when the young idealist was interested in achieving industrial peace through non-hierarchical entrances, was built as part of the new town not far from here. In between is a huge swathe of history, the difference between New Labour's economic and social ideas and the social democratic, Keynesian models it belatedly took to invoking. Alistair Darling recently pledged (perhaps to the relief of a good few architecture firms) that one of the 'public works' that would receive governmental 'stimulus' was the 'Building Schools for the Future' programme. This means a lot more City Academies—200 of them by 2010.

We now have an extraordinary new system, one in which the government lavishes the banks with cash but refuses to impose

Amputated walkways

THE NEW RUINS OF GREAT BRITAIN

policy on them, and at the same time gives a significant amount of control of policy in public education to businesses and wealthy private individuals, in return for a minor amount of the funding. Just about anyone can 'sponsor' an academy. At Bexley it's the property developer David Garrard, but elsewhere the list includes banks, creationists, the *Daily Mail*—as long as they stump up a piffling 8 per cent of the cash. It's astonishing that banks are considered capable of running schools, given their evident inability to run their own affairs. The academies—of which Bexley, designed by a starchitect, is a flagship—are dominated by a deeply corporate philosophy, one in which 'management' and the snake-oil salesmen of 'motivation' are the gods to be appeased. Stephen Bayley recently wrote of an academy where a teacher claimed that, in order to learn history and French, 'we do Napoleon', with the bonus that the pupils 'learn about motivational leadership'.[65] The Bexley Business Academy even has its own 'stock exchange', where hopefully the pupils have been staging their own financial crisis. The Academies are steeped in the vacuous thinking that got us into this mess, and it ought to be terrifying to imagine these pernicious ideas being sold to young people as mere educational common sense.

The gulf between these two structures is that between two kinds of ruin. It's more instructive, though, to look at a noble failure than an idiotic one. West Thamesmead, Greenwich Peninsula, the Heart of East Greenwich: these are already relics of New Labour's New London, a mess of the punitive, the crassly money-spinning and the literally fraudulent. Hence there could be no better place to see the London Blairism built. Go and climb up the Tor in Broadwater Green, look around, and wonder at how so much potential was thrown away. They could have remade London, but they made this instead.

Chapter Twelve

Liverpool: Exit

Coming as I do from Southampton, I have long regarded Liverpool as everything my hometown could have been but wasn't. The port that succeeded it in the 1910s was never interested in emulating its architectural grandeur, and some seem to find this a good thing— both those who fear a Solent City, and the occasional Liver- pudlian sentimentalist. In 1984 Beryl Bainbridge wrote an *English Journey* in tribute to Priestley, and she too started in Southampton. Although she seemed to have spent all of five minutes in the city—at least, unlike in her account of Milton Keynes, she man- aged to get out of her car—she was pleased to find that the port that had 'done in' Liverpool was not, unlike her hometown, some- where big, dark and grandiose, but a mere 'holiday village', jolly and quaint, and good for yachting. Maybe all of Britain could be one big holiday village. Maybe, as Prince Charles once advocated, Toxteth could turn 'back into countryside', as has parts of Detroit.[66] Hell, let's just dissolve the cities altogether, destroy the tower blocks and write off the last 150 years as a mistake.

The great thing about Liverpool is that it, at first sight, has no truck with this whatsoever. It is not a village. It's a dramatic, great city, and at its centre is the most wholly and thrillingly urban envi- ronment in England outside of London. Cliché it may be, but with Liverpool comparisons are never really to Manchester, Leeds, Bristol, let alone Southampton, but to Berlin, Hamburg, New York. Walking round the commercial centre built up around the

Pier Head, there is alternately a crucible of modern architecture, in the form of the steampunk iron and glass experiments of Peter Ellis's 1864 Oriel Chambers or the mutilated 1906 Cotton Exchange; the stripped, classical, steel-framed interwar towers of C. H. Reilly's Liverpool school; bizarre eruptions of sixties modernism, like Bradshaw Rose and Harker's former HSBC Building, a Czech Cubist experiment in black glass; a telecommunications tower of the sort a Canadian or German city would find entirely normal but the English faintly hubristic; and at the head itself, W. A. Thomas's Tower and Liver Buildings, the latter the only English work of the twentieth century to have influenced skyscraper design elsewhere, rather than vice versa. The architectural richness here is so overwhelming you feel almost spoiled by it. Further up, the Georgian terraces and the brilliantly ludicrous competing cathedrals offer views of an astonishing skyline, easily the finest in Britain. It's not enough. The problem is amply demonstrated by the fact that this magnificent metropolis was supplanted so quickly and easily by *Southampton*. Liverpool's recent history is a massive demonstration of the unnerving fact that many don't seem to *want* cities, even one as good as this. The reasons for this are not wholly aesthetic.

A view down to the Pier Head

The Last Days of Municipal Socialism

Liverpool has experienced a resurgence, not necessarily in economic terms—it is still the poorest city in Britain—but in terms of national prominence. Its year as European Capital of Culture in 2008, which left a legacy of Superlambananas and unfinished museums, acquired a certain art-house grandeur through Terence Davies's vainglorious *Of Time and the City*, a sometimes witty but mostly thumpingly banal city portrait, all tourist-board shots of the Pier Head's 'Three Graces' and booming renditions of startlingly obvious poetry half-remembered from school ('Ozymandias', 'Into My Heart an Air That Kills'—you half expect him to intone 'To be or not to be: that is the question'). As Sukhdev Sandhu was almost alone in pointing out, Davies's film said nothing about time other than 'it passes' and nothing about the city other than 'it ain't what it used to be', but with undeniable visual assurance it fixed in celluloid an accepted narrative: the city was betrayed, and betrayed by the planners. So the postwar towers rising from the slums, or from the picturesque ruins left by the Luftwaffe—'we were promised paradise,' he wonderfully intones, 'but municipal architecture, combined with the English

Superlambanana

talent for the dismal, made for something *far from Elysian*'—is mixed in with footage of far more interesting 1930s schemes, when Liverpool's municipal architect Lancelot Keay was considered one of the best designers and planners in the country. What the film doesn't feature is the fact that these schemes nearly all went down in their turn, at the hands of the last great municipal socialist experiment in Britain.

Most recent accounts of Liverpool will mention Militant, along with the Toxteth riots, as an example of the 'basket case' the city had become by the 1980s. For much of that decade, until the 'Liverpool 47' were forcibly removed from office in 1987, the Labour council was essentially controlled by Militant, a Trotskyist organization operating semi-clandestinely within the Party, which after mass expulsions now enjoys occasional moderate electoral success in Preston or Coventry as the Socialist Party. The council's heads, Derek Hatton and Tony Mulhearn, seemed to represent the two stereotypes of both Liverpool and Marxist politics: one a dodgy geezer, whose fame has endured since; the other a quiet, academic figure, still politically active but lacking his former comrade's business ventures and talk radio shows. Regardless, ever since Neil Kinnock ill-advisedly decided that attacking his own

Liverpool Futurism—the Playhouse and the TV Tower

party was the best way to win an election, Liverpool City Council has stood in for failure and chaos, the final death of the long-standing Labour tradition of reforms through local government, at the hands of those who had always claimed reform was impossible anyway. Oddly enough, however, Militant's municipal legacy is very unlike that of its reformist forbears. No Karl-Marx-Hof, no Park Hill or even Byker was left by them, although they built thousands of housing units. The diametric opposite of former Trotskyist T. Dan Smith's *dirigiste* 'Brasilia of the North', in architectural terms Militant's policy was perhaps the widest-scale attempt to give people what most (if not all) always said they wanted—a house and garden, close to their place of work.

Frankly, the effect is bizarre, warping a metropolis into Beryl Bainbridge's 'holiday village'. It's as if the city were straining all sinews to actually become as boring as Southampton. Accounts from the sixties, like that of Ian Nairn, argue that postwar architecture in the city was far less interesting than that of, say, Sheffield, and Davies's footage of some humdrum system-built blocks generally supports this. However, the case is quite different with the 1930s 'tenements', which feature just as heavily in *Of Time and the City* as emblems of far from Elysian municipal architecture. These brick blocks of flats, taking after the more unambiguously municipal socialist precedents of the cities with which Liverpool is rightly compared—Hamburg, Vienna, Berlin, Rotterdam—were designed as an attempt, conscious or otherwise, to make a city in which giant office blocks and cathedrals dissolved into back-to-backs and two-up-two-downs into something more coherent and genuinely metropolitan, giving the working-class areas of the city the kind of dramatic urban grain that the commercial centre took for granted. These too were demolished, first by Militant and then by the various more politically conformist regimes that followed it. One tenement complex in Old Swan went down as late as 2001, to be replaced by a Tesco. By way of comparison, in Glasgow it had been commonsensical for years that tenements were as decent a form of housing as any other, with 'tenement rehabilitation' well into its third decade.

So an experiment in convincing the English to live in low-rise apartment blocks, in making an English city as honest about its urbanity as a Scottish or European one, became another smugly accepted failure.

The reasons for this, however, are easily understandable. Liverpool is the only British city to have really experienced the kind of drastic population drop considered normal in postwar American cities, declining by around half between the 1940s and 1990s, from around 850,000 people to something around 400,000. So what possible need could there be for apartment blocks? If there was enough space and few enough people, why shouldn't every council tenant have their own house and garden? The only counter-argument is aesthetic, due to the incontrovertible fact that as a result of this policy, whole swathes of inner-city Liverpool look utterly ridiculous. One moment you're in Berlin, the next in Basingstoke. Walking along Park Road in Dingle, you can see how Militant took up the theories of 'defensible space' and Alice Coleman's walkway turd-counting, so that the semis are not for the most part arranged in terraces, but in closes and cul-de-sacs, with brick walls screening them from the street and all its unpredictability. In his spirited self-defence *Liverpool—A City That Dared to Fight*, Tony Mulhearn even quotes Coleman's approval of his housing policy, not pausing to wonder why an architectural adviser to Margaret Thatcher might be praising low-density housing in inner cities.

It's horribly sad. They're not bad houses, in their drab way, and residents have often dressed the exteriors up in a manner which would be difficult in the tenements and towers. They cost much less in upkeep than a block of flats, so nobody has to reckon with piss-stained or broken lifts. They cater for the very people—working-class families—who have been designed out of Manchester or Leeds. They have the virtue of being in the centre of a city, rather than in the suburbs from whence they borrow their forms; but they just look so utterly *wrong*. It's not dignified for the city centre to mimic the 'burbs. It leads to depressing juxtapositions —as at the point where the grand sweep of the major surviving

St Andrew's Gardens, designed by John Hughes under Lancelot Keay

Militant semis

Park Road, Dingle

Semis, Metropolitan Cathedral

thirties tenement block, St Andrew's Gardens (now gated student flats) meets a piddling close of nineties semis, with the Metropolitan Cathedral of Christ the King in the background. The scale is preposterous, with the houses seeming to desperately want to be somewhere less dramatic, a murmur of discontent with the idea of getting above your station. It's not for the likes of us. Walk from Dingle to the centre and wasteland punctuates the cul-de-sacs, revealing the sudden howl of Giles Gilbert Scott's other Cathedral, beamed in from another planet, until you get to a set of bungalows. *Bungalows*, for God's sake, you think, as it all

Militant bungalows, next to Liverpool One

becomes a tragicomedy. Why didn't London hit on the idea of building bungalows in Whitechapel? One of the bungalows has 'GRASS' spray-painted onto it. Then you see a black car park, a 'GROSVENOR' sign, and you've entered one of Militant's more unexpected legacies in the city.

The One Is Not

After defeat in the battle over 'rate-capping' with Thatcher's government (put simply, her successful attempt to curb the city's abundant spending on housing and social facilities), Liverpool City Council sold off a swathe of publicly owned land in the centre, around Paradise Street. This in turn was bought up by a developer, who sat on it for years before being bought out by the Duke of Westminster's property company, the aforementioned Grosvenor. The result has been alternately lauded or reviled depending on whether you're reading a newspaper or an architecture magazine. It was criticized before it had even been completed by Paul Kingsnorth in the *Guardian*, for creating a 'mall without walls', a privatized city-district where public rights of way were irrelevant, an enclave shutting itself off and boasting its own private security force and a policy of keeping undesirables off its streets. Anna Minton features it in her brilliant indictment of Blairite urban policy *Ground Control* as a prime example of the creeping securitization and privatization of the British city, motivated by fear and greed. I don't intend to disagree with either of these accounts when I say that my feeling upon entering Liverpool One was not horror at entering a new dystopia, but a sense of relief after so much visual impoverishment along Park Road—some architecture, finally, aside from the distant silhouettes of the cathedrals and the Liver Building. Some planning, some urban coherence, some sense that I was somewhere special rather than somewhere trying desperately not to be special.

Before I went to Liverpool One I spoke to an architect at BDP, the firm that master-planned the scheme and hired a diverse group of architects to design the individual buildings. He recommended

The private city-district

a route where I would not be able to see the join between the
old city and the new roofless shopping complex in its midst, in
response to my Minton-influenced arguments about its exclusive
demarcation between itself and the surrounding area. That might
be the case at one exit, but at all others the screens, signs and fit-
tings immediately announce a rupture. But then why *should* it try
to blend in? The maniacal megalopolis of the Pier Head owed
very little to the Georgiana of Hope Street. More contentiously,
he dismissed worries about the privatization of public space by
pointing out that a local council would be unwilling or unable to
look after such a development, claiming that regeneration schemes
elsewhere—like BDP's own Ropewalks—had fallen into dilapi-
dation because of municipal indifference (it merely looked as
though it had been lived in a bit when I visited). He included most
developers in this too, claiming that a shopping-mall developer
like Hammerson would be far less inclined to treat this area in the
way Grosvenor have done—as if money is no object, which in the
case of the Duke of Westminster it is not, so finishes on the buildings are of a far higher standard than almost anything else built
over the last decade. Feudalism, it seems, is able to achieve results
where neoliberalism or municipal socialism have failed.

BDP were also the designers of WestQuay, and Liverpool One
marks one of the many ways that the Mersey port has taken

revenge on its southern rival. Architecturally, there's no doubt that Liverpool One is good, especially compared with the appalling WestQuay, and some of the attacks on it seem misplaced. Dutch architect and critic Hans van der Heijden of BIQ Architecten designed new buildings for Bluecoat Chambers in a red-brick vernacular attempt to create serious architecture in the midst of Liverpool One's commercial frivolity. Not only is this a misreading of the far from traditionalist architecture of central Liverpool; BIQ's structures actually slot rather well into the panoply of registers and references, and at first I don't realize that they're from a different project. The buildings on the ground are mostly excellent—FAT's sweet-shop kiosks are as garishly playful as one would expect, Dixon Jones's arcades as chic and sober. Even those by often mediocre practices are fine. CZWG's 'Bling Building' is as embarrassing and enjoyable as old men talking about 'bling' tend to be, but more surprising is Glenn Howells' row of shops culminating in a tower, its golden frame the most striking element in the whole scheme—until, that is, you start to traverse the walkways and escalators that lead up to BDP and Allies & Morrison's South John Street. Suddenly, all the walkways that we were told led to crime and desolation are in place, swooping across each other, a Piranesian spectacle in pink and green. The stairs from here lead to a raised park, concluding what

FAT's Liverpool One Pavilion

is one of the very few actually pleasurable walking experiences created by the Urban Renaissance, a school of thought that otherwise remains boringly earthbound. There is more than a ghost of Park Hill or Thamesmead here (the BDP architect I spoke to talks of his admiration for the Smithsons), and it finally injects a bit of excitement into the prosaic act of getting from A to B, a form of planning based on movement through spaces, for once, rather than sitting wanly sipping a coffee. At this point I'm suddenly disarmed. I had expected to hate this place, to see it as the culmination of the idiocies of Blairite urbanism, but in fact, it's almost everything I like about architecture, albeit in heavy disguise.

After the triumph of the walkways and Chavasse Park, the reality of the place begins to sink in, and I notice that some of Liverpool One's architecture is actually quite poor—Aedas's dull Hilton Hotel, Cesar Pelli's silly, strained One Park West tower. I realize that I have absolutely no desire to buy anything, which means that the place is a functional failure at least in my case. To see architecture as good as at least half of Liverpool One is housing Waterstone's and Tie Rack creates a definite bathos. And to praise the buildings and the plan does not automatically mean that the claim by the Stirling Prize judges, that Liverpool One 'singlehandedly reversed the city's fortunes', stops being insulting nonsense. This is still unashamedly designed for consumers from Cheshire rather than Bootle (hence the many car parks), and it's still a CCTV-ridden enclave where civic virtues are secondary to the imperative to spend spend spend. Yet the unexpected brilliance of Liverpool One is perhaps appropriate. Every society erects its finest buildings for what it considers to be the most important function, whether it be the glorification of a deity, of capital, or of council housing. Liverpool One is our finest monument to shopping, to the dazed purchase of Chinese-made consumer goods and the precarious just-in-time production behind them. Its buildings are display fronts, with little underneath—FAT even draws attention to this, with its Liquorice Allsorts wall giving way to a void and an escape staircase. I would love something with this much care and attention to be devoted to

Glenn Howells' tower, Liverpool One

Liverpool One walkways

Liverpool One from Chavasse Park

a function of some genuine worth, but this at least has the virtue of macropolitical neatness.

Over the Wall

To see how little other functions are valued, walk to the other side of the Pier Head, where culture and accommodation are encompassed by some extremely shoddy and banal buildings, and walk from there to the remnants of the docks. First the Pier Head itself, where three very different buildings have been fixed forever as the 'Three Graces' and two new buildings which sum up the problem of British architecture with depressing acuity now share the riverfront with them. One is the Museum of Liverpool, unfinished but nearly complete at the time of writing. Designed by Scandinavian architects 3XN (subsequently sacked, so their design is now somewhat bastardized), it stands as the current mutation of the north European urbanism of which Liverpool was the finest, and arguably only, English example. However, because Liverpool's architecture has not itself kept pace with developments in its fellow northern ports, it is treated as an alien intrusion onto an ensemble fixed in time. But the worry about the appropriateness

The Museum of Liverpool, under construction

Hamiltons' Pier Head Terminal

or otherwise of this building, an immaculately stone-clad, snaking structure standing aside at a respectful distance from the Graces, is perhaps less offensive than the first positive reaction to its presence. That is, the new Pier Head Terminal, by prolific hacks Hamiltons, which is quite precisely a bonsai version of the Museum, only tricked out in a much cheaper stone with additional jagged sub-expressionist windows cut into it, housing a Beatles Museum and a new Terminal, providing an introduction to a city which wants to be a passenger port once again. It stands in front of the Liver Building taking the piss, and was the justified winner of the 2009 Carbuncle Cup, the award for worst building of the year given out by *Building Design*. In its pathetic, Lidl version of the New Thing, it is a new gateway to a servile, provincial nation, unable to produce anything of worth but only cheap imitations of other, less hidebound peoples' ideas.

Further on from here are a cluster of towers, almost all far duller than what would be built in Manchester or Glasgow (as in Liverpool, nobody is looking), by Ian Simpson, Aedas and AHMM. Of the latter's two skyscrapers, one has a certain kitschy, sci-fi joie de vivre, the other is a banal barcode façade. As a cluster, distance flatters it, but up close this is inept urbanism, randomly scattered towers with wasteland and howling main roads in between. That is, until you get to the start of the docks, the kind of port where you can enjoy walking, the opposite of Southampton's vast screened-off container reservation. It was certainly once intended to be seen. The Dock Road runs along the former path of the Liverpool Overhead Railway, an elevated line built in the 1890s, directly equivalent to New York's 'High Line', which was regularly advertised as a tourist attraction, to give a panoramic view of Liverpool Shipping. It was demolished in the 1950s because neither government nor business was interested in funding its refurbishment, one of the earliest of many snubs to Liverpool's aspirations to metropolitanism. That said, the impression that this dock wall was ever permeable by members of the public is anachronistic, and what you can look at here is not a working, living dock—it's a ruin. There are miles of dereliction before you reach the entity which still functions and trades (lucratively enough) as the Port of Liverpool. In the mid nineties, this was the site of one of the last major industrial disputes in Britain, the Liverpool Dock Strike, one of those evanescent moments where a strike stopped being just about Pay And Conditions, but became about abstractions—casualization, de-industrialization, a declaration of solidarity. It disappeared from prominence as quickly as it arose, but Liverpool has a long memory.

It's walled, the derelict dock, but the walls themselves are architecturally detailed, while the gates and the walkable road that

The new Liverpool skyline

AHMM's Unity Tower

The voids of regeneration

The Wasteland on the other side of the wall

runs along them provide constant sights, snatches and views into a seafaring architecture, which even in its most prosaic moments has a romance to it, a feeling of potential escape, the sense that you could just get on a boat from here and get out of Britain—a feeling I have never had in Southampton. The reason is that you no longer feel like you're in Britain here, but rather an international zone, a space where transit is romantic rather than a matter of mere distribution. Along the dock wall you can see a litany of industrial curios with a similar strange power and ruthless ambition to the century-old office blocks in the centre: a cyclopean ventilation shaft like one of Antonio Sant' Elia's futurist power stations, the enormous arch of the Tate & Lyle Grain Silo a rare reminder of the dubious money and Caribbean labour behind the Tate Gallery a mile upriver. Interrupting it all—blocking the road, in fact—is the Stanley Dock, the place where this journey ends.

It's blisteringly, skin-scrapingly cold, in the dead centre of the longest, bleakest winter for decades, a winter which has passed without the expected discontent. Vague, confused anger and despair is the prevalent mood instead, here in Liverpool as much as everywhere else. Fluttering in the wind is some torn police tape, and the mechanical bridge over the dock is blocked by several caravans, with a pink wheelie bin and a pink child's tricycle in front of them. Adjacent to this mobile architecture is the rotting black and red

The other Tate

Caravans at Stanley Dock

masonry of the 1901 Stanley Dock Tobacco Warehouse, reputedly the largest brick building in the world. Just a few yards north of the Warehouse, along a canal, is the Eldonian Village, a housing co-operative built in the politicized mid eighties. Its residents had input into the design, which is, a couple of thoughtful details aside, indistinguishable from any area of outer suburban housing anywhere in the country—it feels like a piece of Berkshire in Manhattan.

Together, the Dock, the Caravans and the Village provide three possible ways out of the Blairite city. At Eldonian Village, still a housing co-op today, there's a scheme which involves all the democratic control and popular politics that are completely absent from today's urban planning, housing the people who are now expelled by hook or by crook from the city centres. It also entails the rejection of urban architecture entirely, in favour of reduced versions of the houses of the nineteenth century, arranged in cul-de-sacs; giving people what they say they want, and in so doing abandoning the idea that the design of British cities can be anything other than provincial and backward-looking—something especially sad in a city which once spectacularly proved otherwise. At Stanley Dock, there is the monumentalism of industry, gigantic creations of production and distribution, the forbears of the giant distribution sheds of our times, only put at the centre of a culture rather than hidden away somewhere off the motorway. And then there are the caravans, homes on which you'll never have to pay a mortgage, a totally modern architecture that is no longer even tied to a fixed site. An old idea of urbanism is utterly ruined, here at Stanley Dock, and you can smell its decomposition. Yet it feels so much less ruinous than the desolate city of property and tourism just a couple of miles away.

Acknowledgements

All photographs are by Joel Anderson, with the exceptions of 0.1, 1.1–3, 1.5, 1.7–11, 1.13–19, 1.22–3, 1.28–9, 3.2, 3.4–5, 3.12, 5.1, 5.3–4, 5.11, 5.13, 5.24–5, 7.19–27, 7.29–31 and 12.1–21 by the author, 4.5–7, 4.12, 5.14, 6.1, 6.16, 6.19, 11.3–4, 11.16–23 by Nina Power, 4.18–4.22 by Steve Parnell and 11.30 by Douglas Murphy.

Like anyone interested in architecture in the UK, I am enormously indebted to the various editions of Nikolaus Pevsner's *The Buildings of England* (and later, Scotland and Wales) published over the last fifty years—the recent series of paperback Pevsner Architectural Guides to individual cities was especially useful. However, this book and the articles that preceded it would have been yet more impossible without the information, recommendations, hospitality and gossip provided by a long list of people, sometimes inadvertently, sometimes through correcting my howling errors, but most often through responding to my online pleas.

So this book is dedicated to the following, though this should not indicate that they agree with any of it. Ordered roughly by city, though there are overlaps. Southampton: Steve Hatherley, Jonathan Raban, Kieran Long, Maggie Fricker; Milton Keynes: Geoff Shearcroft, Iqbal Aalam; Nottingham: Chris Matthews, Anthony Paul Smith, Sophie Sheehy; Sheffield: Steve Parnell, Tom Keeley, Dan Hill, Lisa Cradduck, Ben Morris; Manchester: Penny Anderson, Liz Naylor, Justin O'Connor, Charles Holland,

Scott Neil, Ella Wredenfors; Tyneside: Andrew Stevens, James K. Thorp, Tom May, Ev Cook; Glasgow: Colin Ferguson, Douglas Murphy, Anne Ward, Jon-Marc Creaney; Cambridge: William Wiles; West Riding: Laura Oldfield Ford, Matt Tempest, Alison Sampson; Cardiff: Marc Haynes, Richard King; Greenwich: Mary Mills, Carol Kenna, Nina Power, Frances Hatherley, Alberto Toscano, Carl Neville; Liverpool: Jamie Scott, Matthew Whitfield, Jonathan Meades and the corner shop owner who gave me a lift. Thanks also to anyone who stayed anonymous, and apologies to anyone I've forgotten. Dzięki Pyzik.

Special thanks to the pseudonymous Lang Rabbie, all-purpose architectural deep throat; to Ian Irvine, Daniel Trilling, Paul Laity, Natalie Hanman, Brian Dillon, Caspar Melville, Esther Leslie and anyone else surprised to have found something they'd commissioned find its way into this text; to Rowan Wilson and Tom Penn at Verso; and most obviously to Amanda Baillieu at *Building Design* for commissioning Urban Trawl in the first place, and for humouring my occasional skirting around the edges of libel. Finally, thanks to Joel for providing company, drollery and expertise on all but the last of these journeys, and for enduring, and perhaps enjoying, a multitude of fry-ups and Chinese buffets along the way.

Notes

1 Perry Anderson, *The New Old World* (London: Verso, 2010), p. xii.

2 Rory Olcayto, 'The Mill, Ipswich, by John Lyall Architects', in *Architects' Journal*, 6/10/09.

3 See Adam Wilkinson, *Pathfinder* (London: Save Britain's Heritage, 2009). This report, while excellent on the depressing details of Pathfinder, is somewhat marked by a misplaced sentimentalism about some nondescript housing—and it's notable that the Pathfinder programme in Sheffield, which entailed demolition of less Heritage twentieth-century properties, is not considered worthy of comment.

4 Andrew Hosken's *Nothing Like a Dame—The Scandals of Shirley Porter* (London: Granta, 2006) brilliantly profiles the use of housing as an instrument in class war, but it should be remembered that the policy *worked*—Westminster has been a safe Tory council for some time.

5 The analysis here is indebted to James Heartfield's article 'State Capitalism in Britain', published in *Mute*, volume 2 #13, though this should not imply support for its neo-entrepreneurialist conclusions.

6 Alan Hess, *Googie—Ultramodern Roadside Architecture* (San Francisco: Chronicle Books, 2004).

7 Chin Tao-Wu, *Privatising Culture* (London: Verso, 2002), p. 280.

8 Adrian Hornsby, 'The Sheikhs Mean Business', *Architects' Journal*, 30/10/08.

9 J. B. Priestley, *English Journey* (Harmondsworth, Penguin, 1977). Avoid at all costs the 2009 illustrated edition, which features a set of sentimental photographs of landscapes as different from Priestley's pugnacious descriptions as could be imagined.

10 J. G. Ballard, *Miracles of Life* (London: Fourth Estate, 2008), p. 121.

11 Clare Kennedy, '24 Floors—and the lift does not work', *Southern Daily Echo*, 18/4/08.

12 Jonathan Raban, *Soft City* (London: Harvill, 1998), p. 22. Raban commented on an earlier version of my account here that 'I didn't "go looking for" dystopia, only to find it in Southampton: dystopia, in the form of the

Millbrook estate, jumped up and mugged me from behind a bend in the road. I was teaching at the University of Wales when my father, a priest in the C of E, moved from a parish just outside Lymington to Millbrook in Soton, and acquired the title of "Rural Dean of Southampton"—a contradiction if ever there was one. I remember my first sight of Millbrook, as I turned off the main road: Kafka! Orwell! Christ! I'd lived for five years in Hull—a parallel bombed city, and hardly a byword for architectural elegance, but Millbrook took my breath away with its fresh-out-of-the-box style of brutalism. This was 1965 or '66, and the estate must've been just post-natal.'

13 Jon Reeve, 'City Is Third Most Dangerous Place to Live', *Southern Daily Echo*, 25/8/2008.

14 Chris Huhne, 'Say No To Urban Sprawl of Solent City', 22/10/08, at eastleighlibdems.org.uk.

15 Peter Laws, 'Southampton's Vision of the Future Is Put on Hold', *Southern Daily Echo*, 28/10/08.

16 BBC News, 'Crane Topples Over at Southampton Docks', at news.bbc.co.uk.

17 Bad British Architecture 10/3/09, at http://badbritisharchitecture. blogspot.com/2009/03/millennium-hotel-southampton-by-hkr.html.

18 Peter Walker, 'Botched Council Renovations May Have Caused Camberwell Tower Block Fire', *Guardian*, 6/8/2009.

19 See Elain Harwood's essay on Lyons's council schemes, in Barbara Simms's *Eric Lyons and Span* (London: RIBA, 2006).

20 This wasteland was, incredibly, reserved for another Mall, Watermark WestQuay, a casualty of the recession. It was to be designed by the (now defunct) moderately outré practice Foreign Office Architects, in an unusual bit of daring.

21 See Clive Aslet, *The English House* (London: Bloomsbury, 2008).

22 The latter of whom dismissed the place with a curt 'back-of-an-envelope job' to me in conversation, before going on to explain it as inspired by the welcoming, civic U-plans of 1930s town halls.

23 Lewis Smith, 'Lord Rogers Redesigns the Rabbit Hutch for Wimpey', *The Times*, 3/5/07.

24 Richard Vaughan, 'Watch This Space', *Architects' Journal*, 29/11/07.

25 Ellis Woodman, 'Caruso St John's Nottingham Curtain Raiser', *Building Design*, 13/11/09.

26 Alan Sillitoe, *Saturday Night and Sunday Morning* (London: Pan, 1960), p. 20.

27 'Trinity Square Developer Loathes His Own Scheme', *Evening Post*, 29/12/09.

28 Royston Landau, *New Directions in British Architecture* (New York: George Braziller, 1968), p. 30.

29 J. L. Womersley et al., *Ten Years of Housing in Sheffield* (Sheffield: Corporation of Sheffield, 1962), p. 47.

30 Ian Nairn, *Britain's Changing Towns* (London: BBC, 1967), p. 76.

31 *Britain's Changing Towns*, p. 76.

32 *Britain's Changing Towns*, p. 80.

33 Reyner Banham, *The New Brutalism—Ethic or Aesthetic?* (London: Architectural Press, 1964), p. 132.

34 See Andrew Saint (ed.), *Park Hill—What Next?* (London: Architectural Association, 1996), pp. 37–8.

35 Kelvin was, even more inexplicably, restored shortly before it was demolished in 1995, and is interestingly described in Peter Jones' *Streets in the Sky—Life in Sheffield's High-Rise* (Sheffield: self-published, 2008). A former tenant of all three deck-access blocks in the eighties and nineties, Jones claims Kelvin, the least famous and least publicly lamented of the three, had the warmest sense of community, while the reclad, heavily surveilled Hyde Park was the least enjoyable place to live.

36 Ben Morris, *Sheffield's Housing Timebomb* (Sheffield: Respect, 2007).

37 Crispin Dowler, 'How the HCA Spent £2.8bn in Four Months', *Inside Housing*, 22/05/2009.

38 David Rogers, 'Budget Gives £600 Million Boost to Housing Sector', *Building Design*, 22/4/2009.

39 Nick Johnson, *Park Hill: Made in Sheffield, England* (Manchester: Urban Splash, 2006), p. 75.

40 Michael Foot, *Aneurin Bevan* (London: Indigo, 1997), p. 269.

41 Jon Savage, *Time Travel* (London: Vintage, 1997), p. 361.

42 Comment left on my blog: http://nastybrutalistandshort.blogspot.com/2008/11/so-much-to-answer-for.html.

43 Most recently reprinted in Tom McDonough (ed.), *The Situationists and the City* (London: Verso, 2009).

44 Kevin Cummins, 'Closer to the Birth of a Music Legend', *Observer*, 12/8/07.

45 Comment on my weblog: http://themeasurestaken.blogspot.com/2008/11/icon-fire.html.

46 E. Jane Dickson, 'Making a Splash', *Independent*, 19/9/98.

47 Alice Thomson and Rachel Sylvester, 'Hazel Blears: "We Need Mother and Baby Homes for Teenagers—Not Council Flats"', *The Times*, 13/12/08.

48 See Anna Minton's excellent *Ground Control* (London: Penguin, 2009), which among other things reveals that Salford spends more on the issuing of ASBOs than it does on youth services. QED.

49 Pevsner et al., *The Buildings of England—Northumbria* (London: Yale University Press, 2002), pp. 361–2.

50 T. Dan Smith quoted in Grace McCombie, *Newcastle and Gateshead* (London: Yale University Press, 2009), p. 79.

51 The film can be viewed online at sidetv.net/channel6/.

52 Fittingly enough, the earliest office blocks in London that 'expressed' their steel frames were a direct importation from Glasgow, in the form of Burnet & Tait's Kodak House and Adelaide House, both incongruously futuristic for their place and context.

53 See Nairn's *Britain's Changing Towns*, p. 51.

54 For more on this, see 'Constructing Neo-Liberal Glasgow', by 'Friend of Zanetti' at the Glasgow Residents Network website: http://glasgowresidents. wordpress.com/tag/media/page/5/.

55 Graeme Murray, 'Anger over Gorbals Designer Flats Plan', *Evening Times*, 31/1/08.

56 Outram's essays on the building are at http://www.johnoutram.com/ judge.html and are highly recommended.

57 See Will Alsop, *Supercity* (Manchester: Urbis, 2004).

58 Simon Jenkins, 'Adapt, Don't Destroy—Leeds Is the Template to Revive Our Scarred Cities', *Guardian*, 5/5/08.

59 1949 obituary, quoted in *Edward Wadsworth: Genius of Industrial England* (Arkwright Art Trust, 1990), p. 16.

60 We did not photograph the Titus Salt School. After Joel's Mum said, 'So, you and another bloke, probably also wearing a long coat, are going to stand outside a school taking photographs?' we thought better of it—the suspicion directed at those taking photographs of buildings in the UK takes many forms. For more information on the chaotic design flaws of the PFI schools in Bradford, see Kaye Alexander's otherwise sympathetic 'Titus Salt School, Bradford, by Anshen + Allen', *Architects' Journal*, 28/7/09.

61 *'Common Sense' Regeneration—A Plan to Revive the Fortunes of Bradford and Its People* (Bradford: Bradford Civic Society, 2009). See also Christopher Hammond's useful, droll *The Good, the Bad and the Ugly* (Bradford: Bradford Building Preservation Trust, 2006).

62 Sian Best, 'The Cost of the Cardiff Bay Barrage', *Guardian* 5/1/05.

63 Ruth Bloomfield, 'Millennium Housing Falls Drastically Short of Target', *Building Design*, 29/5/09. The fact that this article, listing the practical abandonment of the failed or never-started seven 'Millennium Communities' of 'high-specification homes built to stringent environmental standards' planned in 1999, claims New Islington as one of its 'successes' is telling regarding just how low expectations have become. It was planned to have created an already fairly minimal 6,000 of these high-spec homes by 2010. Only 1,626 were built.

64 James Gregory, *In The Mix* (London: Fabian Society, 2009).

65 Stephen Bayley, 'There's a Lesson in all this', *Observer*, 13/7/08.
66 Quoted in Patrick Wright, *A Journey Through Ruins* (Oxford: Oxford University Press, 2009), p. 314.

General Index

Page numbers in **bold** refer to illustrations.

Broadway Malyan 36, 103
Brooks, Alison 218
Brown, Gordon 48
Brunton, John 247, 254
Brutalism 87–100, **88**, **90**, **94**, **98**,
   109, 124, 128–31, 160, **160**
Buchanan, Colin 12
Building Design (magazine)
   xviii–xix, xxxi–xxxiii, 67, 345
Building Design Partnership xii,
   41, 44, 101, **190**, 191, 243–4,
   244, 252–3, 277, 339–41
Building Stable Communities
   programme xvii–xviii
Buildings of England, The
   (Pevsner) 4
Bunton, Sam 197
Burdett, Ricky xxx

CABEism xiii, **xiii**
Calatrava, Santiago xxiii, 150
Capita Percy Thomas 272
Capita Symonds 269
Captive State (Monbiot) 35
Carey Jones **81**, 106, 235, 254,
   255–7, 261
Cartwright Packard 80
Caruso St John 66–7
Casson and Conder 223
Chamberlin Powell and Bon 228,
   257, 259
Change We See, The programme
   vii–viii, xxxv
Channel 4 238
Charles (Prince of Wales) 49
Chetwood Associates 296
Chipperfield, David xii, 191
Chtcheglov, Ivan 122–3
Coates, Nigel xxvii, 110

Cobban and Lironi 190
Coleman, Alice 94–5
Collins, Herbert 7
Commission for Architecture and
   the Built Environment xiii, xiv,
   xviii–xix
component fixation xxv
Cooper & Cromer 204
Countryside Properties 218
Cropper, J. W. 247
Cullinan, Edward 225, 229–30,
   303, 304
Cummins, Kevin 126, 129

Darling, Alistair 329
David Morley Architects 251
Davies, John 174–5, 177–8
Davies, Mike 293
Davies, Terence 333, 335
Davis, Mike 307
Deconstructivism xx, xxvii–xxix
Delirious New York (Koolhaas) 19
Denton Corker Marshall 132
Derbyshire, Andrew 83–4, 87
Derrida, Jacques xxvii
Design Group 3, 148
Dilapidated Dwelling, The (film)
   xiv–xv
Disneyfication xxviii
DLA Architects 155
dMFK 141, 143, **144**, 148
Dobson, John 173
Docklands Enterprise Zone
   292–3
Docklands Light Railway 318–20
Dudok, Wilhelm Marinus 286–7
Dunlop, Alan 189

eco-towns 48–9

Index of Places